PASSIONATE WORK

PASSIONATE WORK

CHOREOGRAPHING A DANCE CAREER

Ruth Horowitz

STANFORD UNIVERSITY PRESS
Stanford, California

Stanford University Press
Stanford, California

Printed in the United States of America on acid-free, archival-quality paper.

Library of Congress Cataloging-in-Publication Data
Names: Horowitz, Ruth, author.
Title: Passionate work : choreographing a dance career / Ruth Horowitz.
Description: Stanford, California : Stanford University Press, 2024. | Includes
    bibliographical references and index.
Identifiers: LCCN 2023053782 (print) | LCCN 2023053783 (ebook) |
    ISBN 9781503638860 (cloth) | ISBN 9781503639607 (paperback) |
    ISBN 9781503639614 (ebook)
Subjects: LCSH: Dancers—United States—Social conditions. | Dancers—
    United States—Economic conditions. | Career development—United States.
Classification: LCC GV1597 .H688 2024 (print) | LCC GV1597 (ebook) | DDC
    792.8/0973—dc23/eng/20231215
LC record available at https://lccn.loc.gov/2023053782
LC ebook record available at https://lccn.loc.gov/2023053783

Title page photograph: Evgeny Atamanenko. Shutterstock

Cover design: Daniel Benneworth-Gray
Cover photograph: Samantha Weisburg / Unsplash

CONTENTS

PREFACE   *vii*

INTRODUCTION   The Concert Dance World   1

ONE   A *Nutcracker* Lens   17
       PASSION AND PRECARIOUS LABOR

TWO   Learning the Practice of Ballet   39
       BODY AND SELF

THREE   Career Decision Challenges   73
       ASPIRATIONS AND A STICKY SELF

FOUR   Companies   108
       CORPORATE BODIES/HUMAN BODIES

FIVE   Portfolios   157
       PRECARIOUS WORK AND CREATIVE LABOR

SIX   Distancing from the Performing Self   202

SEVEN   New Work   229
       NEW IDENTITIES AND ADAPTED SELF

CONCLUSION   Passionate Work in Perspective   258

GLOSSARY   267

NOTES   273

REFERENCES   285

INDEX   295

PREFACE

This is a book about dancers' careers. I am not focusing on performances or styles of dance but on dancers' work careers. It is about the fascination with dancing that brought gifted strivers to the stage, the dedication and grit that sustained them through the years of rigorous training, the artistic sensibilities and ambition that kept their dance careers going, and the adjustments they make after transitioning to the post-performance phase in their life cycle. They face many challenges. Unlike professional athletes who often earn large salaries, only a tiny handful of very famous dancers make enough money to live on and save. But both dancers and athletes must retire when the body can no longer do what it must. And unlike other artists whose careers can persist over many decades as they chase recognition, dancers have only a short time to do so. Most stop performing between the ages of thirty and forty.

Many dance books are autobiographies, biographies, or interviews with well-known dancers and choreographers. All are names dance fans easily recognize: Rudolf Nureyev, Margot Fonteyn, George Balanchine, Mikhail Baryshnikov, Jacques d'Amboise, Gelsey Kirkland, Jerome Robbins, Allegra Kent, Suzanne Farrell, Edward Villella, Merrill Ashley, Mark Morris, Martha Graham, Merce Cunningham, Twyla Tharp, La Nijinska, Alexei Ratmansky, and Patricia Wilde, among others. Collections of interviews by John Gruen, Barbara Newman, Joysanne Sidimus, and Nancy Upper tell us more about the lives of largely well-known dancers.[1] Some recent autobiographies are narratives of difference and fighting the odds, racially (Misty Copeland and Michaela DePrince) or recovering from injury (David Hallberg). The status of this roster is similar to that of all-star baseball players or those elected to the hall of fame.

Some write about performances, but as a visual art, it is difficult to describe performances using only words. I would love to be able to describe movement when I see dance. I am having difficulty even describing a *rond de jambe*, a single ballet movement, but I can show you. It won't look good when I do it, but you will have a better idea than what I can describe. David Hallberg's wonderful account of his life as a principal dancer describes a *tour jeté* as "a leap into the air springing off one foot, then executing a half turn and landing on the opposite leg."[2] I doubt most people who have not taken ballet or seen this movement could execute it from a description alone. Alastair Macaulay, the former senior dance critic for the *New York Times* who writes eloquently about dance, when giving a lecture before several hundred people, *bouréed* out from behind the podium to illustrate a point. It is an art form requiring serious training of the body that communicates a story, relationships, emotions, or intricate patterns through movement, rarely words. I turn to dance writers and critics to describe dance performances. Few can write about dance and the feelings one gets while dancing better than Alma Guillermoprieto in *Samba* and *Dancing with Cuba*, and Marina Harss's biography of Ratmansky and description of his dances encouraged me to reexamine his choreography. All taught me much about dance, dance performances, and dance history, but live performances are required to see what dance is really about; film tends to make everything look flat, or you miss something while the camera is on someone's face. You can't hear the dancers breathing on film.

Few books investigate the lives of the dedicated dancers outside of the very elite circles except for Toni Bentley's *Winter Season*, a corps de ballet member in the early 1980s of the New York City Ballet (NYCB) and Barbara Milberg Fisher's *In Balanchine's Company*, an early soloist with the NYCB who became a professor of English. In 2003 Bentley wrote in the new preface to her book, "Dancers didn't write unless they were stars—only then did they have a story worth telling, the story of success."[3] I think that she and other corps de ballet members who mostly dance the ensemble work have stories worth telling as, without a strong corps, classical dance suffers.[4] Dancers in smaller companies and project-based groups create memorable evenings of dance and lead different lifestyles than members of large companies. They often dance with several groups and also need to find additional paying work. They put together portfolios of work; hence I refer to them as "portfolio dancers."[5] Their struggles are worth telling.

Life is different for the corps de ballet and for most portfolio dancers who perform before small audiences. It is not the life of the principals of major companies who appear from behind the closed curtain to bow again, hear the roar of the crowd, and receive flowers. I remember an American Ballet Theatre (ABT) performance when Angel Corella, who was later appointed artistic director of the Philadelphia Ballet in 2014, danced Ali, in *Le Corsaire*. After the performance, a group of young ballet students (in the language of today—bunheads) sitting in the orchestra section rushed toward the stage throwing flowers when he took his bow. I felt like we were attending a rock concert. Wendy Whelan, after thirty years with the NYCB, continued to perform for contemporary choreographers and as a solo dancer for two evenings at the Joyce Theater in October 2019. She had already been appointed associate artistic director of NYCB.

This doesn't happen for the corps de ballet, even in our biggest companies, who tend to dance in large groups and are the lowest rank. Most are unknown except to a few balletomanes (regulars) who attend many performances and sit in the first rows. It is difficult to identify most corps members, certainly not when wearing wigs or swan feathers. These are classical or neoclassical ballet dancers. Small company members, often contemporary dancers, perform most often before smaller audiences and are known largely by other dancers and stalwart dance fans. I am on their email lists now, so I learn where they perform. But times are changing, and the less-than-famous often speak out too. Although their pictures are not in the program, photos and often videos of the corps de ballet in large companies and small-company or project-based dancers are available on social media. There you can find a curated self—dancing and doing a variety of activities outside the theater.

Passionate Work is about dancers who didn't become stars. Some decided not to become professionals, and others stayed committed to professional performing using their savvy and hard-won skills to secure a place in the concert dance world in a corps de ballet but rarely made it further, or danced in the world of small companies and projects where taking on extra work is necessary to survive economically. They all remain passionate and continue a meaningful existence.

Readers may wonder how I became interested in such a project. Although I am not a dancer, I have been a hobbyist for many years—modern as a kid (Mary Wigman-modern style through classes with Jan Veen) and in college (more Wigman with Hellmut Gottschild and some Graham).[6] Then I skipped many years while I was a graduate student and assistant professor of sociology—too much to do. When I received tenure, I started to breathe again and looked around for some modern classes. I found none locally, but there was an excellent ballet studio a few blocks away that produced several professional dancers and had adult classes for the hobbyists. Thank you, Jamie Jamieson. I moved to New York, and one of the first things I did was locate a ballet studio that welcomed hobbyists. Cheers to you, Andrei Kulyk and Stephanie Godino for creating a wonderful community of hobbyists. I love watching professionals, but I never wanted to take up space with them in the room. Then came COVID-19 and classes were online, and no one could see my efforts. Complicated center combinations or across the floor were limited as many were dancing in New York City apartments. Gabrielle Lamb and the NYCommunity Ballet teachers—I am forever in your debt. And thank you Jennifer Homans, John Michael Schert, and the Center for Ballet and the Arts at New York University for suggesting I take on a dance project.

To understand the careers of dancers into and out of performing, I spoke with eighty-seven dancers. We talked about their first experiences with dance, their families, their important decisions, their years as professional dancers, and their decisions to stop performing and transition to new work. Most began with intensive ballet training even before they were teens, especially the women. Some exited after high school, others continued dancing in college, and still others tried out for companies, some successfully, without attending college. Others moved in and out of performing. Some made it to major companies, but few made it beyond the corps de ballet of those companies. Many danced in the small company and project market, using their energies to locate and create ways to perform and eat. Dancers make decisions about taking paths that shape their performing careers. Sometimes decisions are made for them by people in control of organizations. Some have more choices than others, not only because of skill and artistry, but because of their bodies and prior decisions about training.

The dancers I spoke with do not represent all, or even most, dancers as I did not include Las Vegas style, tap, folkloric, backup dancers for popular music videos, or hip-hop dancers.[7] With a small number of dancers that is impossible, but I have worked to generate as diverse a sample of concert dancers (not for profit) as possible. Almost all started with a serious commitment to ballet classes, but those who became professionals did many styles of dance from classical or neoclassical ballet to contemporary with pointe shoes, with socks, or barefoot. A few called themselves "experimental" dancers. Some danced in Broadway musicals, but that wasn't their first choice. Some were just starting out, while others had stopped performing long ago. They ranged in age from twenty to people in their eighties. Sixty-three were women and twenty-four were men, reflecting most estimates of the gender balance in dance. When I spoke with them, fourteen had decided not to follow a career in dance, ten were dancing in or had recently left major companies, thirty were creating portfolios, five danced on Broadway, and twenty-eight were pursuing a new occupation after performing. Despite my efforts to designate what they were doing when interviewed (between 2016 and 2019), some changed course several times since then. Collectively, their experiences and the decisions they made are the focus of this book.[8]

I used a process to find these dancers that in sociology we call a "snowball sample." I started in many places: schools and studios of dance, dancers at choreographers' showings at the Center for Ballet and the Arts (CBA) at New York University, dancers I spotted at events around New York City, friends of friends and my students, and participants at Career Transition for Dancers, which helps dancers transition from performing. I asked each dancer to recommend others. Most danced, trained, or retired in New York City, but not all. During the years I worked on this project I attended many performances—from those by the major companies to performances by small groups in Brooklyn and Queens, in lofts and in former factories, in studio spaces, in small theaters that I hadn't known existed, in parks and on sidewalks, in hotel lobbies, in parking lots, and even in rooftop gardens. I also had opportunities to watch choreographers create new dances and rehearse. I often spent time with dancers after performances, when I saw them in class or after rehearsals.

I have given pseudonyms to all the dancers I spoke with and will not refer to the companies with which they danced by name. When I have attended a public performance or am quoting from a public source, I use the real name of the person or company. I refer to companies as "major ballet companies" if they have at least forty dancers and long seasons, and then "major contemporary companies" that tend to be smaller, mostly under twenty dancers, except Alvin Ailey, which has about thirty dancers. The smaller ballet companies I have referred to as "small ballet companies" though some have only slightly fewer than forty dancers and some have national reputations. Many tiny companies, especially of contemporary dancers, dot the landscape of the dance world too. They have shorter seasons, some travel, and many of their dancers perform in projects too. Some project-based companies perform just a few weekends a year. Think of it as a continuum from large to small and classical ballet to barefoot contemporary. The landscape of "companies" keeps evolving. Each state has its own mix, but New York City has the largest number of dancers in the country and is the only city with two large ballet companies with training schools, many smaller contemporary and ballet companies (several with training programs), a conservatory, and several college dance programs.

REAL-TIME REFLECTIONS ON DANCE AND COVID-19

COVID-19 changed much about the dance world and affected me and some of what I had begun to write. The arts community along with most other businesses and organizations moved online in March and April 2020. Many arts organizations showed older films on internet sites, providing hours of viewing for those sheltering in place.

Portfolio dancers went from low income to zero income overnight in March 2020. Some stepped up immediately with dance classes on Zoom for which they were asking five dollars, if you could afford it. I began to take six classes a week. They were serious classes, not for beginners. The community of dancers started to join in from across the country and around the world. They taught from kitchens and living rooms and some danced in bedrooms. Sometimes ten people Zoomed for a class but other times as many as fifty. All worried about flooring and what dancers would have to do to ensure that they had enough space to dance. By the end of March, most teachers had figured out the best place to stand relative to their computers or phones in order to demonstrate, and how to run their music and talk over it, giving the class instructions. In more than one instance, the internet malfunctioned. By the sixth week of sheltering in place, I suspected we would be on Zoom for a while. When rehearsals and performances could recommence was the question. Zoom classes were keeping me sane.

In May and June 2020, I was still taking Zoom classes, up to eight a week, and watching with great interest the videos being created by dancers and dance companies around the world. I particularly liked the Paris Opera Ballet's video of dancers at home, dancing with pets, children, and in great Paris apartments. It made me laugh happily. The Guggenheim's Works & Process series had commissioned short individual dance videos, many filmed with cellphone cameras of dancers alone at home or in city parks. I watched them immediately when a new one arrived in my inbox. I loved the films of ballets released by NYCB, Dance Theatre of Harlem (DTH), and American Ballet Theatre (ABT). And New York City Center's videos of coaching by prominent former dancers were among my favorites along with those coached by Christopher Saunders of the Royal Ballet.

By July and August 2020, everyone was itching to get back into the studio so we could move. I was tired of hitting my toe on the sofa bed on one side and the chair on the other. My desk chair was getting worn from facing the computer screen and use as my barre. I discovered my body couldn't really do eight classes a week.

But the dancers wanted to perform—they really wanted to. Some choreographers were working on Zoom with their dancers, creating and performing in New York City's parks with masks and separated by six feet. I caught Barry Kerollis's Movement Headquarters group in Washington Square Park rehearsing in sneakers and trying out several locations. They estimated how the dance had to change in the different sections of the park.

I also saw Gabrielle Lamb's Pigeonwing Dance in Madison Square

Park performing on her five by eight rug, which she toted around the city on the subway, along with the squishy underflooring she used to save hers and the four dancers' knees and hips as they danced barefoot. They wore matching flip-flops while awaiting turns to perform on the rug. At the end of each solo, they communicated, at a distance and masked, with the next dancer. Lamb used four different music types with the four performances they danced in each site. The music changed the quality of the movements. People stopped, engrossed by the organic movement and the interesting ways the Pigeonwing dancers were able to move their bodies—no jumps, but twists of arms and legs, long-legged extensions, and upside-down stances. Very mobile joints and straight long legs with pointed arched feet were required, as was the ability to improvise.

The audience was varied in each park and performance of the Pigeonwing dancers; two park workers stayed for an entire performance, several older women pushing carriages watched, turning the carriages so that children could see. One father held his son, about three years old, on the low side wall of the circular well (a dry fountain) where they danced. The child looked mesmerized and cried when the dancers ended their performance. Two small girls of about seven or eight tried to move as the dancers did. One had amazing ability to shape her body. Another child escaped her mother's arms and ran to the rug and started dancing. She protested as she was moved away. Several people posted contributions to the Venmo site (the only source of income), and one posted a photo on Instagram before Pigeonwing packed up as it was getting dark. Pigeonwing continued its twice a week rotation through New York City parks until the end of September 2020. But they did not make enough from the Venmo contributions to cover the small fee Gabrielle Lamb (choreographer) paid for the four dancers.

Another project-based contemporary group, Konverjdans, had two creative performances, one on a rooftop (with live music) with a few on-site observers and a live YouTube feed. Earlier, they gave a live performance on Zoom with film, live dancing, and music. It almost felt like being in a real audience with others. Everyone used "chat" to congratulate the dancers. Dancers were beginning to figure out things that they could do with film that they couldn't do in a live performance, such as looking as though they are walking on the wall of a room. Several

ABT dancers, some from the corps, shot short films with stories, as well as dancing. College dance programs were trying to adapt, and choreographers not only had to choreograph for them on Zoom but teach the students how to film themselves. Kaatsbaan, an estate in upstate New York, had weekend performances outdoors: new works, dancers from different groups, and dances created by and for people quarantining together. It was a beautiful evening for those lucky enough to snag one of the fifty seats.

By winter 2020-21, the sadness was turning into nervousness as fundraising took on a pleading tone. Companies, large and small, sought contributions to enable them to do new films of bits of the *Nutcracker.* Some had versions from past years. Dance Theatre of Harlem created some scenes using Duke Ellington and Billy Strayhorn's version of Tchaikovsky. The jazz score and choreography lifted my spirits.

Winter to spring of 2021 I would describe as desperation. Some dancers had returned to New York City, and I saw fewer in classes. Claudia Schreier created a wonderful dance for the Miami City Ballet and another for Dance Theatre of Harlem on Zoom. The big companies were producing work for film, some of which I really enjoyed. But they still weren't live performances. Some studios had a few masked students in class and the rest on Zoom. Several companies were dancing upstate with strict protocols. "Ballet bubble" was a new concept that allowed them to work together safely.

In summer 2021, we had more live performances outdoors! Predicting rain became an important skill. Gabrielle Lamb's Pigeonwing dancers performed *The Carpet Series* in twenty-nine locations around the city. In one venue, they performed in an art center's parking lot in Long Island City. They danced on a raised platform between two shipping containers, which served as dressing rooms. A 1950s pickup truck was pulled up to the side of the stage in front of one shipping container. The violinist played Bach while standing on the back of the truck. The evening was totally cool. The rug fit nicely on the stage. Typically, in parks, when the dancers finished their sections, they moved to the side, blending in with the audience. Here, they could not and had to stand on the side of the raised stage, fully exposed. They looked a bit uncomfortable. The raised stage required some new choreography.

In October 2021 we had seasons for the vaccinated and masked! You could feel the energy of the dancers and audiences. But by December 2021, Broadway shows were closing, and some *Nutcracker* performances were canceled.

Although COVID-19 has petered out as central to our health concerns, the audiences have been slow to return, though our hobbyist classes are maskless and seem full. The Pigeonwing dancers are performing on a larger rug outdoors around the city for the third and fourth summer. Many of the dancers shouldered through the long period of no performances and returned to New York as the companies tried cautiously to restart classes and performances. Others retired and started working toward new careers. Many of the performance arts are still suffering from less funding and lower attendance as of this writing.

I would like to thank my sociology friends who have read sections of this manuscript; Lynn Chancer, Dan Cornfield, Paul DiMaggio, Kathleen Gerson, Lynne Haney, Ann Morning, Dmitri Shalin, Michaela Soyer, and Iddo Tavory. Lynn Garafola, chair of the Columbia University seminar "Studies in Dance," invited me to attend, and I have learned much about dance from the interesting and knowledgeable participants. Martha Coe provided useful comments on the manuscript as did Marie Peterson, a former honors student at New York University. My nieces—Sarah (special collections librarian) and Rachel (archeologist)—frequently received entire rundowns of what I was learning about dance and dancers and never complained, as they too are dance enthusiasts and hobbyists. My dance hobbyist buddies—Gigi Abrantes, Ava Dawson, Vanessa Dimapilis, Hirono Ota, and Beverly Winikoff—are owed a special thanks along with our ballet teacher, Stephanie Godino. Marcela Maxfield and her team at Stanford University Press, especially my copy editor Jennifer Gordon, have made excellent suggestions as they shepherd this manuscript through the publication process. Most important are the many dancers with whom I spoke who shared their stories.

PASSIONATE WORK

INTRODUCTION

THE CONCERT DANCE WORLD

Having a passion and turning it into a career involves complex, diffi-cult work and processes, and only some are able over time to continue to nurture that passion and successfully sustain it. Following a passion presents people with many challenges, some beneficial and others det-rimental. This doesn't develop without the involvement of institutions, such as schools and places of employment, and families, teachers, and employers who actively work to sustain those careers and also serve as gatekeepers to exclude. Concert dancers—whether ballet, modern, or contemporary—begin with early training like gymnasts, football players, or musicians. Like professional athletes, dancers require a co-operative body. Dancers also have body size requirements along with movement abilities, understanding of music, and ability to communi-cate using the body. Assessments of dancers' bodies begin early on and continue until it is time for professionals to retire from performing.

The concert dance world—created by dancers, choreographers, artis-tic directors, musicians, and many others—has evolved and continues to do so. Howard Becker in *Art Worlds* describes these worlds as porous, with actors making decisions, and people coordinating their activities, sometimes fighting and other times cooperating without question.[1] What is danced (style and content), by whom, who leads the groups, and who pays varies with the historical and national context and has evolved with changes in gender, racial, educational, and work conventions. People who dance, choreograph, and run companies also incorporate, transform, and counter what is going on in other social worlds.

The seventeenth-century French king, Louis XIV, valorized aristocratic demeanor and magnified royal opulence and absolute power that rightfully belonged to the king; ballet's highest goal was "to elevate the nobility to serve the king."[2] Louis XIV also created the Académie Royale de Danse and codified ballet steps. Dance performances at the time served to entertain members of the court, and dancers included Louis XIV and court members. The guild of musicians and dancers challenged the king, claiming he was removing music from dance, which "robbed it of all meaning."[3] As the power of the king ebbed at the beginning of the eighteenth century, what became the Paris Opera Ballet produced shows in theaters with professional dancers who were often from poor families looking for employment. The professional dancers, especially the corps de ballet, were inadequately paid and were expected to show deference and cater to whims of wealthy patrons who funded dance performances and sometimes the clothing and housing of the women dancers. One can imagine that the court personnel when they retired received a royal reward, but that the professional women dancers could only hope for continuing support (housing, clothing, and food) from the men who frequented the ballet.[4] Various versions of ballet steps developed in the nineteenth and early twentieth century associated with different national schools: Agrippina Vaganova in Russia developed her system built on an amalgamation of Russian, Italian, and French styles; Enrico Cecchetti was one of several pedagogues in Italy; and August Bournonville consolidated several national styles in Denmark. Although the styles were different, trained dancers could, and did, take class anywhere.[5] In the nineteenth century, ballets with romantic stories were popular, and dancers and choreographers traveled around Europe and Russia. One of the best-known choreographers, Marius Petipa, was French but gained his fame in Russia.

By the twentieth century, Diaghilev's Ballets Russes excited Europe with its innovative movement, stories, and collaborations with well-known composers and artists. Nijinsky, already a renowned dancer, scandalized Europe with his *Afternoon of a Faun*, regarded as a sexually explicit dance.[6] But, Lynn Garafola explored why critics and audiences failed to give his sister, La Nijinska (1891–1972), the recognition and accolades for her choreography and dancing while her brother's choreography and performances made him famous. Gender mattered for leading companies and choreography.

Concert dance in the United States developed differently; locally grown civic ballet companies were initiated by women after modern dance was firmly established. In the United States, the modern dance form developed in the beginning of the twentieth century, also by women. Gender was more complicated in the United States where civic ballet companies often had women founders, directors, or choreographers, in contrast to ballet in Europe, where artistic directors and choreographers were men. The new modern dance had grounded movements rather than the upward thrust of ballet, and choreographers rejected pointe shoes and ballet positions. Each modern dancer developed her own technique, company, and school. But Isadora Duncan (1877-1927) left the United States at the age of twenty-two for Europe and Russia, creating her new dance technique of bare feet and natural movement.

Although many of the pioneers who started modern dance companies were women—such as Martha Graham (1894-1991),[7] Ruth St. Denis (1879-1968),[8] Doris Humphrey (1895-1958),[9] Helen Tamiris (1902-1966),[10] and Katherine Dunham (1909-2006)[11]—they were often followed by men as artistic directors and choreographers.[12] Each developed her own style of movement and subjects for their dances—for example, from the contraction and release and Greek myths of Martha Graham to the Afrocentric movements and dances raising issues related to race of Katherine Dunham. With the exception of pioneering modern dancers and a few hardy women on the commercial stage, women choreographers were marginalized, especially in the ballet world.[13]

Ballet largely arrived in the United States from Europe and Russia at the beginning of the twentieth century as small groups of European and Russian ballet dancers came, sometimes in search of adventure and more often fleeing the disruption that followed the Russian Revolution.[14] Some of these dancers set up ballet studios in major cities. George Balanchine, a Russian who spent nearly a decade working in western Europe, was brought to the United States by Lincoln Kirstein in 1933. They started a ballet school in 1934 and then created the New York City Ballet (1948) with Balanchine's unique ballet technique and choreographic vision.[15] Women did officially, nevertheless, start several ballet companies that became the large companies of today: Lucia Chase (American Ballet Theatre), E. Virginia Williams (Boston Ballet), and Barbara Weisberger (Philadelphia Ballet); these women were replaced by men as artistic directors. Despite the changing position of women in the 1970s, ballet company artistic directors were largely men until the second decade of the twenty-first century.

Who dances professionally and what happens after performing ends has evolved with the changes in conventions. In the twenty-first century in the United States, many middle-class youth attend college at eighteen, women are more often employed than in the past,[16] young people are encouraged to seek "passionate or meaningful work,"[17] and freelance/contract work involves a larger percentage of people employed.[18] Workers are more likely to change jobs or to work on contract while holding onto their occupational identities rather than company identities. Others change type of work. Issues concerning the underrepresentation of traditionally excluded groups in many lines of work and sexual misconduct have been foregrounded by Black Lives Matter (BLM) and #MeToo. Long before BLM, Misty Copeland, principal dancer with American Ballet Theatre, had done much to promote the hiring of Black dancers, and she is known beyond the dance community for her efforts. These changes have influenced dancers' perceived options, choices, and trajectories. In the twentieth century, women dancers, upon retirement, often married men with steady jobs and then had children, a common path throughout the 1970s; finally, in the second decade of the twenty-first century, women began to take more leadership positions in the dance world. Men struggled more if they had to support a family in the twentieth century, but they had more access than women to work as artistic directors, choreographers, and other staff positions of companies upon the end of a performing career. And acknowledgment of some of the problematic sexual behavior in companies did not occur until the second decade of the twenty-first century.

While large ballet companies have been slow to become more racially inclusive, small and project-based companies with more contemporary styles often choreograph stories about social and political issues. These tend to be more inclusive, and some are directed by persons of color, such as, Kyle Abraham's A.I.M. Company, Alonzo King LINES Ballet, Dance Theatre of Harlem, and Ballet Hispánico. They face challenges of their own with fewer than twenty dancers, small staffs, and little funding. Companies with about eight to twelve performers such as the L.A. Project, BodyTraffic, Whim W'him, Complexions, Hubbard Street Dance, and BalletX are directed by people known for their efforts to hire choreographers with diverse ethno-racial backgrounds who challenge a more diverse group of dancers to experiment with fresh dance forms and ideas. Mark Morris Dance Company has a diverse group of dancers, and older companies, such as Martha Graham Dance Company and Paul Taylor Company, now hire choreographers who can add to the existing body of their namesakes' works. These companies have reasonable-length seasons, but most of the small companies have shorter seasons, are run by their choreographer, and have fewer resources to diversify their offerings, which make it difficult to employ dancers on a long-term basis. Many companies are project based and have performances irregularly.

What gets danced in smaller companies also reflects greater racial, ethnic, and gender diversity. Groups such as Alvin Ailey American Dance Theater (about thirty dancers), Ballet Hispánico, and Dance Theatre of Harlem produce evenings of performances that deal with racial and ethnic issues and conflicts. Other smaller, often project-based, groups offer a great variety of performances. Tabula Rasa Dance Theater choreographed an exciting and heartbreaking evening performance about imprisonment. Christopher Williams explored gender in several dances. Both Tabula Rasa and Christopher Williams's projects were performed at New York Live Arts (NYLA) directed by the choreographer Bill T. Jones co-founder of the Bill T. Jones/Arnie Zane Dance Company. Kyle Abraham has created many dances both for his company (A.I.M.) and others on Black experience and racial issues. His *Runaway* for NYCB with Taylor Stanley, principal dancer, brought out much in that dancer that performing Balanchine had not. Small companies are even exploring today's issues such as the environment. COVID-19 encouraged more dances critical of the social world and embraced difference by some of the large ballet companies. This is a very abbreviated list of subjects, styles, and companies.

Different dance styles are now included in dance concerts[19]—styles that do not involve traditional training.[20] "Street dance" has begun to be incorporated in traditional theaters and on stages. Rennie Harris brought in a more diverse audience to the Joyce Theater in New York

City than is typical for his *Rome & Jewels,* an adaptation of *Romeo and Juliet,* performed by his group of hip-hop dancers in February 2023. Many of his dancers are not trained in standard ballet or modern dance classes but in places where street dancers hang out and compete. Several current directors of dance festivals have brought new styles of dance and dancers into the concert world. Major festival directors—such as Damian Woetzel, former principal dancer for the New York City Ballet and president of Juilliard—brings together different groups, creates new ones, and integrates several styles of movement: tap, jookin, and ballet; dancers often dance them all in one dance for Vail Summer Dance. Arlene Shuler—a former Joffrey Ballet dancer, lawyer, and president of City Center (retired 2023)—organizes companies of a variety of dance styles, including tap, folk, and street dance,[21] along with major ballet and contemporary dancers in "Fall for Dance" programs. These performances bring in a more diverse and very enthusiastic audience; the price was typically about twenty dollars a ticket.

The above are major ventures. Smaller ventures also bring together a diversity of groups, not generally seen as concert dance, such as Jonathan Hollander, the creator of the Battery Dance Festival that is performed on a stage next to the Hudson River with many international groups, some of which are closer to the countries' traditional dances. The Hudson River Dance Festival, organized by the Joyce Theater Foundation, in June 2023 included Ayodele Casel (creative tap), The Missing Element (beatbox and street dance), Complexions Contemporary Ballet, and Paul Taylor (modern). The diverse large audience stayed through one rain break, but after the Paul Taylor Company took the stage, another downpour canceled the performance. No one can dance on a slippery wet stage. The Missing Element was one of the most innovative and exciting performances I have seen recently.[22]

Even what a location *is* for concert dance is evolving. A summer convention of free outdoor concert performances on stages, open to more diverse groups and dancers, expanded to performances outdoors without stages during the pandemic. Several small companies took to the streets, parks, and waters' edge to perform as did the dancers who made short films for the Guggenheim's Works & Process series. Some groups continued to perform in a variety of public spaces after the theaters reopened. Dancers also perform on rooftops, at the opening of nightclubs, and in churches. In sum, concert dance is porous and changing. It has incorporated street styles, street dancers, and unconventional spaces.

One element that makes dancing different from painting or writing, but similar to acting, is that a dance performance is typically collective. While painters need gallerists and reviewers and writers require editors and publishers, most performances require many people with different skills—many more than just several dancers and choreographers are needed even to put on a small performance.

The need for cooperation of not only the dancers onstage but the behind the scenes workers is revealed during dress rehearsals. Sometimes conflicts arise. A principal dancer stopped and stamped her foot. Her leg, she said, kept getting caught in the folds of her new tutu. The costumer would have to make changes before her performance the next evening. On other occasions, the lighting was too dark or the spotlight didn't follow the dancers. It needed adjustments. Cinderella's coach failed to move on cue, and stage crew members dressed in black rushed to solve that problem. Sometimes the orchestra and dancers had different ideas about the speed of the music. One dancer stopped and said loudly that the music was too fast. During one dress rehearsal, the orchestra, following union rules of time between rehearsal and performance, walked out of the pit, and stagehands seamlessly rolled a piano onstage along with the pianist who picked right up so the rehearsal with the dancers could proceed.

Costumes can contribute to the performance, but many small groups can afford only basic clothing such as stretch jeans. When the costume team of Reid Bartelme and Harriet Jung designed costumes for two freelance choreographers for a Guggenheim Works & Process performance, it revealed much about the relationship between costumes and dance; dancers in one section of *Daphnis et Chloé*, choreographed by Christopher Williams to the music of Ravel, had beautiful, draped fabric attached at the waist that made turns look faster, making the dance more fluid. The second piece involved a dance created for the costumes; stretchy fabric encased the dancers, as is the dancer in Martha Graham's *Lamentation*. Netta Yerushalmy choreographed the work; here the dancers shed their covers revealing silkscreened leotards—caterpillars turned into butterflies, perhaps, with the freedom to move in any direction. As a visual art, costumes are important.

Additionally, someone needs to write the description of the dance for the program, build the set, change the scenery between acts, rent the theater (contracts), raise the money, attach the hair pieces or wigs, promote the performance, make travel arrangements, sell tickets, and get the patrons to their seats. Others need to ensure the company members' bodies are ready to perform: lead daily class, rehearse the dances, massage the aches, and examine and work with injuries. In small companies many of these tasks are done by the same person or they don't get done. Most groups do not have specialized people to do much of this work.

What is danced, *how* people dance, *where* people perform, and *who* performs changes, but in all periods, significant backstage workers and musicians up front are part of the process of creating a performance for an audience. To develop people who perform requires dance schools and parents to take kids to classes and pay for them.

PASSION, REWARDS, AND CHALLENGES: THE LABOR OF DANCE CAREERS

How do you turn passion for dance into a career? How do teachers and parents, then artistic directors, choreographers, and ballet masters, work to support or undermine a career? Although performances are collaborative, relying on a complex series of actors and materials, they importantly rely on the work of individual dancers. How do dancers turn passion into a career?

Dance has always been precarious labor.[23] There are too many dancers, artists in general, for the paid work available. Between 1970 and 2000 the numbers of dancers increased even faster than the number of paid positions as it did in much of the art world. Dance in the United States is financially precarious and dependent not only on paying audiences, but both public and largely private funding.[24] Companies, large and small, rarely have enough money to pay dancers for an entire year; most have short seasons. So how do young people who worked so hard to develop their bodies and selves for dance make professional careers in dance? How then do they transition to something else when they leave performing? Why, given these circumstances, would people try to make professional careers in the arts and dance, in particular?

Pierre-Michel Menger, a sociologist, identified three possible rationales for making arts careers: passionate commitment to the arts; willingness to take risks given the uncertainty of finding work; and value placed on social rewards apart from financial gains.[25] My findings from the dance world suggest that these rationales also apply but with added nuance. First, especially in the dance world, I found that what many might see in situations as risks, dancers see as challenges—they don't calculate the pros and cons of choices as much as ask "how can I do that?" Second, I posit that all three rationales are necessary to sustain a dance career. When one weakens—often signaled by the body, outside interests, or artistic directors—they begin to think of leaving performing.

Passion, social and emotional rewards, and the ability to deal with risks as challenges influence all the arts. One additional element is important. Dance, like most acting, opera, and music, is learned and performed with others, typically in some form of organization. In different organizations the lives of the dancers, the performances, and the audiences who see them are distinctive, and the dancers have different identity, body, economic, and social challenges. Therefore, to understand dancers' work lives and their transitions, I focused on the types of organizations where they train and then labor—in which their lives are embedded—the challenges they faced, the precarity of their labor, the shifting rewards, the maintenance of their passions, and their understandings and experiences of their evolving lives. So I looked at their lives as a process, a career approach. How did they develop and change? How did they talk about making the many decisions, step by step in their careers? What did they say about their "self-fulfillment" and creativity? I was interested in their narratives of their experiences: how did they see their training, the gatekeepers, their peers, and their decisions about their lives? Their perspectives were expressed in their interviews.

Passion

First, though many talk about art as a passion, dance is work too.[26] It is very meaningful, but it is work. One way to look at work, which is the focus of many sociological studies, is as alienated labor. Artists may not be seen as "working" because they are intent on following their passions and maintaining control of their labor.

Eliot Freidson argues, "Being freely chosen, they [arts] can be part of the worker's nature and allow self-fulfillment."[27] Nevertheless, "freely chosen" seems to imply that it came out of nowhere, but people develop passions for and commitment to activities, shaped in relationships and institutions. Even those who work in the dirtiest of jobs often enjoy some aspect of the work, and we also know that artists suffer in their work and have only some control over their own labor and its products; they experience some alienation despite passion for their art.[28] How do we uncover what is going on? While passion can continue throughout a career and be expressed in performance, can it also blind dancers to the poor behavior of others in some organizations?

Today, many young people don't envision jobs with bureaucratic routines and careers in large corporations, instead seeking something more exciting and intrinsically rewarding. This is what Angela McRobbie calls "passionate work," whether religious leaders, doctors, lawyers, professors, or artists.[29] Work/passion is a false dichotomy as it presupposes an either/or binary.

Passion may be partially a cultural schema today, as Erin Cech argues: a sense of moral, cognitive, and emotional connection that many young people are told they should use to find employment.[30] For dancers, passion also involves their bodies. They talk about falling in love with how movement feels "in their bodies" and dance movements go "in their bodies." Runners and other athletes talk about "runner's high." I suspect that this is similar. Also, when people are doing something they love from the time they are very young, forgoing activities and relationships for it and with teachers who continuously demand more and parents who support or work to deter it, dance becomes an activity that forms the core of their identity.[31] But at each life stage, passion is expressed differently and is differently shaped by self, body, and responses of others.

Either viewing work as alienated labor or passion as non-work fails to acknowledge that work, even art, especially performance art, takes place in both training and performance organizations.[32] Some are more formal, including schools for learning dance and companies for dancing with almost full-time employment; others are at the other end of formality, such as small project-based groups thriving in the niches of the dance world with performances a few times a year. They are temporary organizations.[33] All have gatekeepers who sift through the applicants. All arts are to some extent collective and require training, cooperation, and organizations.

Those who become professional dancers have varied experiences in big and tiny companies.[34] The hierarchy, dance styles, repertories, contracts, number of performances, and relationships among people vary. It should not be surprising that dancers, all "passionate" about performing, have different experiences. There are differences in control over their labor (creating bodies and choreographing) and its products (performance) between working as corps members in a large company and as portfolio workers. Different companies, choreographers, and dance styles allow different expressions of uniqueness and self-fulfillment.

Rewards

As Menger acknowledges, the financial rewards are few. Dancers seek other rewards. Although the precarity of dance labor affects all dancers, it is different in large companies and among portfolio workers.[35] What academics mean by "precarity" varies, but sociologists around the world argue that employment is increasingly precarious: "uncertain, unpredictable, and risky from the point of view of workers and in which employees bear the risks of work (as opposed to businesses or the government) and receive limited social benefits and statutory protections."[36] The funding for the arts in the United States is limited, and much depends on individual or corporate giving and bringing in a large audience. Even the few "full-time" positions are rarely fifty-two weeks a year, and contracts are only for a year, even for the unionized companies. These contracts are for the royalty of dancers. Most dance in smaller companies with lower salaries (or hourly rates) and are offered at most twenty-six weeks of work with many more contracted for perhaps only a few weekends. Hence, multiple companies and jobs in other lines of work are essential: a work portfolio.[37] Precarity has always been the norm for dancers: like many physically intense jobs, dance is hard on the body, and injuries or just aging bodies mean the end of a performing career; then people need a new source of income. But how do they experience precarity and what allows them to manage?

Thus, except for a handful of jet-setting principal dancers from around the world, financial rewards are limited.[38] Most dancers seek other rewards such as friendships, community, and the emotional and social rewards from performing before an audience. I am sure the dancers could hear the audience excitement expressed during the first performances in fall 2021 after the pandemic. The rewards of working with a big company, but in the corps with all the decision making in the hands of the artistic director, are different from dancing in small venues with small audiences whom dancers can see and feel and also where it is possible to experiment, create, and diversify. For many, the rewards change over the course of a career as a performer, and they do begin to disappear with an aging body.

Challenges

Menger's third rationale—the uncertainty of "making it"—means artists need to assess the risks they take of not making a success as a professional. Dancers ask, "How do I do that?" A career approach allows one to see how dancers learn to deal with challenges from an early age, which better expresses how dancers learn to understand, talk about, and respond to difficult tasks, relationships, or situations. Dancers tend to see most difficult or dangerous situations—such as training in Russia at sixteen, or flying into the arms of another dancer, or auditioning continuously—as challenges and as exciting.

Challenges are different for professionals who have almost full-time work or who have to put together portfolios. What different types of strategies do they use to manage and protect identities? Dancers talk about preparing to confront challenges—physical, social, psychological, or financial. Growing up, they learn strategies that ready them for the challenges ahead. Nevertheless, at some point and under particular conditions, challenges do become risks, sometimes even before their careers take off.

Social scientists argue that the twenty-first century shows major shifts in labor markets and careers—from bounded careers evolving in a single organization, up a hierarchical ladder to fluid, boundaryless careers of continual unproblematic worksite and organization changes.[39] Others, however, view the work shifts as "ruptured or fragmented careers," with disappearing jobs requiring major transformations of self and skills. "Boundaryless" is really too blunt a metaphor to understand current career shapes and transformations.[40]

By examining the challenges faced by dancers in the different labor markets of "making it" in the company and portfolio worlds, and then transitioning to new occupations, we can see the different types of boundaries that are created or crossed by self and others. How do dancers see these boundary challenges both in their careers as performers and when they need to find different work after their performing careers end? This study considers the major dimensions of a career in a performing art—passion, challenge, rewards—to be institutionally grounded and socially constructed. It documents how these dimensions manifest themselves as narratives at each stage in a dancer's life and what identity work the dancer engages in to achieve the sense of biographical continuity in the world often marked by discontinuity and barriers created by gatekeepers. How do dancers make sense of their experiences and shape their identities?

CHAPTER OUTLINE

Chapter 1, "A *Nutcracker* Lens: Passion and Precarious Labor," looks at the *Nutcracker*'s importance both as an inspiration to dance, a beginning expression of passion, and a peak into the world of professional performance for the young dancers who perform it. It is also a financial vehicle for companies, schools, and professional dancers. *Nutcracker* performances have increased exponentially in the last fifty years with the growth in the number of training schools, ballet students, and ballet and contemporary companies. It contributes to that growth too. These performances fill the coffers of companies large and small, as well as the dance schools with companies of their older students. Professional dancers "guest" with companies and schools to add to their income and dance roles they might not otherwise.

Chapter 2, "Learning the Practice of Ballet: Body and Self," asks about the challenges that aspirational dancers face as young people with a passion for dance. Passion, as described later by dancers, seems to appear in their first classes, but, with increasing challenges created by dance teachers, families, their bodies, peers, and academic schools, young people develop dedication, persistence, and learning so they can compete gracefully, sustain their passion over time, and deal with adversity. They also learn to defer to teachers. Parents play a critical role in shaping dancers' ambitions by carting them to classes and rehearsals often six days a week, paying for classes and pointe shoes, and requiring balance between dance and academic education. It is somewhat different for men. With the shortage of males, they are often given more social leeway by dance teachers and receive scholarships, but they are often teased by academic classmates. All young dancers must balance the competing demands of fitting into the world of everyday life and sculpting themselves into dancing bodies. Competition for plum parts and prestigious summer training programs looms large. The reward system especially of performance must keep pace with the dancers' progress, propping up their artistic passion and feeding ambition. Absent parental and institutional support, ample rewards, and a body for dance, other interests take over, and the aspiring performer's dance career comes to an end before taking off for most who start to dance.

Chapter 3, "Career Decision Challenges: Aspirations and a Sticky Self," focuses on critical decisions made by young people at fifteen or sixteen, their parents, and, especially, the gatekeepers of the major schools—either to train away from home at a major training center or to continue at home. By eighteen, some decide to try out for companies; some make it and many don't. Others decide to attend college with a dance major or a conservatory. A third group attends college without a dance major. But young people don't always stick with their first decisions. How they make these decisions and with whom is the focus of this chapter. For those who remain in the field, passion involves increasing dedication, dealing with increased competition, the development of collaboration, and, especially for those in college and conservatory programs, many of which emphasize contemporary dance, the challenge of new body work. For those who leave their aspirations behind, the challenge is to reconcile their sticky dancing self with the realities awaiting them in the world less touched by artistic sensibilities.

Chapter 4, "Companies: Corporate Bodies/Human Bodies," examines the lives of those chosen by gatekeepers to join the few companies that are financially secure enough to have almost full-time work with one-year contracts, but they are kept in the corps. In a world where dancers are primed for hard work and have aspired for the ideal since they were young, the dim prospects for promotion are a constant reminder about the organizational hierarchy and the limits of one's ambition. Ballet companies are "greedy institutions" that need to ensure loyalty just as they devour the lives of their subjects.[41] The "company as family" trope reflects the camaraderie, intimacy, and friendship across ranks, but it doesn't obviate the artistic director's strict control and discipline inside ballet institutions. The family rhetoric sometimes blinds dancers to the power that the artistic director wields over their assignments and long-term prospects with the company. But companies need to fill soloist roles, and that offers opportunities for corps dancers to reap greater rewards as artists, to obtain self-fulfillment and some acclaim. Corps members work to figure out how to deal with their failures to gain promotion. What helps performers to stem disappointment in such situations is the performance collaboration, staying with the flow, and the sense that everyone con-tributed to artistic success.[42] With little control over creative decisions and scarce opportunities for individual expression, corps members work hard to create self-identities consistent with their aspirations.

To what extent does the portfolio market liberate dancers to be "true artists" while navigating precarity? Chapter 5, "Portfolios: Pre-carious Work and Creative Labor," argues that dance portfolio building is different from many other types of freelancing, insofar as it does not permit working from home and offers limited control over schedules. While liberating dancers from rigid performance schedules and stale dance routines, the precarious work environment forces these dancers to be constantly in search of new creative opportunities. As a collective art, dance requires precise scheduling, and, for most, some periods of too much work and others of little or none. They, along with many art-ists, need to shore up their income with extraneous engagements that help pay the bills and provide the necessities—something software engi-neers or editors are less likely to be forced to do. They are on their own to keep up with diverse dance idioms, while working on projects of their own in search of self-expression. Some turn themselves into cultural entrepreneurs, creating their own projects. Keeping a side job such as teaching, catering, or babysitting leaves a mark on the dancer's self, and it requires identity work to keep the performer's core passion alive by creating boundaries to separate financial and passionate work.

All dance performing careers come to an end, typically between the ages of thirty and forty, long before the conventional retirement age. Chapter 6, "Distancing from the Performing Self," focuses on how per-forming careers end and the challenges to adapt the self and develop new skills and relationships. The lack of rewards or of new challenges, injured bodies, the prodding of artistic directors, and new potential passions all push and pull them toward exit. The decision to bow out is different for portfolio dancers, who can slow down and often have college degrees, than it is for performers in major dance companies who are either in or out, have little experience of side employment and entrepreneurial activity, and, until recently, little college education. Most have difficulties during the transition; it is a process. Having the luxury of a liminal period of betwixt and between—school, therapy, or an apprenticeship—makes the process easier and encourages the development of new skills and styles of interaction, which will be needed as they ready themselves for new career stages. Others must do it on their own.

Today many need to find new types of work as industries decline, job markets change, and even accomplished professionals may find themselves unemployable after age forty. In Chapter 7, "New Work: New Identities and Adapted Self," two perspectives are relevant for our project in this respect: one that frames professional careers as boundaryless, fluid, and occasioning transitions to new worksites and occupational pursuits; the other conceptualizing careers as subject to ruptures or fragmentation, leaving workers in a state of shock and perpetual adaptation. To unpack this point, I single out three work options available to dancers transitioning from performing: (1) capitalizing on their bodily skills, (2) honing their artistic sensibilities, and (3) utilizing their analytical abilities. I argue that in the course of their careers, dancers form life skills and develop habits that help them navigate the post-dance challenges. Boundaries between performing dancer and dance teacher appear to be permeable and fluid; those boundaries between being a dancer and being a lawyer appear to be more significant. But all dancers face challenges; they need not only new work skills and behaviors, but new types of relationships with others, whether becoming doctors or Pilates instructors. This chapter explores what habits get in the way as well as what habits they are surprised to find useful and what connections they can make with their dancing past. Challenges vary somewhat among the types of work.[43] But the habits of persistence, dedication, challenge, and collaboration to support their passion serve them well; the performing self recedes in importance but remains in the body and rarely disappears.

CHAPTER ONE

A *NUTCRACKER* LENS

Passion and Precarious Labor

The *Nutcracker*'s first performance was at the Mariinsky Theatre in St. Petersburg on December 18, 1892. Its first full-length U.S. production was by the San Francisco Ballet in 1944. But it was George Balanchine's version for the New York City Ballet in 1954, based on his recollections of performing it as a child in Russia, that made it a holiday ritual.

A quick internet search for *Nutcracker* performances in 2017 yielded a list of at least 300 different productions in the United States.[1] The search results included New York City Ballet's major production, smaller ballet companies such as the Pittsburgh Ballet or the more contemporary Aspen Santa Fe Ballet,[2] and local groups and schools that work hard to produce several performances. Some small companies tour their region such as the Eugene Ballet Company (Oregon), enabling more people to see live productions.

Let's start with the puzzle. Why are there so many *Nutcracker* productions and what does this proliferation of performances suggest about the world of dance? I propose that there are multiple reasons *Nutcracker* is the best-known and watched ballet in the United States, likely because the audiences had children or friends' children dancing in it, they danced in it, or they wanted a child to see that sparkly fantasy world during the winter holidays. *Nutcracker* shows bring in audiences. It is a way for children to fall in love with dance and learn performing; for professional dancers, it often inspired their careers as dancers, and for a few dancers retired from performing, it is a way to stay involved by dancing the adult roles. It exposes the labor of love.

Few dancers or dance institutions are motivated largely by profits. Watching and performing in the *Nutcracker* is glamorous, creating a source of wonder and excitement, and, for young people, it allows a glimpse into the world of dance. What would December holidays be without the *Nutcracker* and what would it be without the large Christmas tree? Gia Kourlas wrote in the *New York Times*, "And as for that glorious tree? It weighs one ton and grows from 12 to 40 feet. . . . The ballet, he (Balanchine) insisted, *was* the tree."[3] Some enjoy the delicacy of "snow" with snowflakes fluttering down or perhaps the more exotic Tea (Chinese) or Coffee (Arabian) variations that are now being challenged for their use of stereotypical movements and costumes. There is something for everyone including a ferocious battle scene between the soldiers and mice (or rats in some productions) and Tchaikovsky's enchanting music. For some families, it means watching their offspring wobbling just a bit in their first performance on pointe or playing a soldier. Jennifer Fisher writes in *Nutcracker Nation*, "The dual personality of *The Nutcracker* surfaced again and again—it was elite but accessible, serious but fun, decorative but meaningful."[4]

The other part of the answer is that the *Nutcracker* is intimately linked to the finances of companies and schools that produce them and to the professional dancers, who as guest artists use it to make ends meet. They are paid to perform the major roles in smaller productions and schools. *The Nutcracker* provides a lens to examine diverse issues: the financial health and proliferation of companies; the growth of project performances and numbers of performers; the growth in the number of schools and colleges where dancers are trained and former performers teach and produce *Nutcrackers*; and work for company members, portfolio dancers, and retired performers. The increase in *Nutcracker* performances contributes to the creation of the labor market for dancers and to the experience of youth being swept away by dance, auditions, rehearsals, and the desire to dance professionally. Without the proliferation of dance schools and companies, there would be fewer productions, students, professional dancers, and jobs. It is the expansion of the

Nutcracker that allows many companies, schools, and dancers to survive economically and contributes to the creation of the (over)supply of professional dancers. These issues may sound pedantic regarding an art that can be transporting both for dancers in performance and for the audience watching them, but dancers need to be trained, and as artists they require artistic nourishment, and also food, medical care, and shelter. *Nutcracker* contributes to the precarity of dance labor by creating a significant supply of dancers, but it also mitigates the precarity by creating work.

NUTCRACKER INSTITUTIONS: COMPANIES AND SCHOOLS

American ballet companies are rather new; some modern companies, still in existence, such as Martha Graham Dance Company (1926), José Limón Dance Company (1946), Paul Taylor Dance Company (1954), and Alvin Ailey (1958) predate many large ballet companies that still perform. Most of the largest companies today were local civic ballets before the "official" dates found on their websites that are provided here. Of the largest ballet companies today, only the San Francisco Ballet founded in 1933 and American Ballet Theatre founded in 1939 precede the New York City Ballet in 1948: Boston Ballet (1963), Pennsylvania Ballet (1963, renamed Philadelphia Ballet), and Ballet West (1963).[5] These companies—along with the Joffrey Ballet (1965), Houston Ballet (1969), Pacific Northwest Ballet (1972), and Miami City Ballet (1985)—are the only ballet companies with at least forty dancers, expenses greater than $15 million in 2013, and contracts that generally promise about forty weeks of work for their dancers. Most other ballet and contemporary companies employ their dancers for fewer weeks and tend to have fewer than forty dancers. Major contemporary and modern companies such as Ballet Hispánico, BalletX, Complexions, L.A. Project, Martha Graham, Mark Morris, and Paul Taylor have twenty or fewer dancers. Alvin Ailey has about thirty dancers.

A few of the smaller ballet companies developed before or at the same time as today's largest companies, for instance Atlanta Ballet, Kansas City Ballet, Ballet Austin, Pittsburgh Ballet, Milwaukee Ballet, and Dance Theatre of Harlem. These smaller companies have expenses that range from $5 million to under $15 million. Many companies are much smaller and have shorter seasons and lower budgets. Without companies and their dancers to spread the interest in *Nutcracker*, fewer would be performed and fewer dancers would have the experience of dancing in *Nutcracker*. The growth of U.S. companies and schools accelerated in the second half of the twentieth century, and the increase of professional dancers slowed nationally only in the 1990s.[6]

Nutcracker productions are diverse in their storytelling and styles of dance, depending on the late twentieth-century expansion of schools and companies. Each company needs funding to survive, and each has its own style of *Nutcracker*. Even among ballet dancers in large companies, some studied Balanchine's neoclassical style and others are trained in Vaganova or Cecchetti styles (classical).[7] Today many dancers consider themselves contemporary, especially portfolio dancers who may dance for several small companies and for different projects, each with a different style of movement. Most of the dancers I spoke with equated modern or post-modern dancers with people who developed specific movement vocabularies taught in their classes in the twentieth century—such as Martha Graham, José Limón, Paul Taylor, or Merce Cunningham—whose styles are still taught today.[8] Companies and schools want a distinctive *Nutcracker*, one that reflects their dancers' styles, a different version of the story, a new setting, or choreography mindful of the skill level of the student dancers.

With all the different styles of productions and public interest, dance critics and writers discuss the relative artistic merits of Balanchine's (NYCB), Ratmansky's (ABT), or Pacific Northwest's *Nutcracker* versions or debate who performed the Sugar Plum Fairy (leading role) more capably or whether to call the little girl "Marie" or "Clara," though in some versions the role is danced by an adult. Some like the traditional versions, while others enjoy more contemporary performances such as Mark Morris's *Hard Nut* or the Bang Group's *Nut/Cracked*. Some find the *Nutcracker Rouge* amusing, and others find it tasteless. I admired the series Alastair Macaulay wrote in the *New York Times* in 2010 after seeing twenty-three *Nutcracker* performances in a single season and finding something to say about each.[9] A debate rages about whether the Sugar Plum Fairy fosters a traditional view of the role of women as she leans on her escort or is a strong ruler of her nation of sweets—the variations in the second act. Jennifer Fisher argues in *Nutcracker Nation* that young dancers are able to see the difference between a submissive female ballet role and the ballerina as a dancer who is strong, employed, and independent.[10] Lauren Kessler flew across the country to see many *Nutcracker* performances and then took classes with the Eugene Ballet to perform in their *Nutcracker* so she could write *Raising the Barre*.[11] Others are concerned that the *Nutcracker* has become the most popular ballet in the United States. I leave these issues to the dance writers, critics, and fans.

Change is also reflected in the *Nutcracker*. If the *Nutcracker* is the dance world in a nutshell, the dance world also is embedded in the society at large.[12] Increasingly challenged by people both inside and outside the concert dance world who are concerned with diversity and representation, in the 2021 and 2022 seasons some ballet companies adapted *Nutcracker* variations to avoid stereotypical portrayals.[13] A hip-hop version was added in December 2018 at the New Jersey Performing Arts Center, originally choreographed by Jennifer Weber in 2014. At every historical juncture, dance has been shaped by powerful social forces, with dancers, choreographers, artistic directors, and organizations actively adopting artistic and everyday roles that are increasingly consistent with the economic, political, and social crosscurrents of the time.[14] In turn, dance affects the world around it.[15]

Companies

Performances of the 1954 NYCB's *Nutcracker* at City Center sold out and, when Lincoln Center opened in 1964, NYCB danced the *Nutcracker* on an enormous stage to an even larger audience:

> "It was very exciting," says Gloria Govrin, who that day unveiled a sinuous new version of the Arabian Coffee dance in Act Two. . . . "I remember the reception of doing it," says Govrin, "because nobody knew there was going to be a change. It got a huge ovation, several bows. In the middle of *Nutcracker* it's kind of unusual to have one or two more bows."[16]

Govrin affirms both the financial and artistic success of the *Nutcracker*. In all its forms, it provides a window into the financial world of dance schools and companies. To perform it in a reasonably traditional manner requires a large cast, but who dances—children, company members, portfolio dancers, parents, and performers in retirement—varies among the different companies and schools. Schools and local companies often use children and teens for most of the roles, while large companies involve children from their schools in several scenes. Only the largest companies can do it only with their own dancers and children from their schools. The New York City Ballet uses sixty children in each of two casts. The smaller companies and schools often pay guest professional dancers for major roles, but they rely on students for most roles. Aspen Santa Fe Ballet, with about fifteen dancers, hired many portfolio dancers who considered it one of the best gigs; they were paid for rehearsal time and performances. I watched one performance of several *Nutcracker* variations in a studio with about twenty wide-eyed tiny girls, who took ballet classes from the performers, along with their mothers. Most performances use a large number of reliable students; the more children dancing, the more families and friends fill the audiences. It can be performed on an elaborate scale with a full orchestra or with recorded music, but some performances are very small. What it always needs is conviction and community support.

A simple answer to the expansion of *Nutcracker* performances is companies and schools are constantly searching for funding, and *Nutcracker* performances make money. Most companies and schools dance multiple *Nutcracker* performances to help their finances; some companies hold performances from just after Thanksgiving until New Year's. The New York City Ballet has about eight performances a week in a 2,755-seat theater (potentially, over 130,000 seats sold and about 45 percent of the year's box office receipts), and Ballet West had twenty-three performances with a new $3 million production in 2019.[17]

Other companies travel for a month, and local companies and schools mount productions for a weekend or two. When children swell the ranks of dancers, their families and neighbors buy tickets. Companies make profits from ticket sales, and small companies and schools that have "companies" of their older students try to make enough to support additional performances in the spring. A small company with seventeen dancers, the Eugene Ballet, has a *Nutcracker* tour of five states with twenty-five performances. It has a $1.8 million budget—of which 60 percent is earned income (not from contributions) and 44 percent of that is from *Nutcracker* performances.[18] Atlanta Ballet has thirty-two dancers and does nineteen performances of *Nutcracker* that earn more than $2 million according to their July 2017 annual report, making almost three times more than all their other ticket sales (27 percent of their revenue).[19] For the NYCB, the *Nutcracker* ticket sales brought in over $13 million, which is about 18 percent of NYCB's total annual budget for the 2014 fiscal year.[20] *Nutcracker* performances matter for the budget of large and small companies, and schools.

Boston Ballet, for example, was dependent on *Nutcracker* ticket sales to finance other productions. Unlike the NYCB that has its own theater, many dance companies have to rent performance space. When, in 2004, the Boston Ballet was bounced from the large Wang Theatre (3,600 seats) for a Rockettes show, the situation appeared dire, according to Christine Temin in *Behind the Scenes at Boston Ballet*. The sets and staging were too big for the other Boston stages, and they wouldn't be able to sell as many tickets (1,600 at the Colonial in 2004 or 2,600 in the Opera House). They lost $4 million in revenue the first year. The debt of the company by 2007 was $8 million. Boston Ballet's financial situation was particularly bad; in 2008 they fired dancers and administrators.[21] *Nutcracker* performances are financially critical.

Schools

The number and types of schools for training dancers have grown substantially since the 1950s. Not only did most large companies develop schools of their own, but many more towns now have schools, often started by former performers from the expanding number of companies or students of company schools who danced in *Nutcracker* as children.

A good many School of American Ballet [SAB] students who were not lucky enough to get into the company [NYCB] after school have scattered across the U.S. to teach in some of today's 2,000-odd schools where ballet is offered. Their futures look secure: the enrollment of such schools has doubled in the past decade, now totals about 200,000.[22]

They want to produce *Nutcracker* for their students to learn performing and to make money. As dancers retire or do not get company jobs, some open more ballet schools.

Where else do the professional dancers train? BFA and BA programs in dance performance have also expanded, especially in the 1970s (before then, few universities offered degrees in dance performance).[23] Colleges and conservatories create future performers and teachers of dance.[24] They also expand the job market for former performers to teach and choreograph.

The University of Wisconsin housed the first dance major in 1926; it was organized "to encourage the dancers' well-being and capacities for self-expression, not to prepare them for the stage and public entertainment."[25] Nevertheless, students pushed for performances to showcase their skills. By 1936 their graduates were beginning to offer classes in a number of universities. The post-WWII cultural shift that expanded the desire for a college education also prompted parents to encourage their offspring to attend, even to pursue a dance major. University or conservatory degrees in dance developed slowly. Juilliard started its music conservatory in 1905 and its dance program in 1951. Most universities, if they had dance, had modern classes in the 1960s, often taught in the physical education department. A few well-known modern dance departments such as Bennington's (1936) developed new choreography and forms of dance in its own autonomous department, but expansion of dance programs developed later.[26]

Currently, over 200 universities and conservatories offer a BFA or BA in performance dance.[27] Others train dance teachers. With the growing interest in dance and the era's emphasis on the importance of a college education, universities saw a chance to expand their arts curricula. This increased the labor pool of dancers as well as providing work for former dancers by hiring faculty with BAs, BFAs, and MFAs. But where do all these BAs and BFAs dance?

EMPLOYMENT REALITIES AND THE ECONOMIC LANDSCAPE

Nutcracker performances provide the money for companies to support their dancers and schools and small companies provide additional pay for larger company dancers and portfolio dancers as "guests." Few dancers have ever been well paid yet young people want to be dancers. Even before the Great Depression, the Martha Graham dancers worked as waitresses and shop assistants to survive.[28] The government collects two kinds of information that help us understand the dancer and choreographer labor market. The Occupational Employment Survey, conducted by the Bureau of Labor Statistics (BLS), surveys employers annually and includes estimates of the number of employed dancers and choreographers nationally and by state and metropolitan area.[29] The American Community Survey (ACS) is a large nationally representative Census Bureau survey of households that includes self-reported information on an individual's occupation and other employment characteristics. Using the ACS, it is possible to identify individuals, whose primary declared occupation was "dancer or choreographer," who worked in the "performing arts industry."[30] Neither organization predicts an increase in employment opportunities for dancers and choreographers in the foreseeable future.

Employers in 2018 were asked how many dancers and choreographers they employed (BLS); 9,720 dancers (30 percent self-employed, 27 percent in performing arts, 9 percent in education, and 6 percent in spectator sports) and 5,090 choreographers (48 percent in education, 30 percent self-employed, and 16 percent in performing arts) with a median wage of $16.31 for dancers and $18.75 per hour for choreographers. This number decreases with the number employed in performing arts companies (3,790 dancers and 1,180 choreographers).

The ACS estimate is 28,317 who said they were choreographers and dancers, but only 18,447 were in the performing arts. The others were employed in gambling, education, personal services, travel services, among other places. But of the 28,000, 5,502 dancers and choreographers said that they were not employed during the past year. Men made up about a fourth of the respondents. That the numbers were so much larger when people were asked to identify their occupations rather than where they were employed should not be surprising as so many more dancers and choreographers are unable to find much work in performing and work at a variety of jobs. Their work as portfolio dancers may not be included as the survey asks where they worked the most hours in the last week, which may mean babysitting or teaching. Thus, the reliability of these numbers is problematic.

The New York City metropolitan area employs about 1,500 dancers and 70 choreographers, which includes Broadway, teachers, and others.[31] Nevada employs 670 dancers and San Francisco, 730. These numbers are estimates, but they give us some idea about the employment prospects for dancers. I suspect that they underestimate the number of portfolio dancers who earn much of their living working at something other than performing; the prospect of earning a living from arts performing is small.

Many who said they were a dancer or choreographer (28,317) did not work throughout the year and also had non-dancing work. And much of their work was not in the performing arts.[32] Most worked less than fifty weeks a year, and their mean annual earnings was $20,431. For those who were full-time workers, salaries were closer to $40,000. Much of that income is likely not from performing. Choreographers earned a bit more than dancers.

Nutcracker performances around the country provide funding for companies, schools, and professional dancers. And *Nutcracker* also provides entertainment and creates a sense of wonder for the audience and unforgettable experiences for those who participate as children, whether or not they become professional dancers.

NUTCRACKER AND THE DANCE CAREER: PASSION AND PRECARIOUS LABOR

Binge watching four or five TV *Nutcracker* productions in the month of December won't really give you the best idea of the *Nutcracker*, though it will provide an idea of the range of performance styles, choreography, and ways companies tell the story and dancers interpret the roles. The flat screen doesn't capture dance fully with the close-ups then pullbacks, lack of depth and perspectives. It loses some of the magic. Every performance is different, even with the same dancers, although it may take a reasonably trained eye to distinguish among them. Dancers talk about the small nuances they use to create a different take on their character. Watching coaches work with professional dancers to bring out those nuances shows how astonishingly detailed dance is.

Despite variations in *Nutcracker* productions, some stories bridge many productions, such as dancers sliding in the snow scene on whatever material the production uses when "snow" lands on the stage. That problem is so much a part of the lore that when David Parker, the Bang Group's artistic director and choreographer, has his dancers artfully slide to the ground and dance around an imagined slippery spot on the

floor in *Nut/Cracked* (a comedic version), the audience chuckled, aware
of the reference.

The *Nutcracker* provides a lens into the experiences at different
career stages. The excitement of many upon seeing a production of *Nutcracker* is enough to inspire young people to want to dance; they "had"
to take ballet classes. Early performances also teach young people about
dealing with competition in the audition process, cooperation, the importance of bodies and size, and perhaps most significant, the excitement
of performing. Most children who enthusiastically embrace dancing in
Nutcracker don't dance professionally. Other interests become more important, or their bodies don't cooperate. Many are left with vivid memories. For company professionals, it means doing performances many
love, but it also allows earning extra money guesting—helping a former
teacher put on a production or dancing a role they would not be asked to
do in their own company. For many portfolio dancers it was the highest
earning period of the year. And for contemporary dancers, it sometimes
means retraining their bodies for pointe shoes and dancing in the style
they learned growing up. The wonder of the *Nutcracker* ballet remains
and reinforces the labor of love. Although I never asked specifically
about the *Nutcracker*, almost everyone I interviewed provided at least
one story about that experience.

Sitting in the audience brings the excitement of ballet to many young
children, especially little girls. The dancers wear beautiful costumes,
and the varieties of dances may keep even the most bored awake. The
music contributes to a mood that many find transporting. When dancers talk about the *Nutcracker*, they recall it in a way that connects their
origin story with the ballet. For some, they ascribe to it the inspiration
for taking their first ballet class; for others performing it breeds interest. Eileen pushed for classes:

> My mom took me to see the Pennsylvania Ballet's *Nutcracker*. She
> said I sat there without moving the entire time. Then I begged her
> for ballet classes until I was old enough to go. She had never seen me
> sit so still before.

Morgan, as a child in a small professional company's performance, describes her fascination:

I loved it. I loved performing. I loved the lights. I loved the stage. I
loved dress rehearsal and the costumes in there. Since it was a professional company, we had real costumes, and they had people doing
our hair and makeup. It was just a really, really great experience as
a child. I held onto that. From the wings, you're watching the professional dancers do Sugar Plum Fairy and all the lead roles. It's just
breathtaking, and you're completely in awe. I think that helped to
continue my motivation.

Even principal dancers of major companies have fond memories
of first roles. Deborah Bull, a former principal dancer with the Royal
Ballet who trained in their London school, describes her first *Nutcracker*
after not getting a part for two years:

> [A]long with eleven other girls from my class and the one below, I
> finally made it. As a rat. Aged thirteen, and we were performing . . .
> alongside the dancers I'd admired every Christmas. . . . It was our
> first taste of life with the professionals. . . . [M]y parents made yet
> another eight-hour round trip to London to watch *The Nutcracker*
> and to keep their eyes peeled, as instructed, for the second rat to
> appear. . . . When my Mum died a few years ago, I found the pro-
> gramme.[33]

The excitement and joy of performing is palpable; it rests in memories
of older dancers and their families. Principal dancers recognize this
when dancing the lead roles as Christine Shevchenko, ABT principal,
acknowledges in her Instagram feed: "I always forget how inspirational
these performances are for the kids involved in the production, to see
the excitement and joy on their faces is worth everything."[34]

First experiences are remembered fondly, with nostalgia. But performing *Nutcracker* is also about learning to deal with challenges. Competition is entwined with American culture, as is what it takes to pursue
a dance career. Young students begin to learn about managing competition for the "best" parts. Some parts have only a few dancers onstage,
while others include many and require head to toe covering. "Snow"
is desirable in many schools as it is generally danced on pointe and in
professional companies, by professionals. For a girl, often about age ten,
the role of Clara, some productions call her Marie, is the most desirable.

The changing room is often crowded when roles are posted with some excitedly saying "I got it," while others look down, trying not to cry. Self-doubt creeps in. "Why did I not get the role I thought I should? Am I too big or just not good enough?" To continue training they have to learn to deal with failures. Competitiveness is learned early, but for some dancers who were successful early, learning to deal with competition may not start until auditions for summer intensives or year-round company programs.

By high school, Jamie began to understand the competition and sources of positive rewards in dance:

> I think around thirteen or fourteen, I got Party Girl, so we got to dance on pointe, so that was a big deal. Then I got a Snowflake, which was also big. But we had Snowflakes and then Snow. Snowflake is the first kind of entry Snow person. Then, as a Soldier, and then the year after I got Spanish, which was really big. I was Clara and our Clara was a mature Clara who did the whole show, so that was a huge like, "Oh my gosh! I can't believe I got this." Also, our production was the biggest in the state. We do it with a symphony. It's in front of a 2,000-person audience, which is really quite large. That was also when I was like, okay, I might actually have potential here and wanna keep working. My teachers weren't super free in their affirmation, so when you would get one [role], you would tend to eat it up. That fed me, I guess, or that was their way of saying that I was talented.

But when dancers enter a major summer intensive or company school, these same young women immediately notice the difference. Some, such as Justine, see this as a challenge to work harder and improve, whereas others are overwhelmed:

> All of a sudden, it's like everybody was Clara in their school's *Nutcracker*. It's like the top of all the regional schools are there. You come and it's very inspiring, because everyone is extremely talented. It's intimidating because everyone's extremely talented. You know that at the end of the day, you're chosen to be there too. Right?

The Nutcracker also teaches much about the importance of the body for ballet beyond technique and movement. How bodies look is critical. Bodies dance, and the dance world wants particular styles of body, though variations exist in what artistic directors or choreographers like. Some aspects of size may be partially malleable such as weight and pliability, but not height or bone structure. Sometimes it is even the size of existing costumes that matter. Learning size matters is difficult, but sometimes a dancer gets lucky with others' bad luck. Lara described her daughter's experience as Clara's understudy in a major company, who was asked to perform in an emergency situation:

> There was illness running through the cast. One prince was sick, the taller kids. The other prince, they call him. He's sick. They call me, "We have no choice but to put the short cast on," because the other taller girls couldn't do it with a shorter boy. They were like, "We need them now."
>
> They'd never had a stage rehearsal. I had to go pull her out of school. I was shaking, "You're on." She was like, "Oh my god." They had a rehearsal with the company. They could get kicked in the head. [The choreographer] was in the audience. I went up to him during intermission. He's like, "They are amazing."

This young Clara, in the hemmed costume, had a chance to dance twice, but the following year she lost her place in the prestigious school; her body wasn't developing as they wanted. Pressures to conform to body type begin early. Some who are too tall, too short, or too muscular for ballet companies may still want to be dancers and find a place in the contemporary dance world. As children they may have performed the same parts and received encouragement, but with puberty, when they may lose their "perfect" bodies, they may begin to see no future in dance. Some are torn, as they want to enter a classical company. Briena was considered too tall and large boned:

> I was so excited [dancing Clara]. I still, to this day, am like "if I could go back and do any role, that would be the one I would do again. Because it was so much fun." I remember she [teacher/*Nutcracker* director] told my mom that she wanted me to lose like five pounds. My mom told me that, and was like, "this is how you should eat." From a very young age, I was aware of this concept of, "Oh, I'm not svelte enough for this world." It caused some turmoil later, but at the time it just was a cue.

Like body size, gender and race matter in casting in the dance world. What steps and how they are done differ between men and women, particularly in the world of classical ballet. Moreover, many fewer men enter the ballet studio than women, especially when young. Boys often start later than girls. Even David Hallberg, one of the great ballet dancers of the early twenty-first century, started in tap and then ballet at eleven, but says he was not serious about ballet until high school.[35] *Nutcracker* roles that "require" boys illustrate the problems of finding boys to participate and their different experiences. Even roles such as the soldiers are often danced by girls. Matthew discussed how teachers attempt to entice boys into ballet and *Nutcracker*:

> How do they get boys into a suburban studio? She [the teacher] saw an opportunity to possibly get some boys, so asked the [martial arts] group if they could collaborate on *The Nutcracker*. She's a super smart woman. She asked if she could have four of his top students come and take classes for the fall semester, and perform a battle scene, so that we'd be fighting the mice. Four did that, and then afterwards two continued dancing, and she kept us on scholarship. I fell in love with dance. I've done *Nutcracker* practically every year, unless I was injured. I couldn't even count. I've done every role in *The Nutcracker* that a male could possibly do.

An inexperienced boy, attending a public arts elementary school, achieved a major role with only a few months of dance and no ballet training. I never heard a Clara story like Philip's narrative:

> Somewhere within that first two months of school [dance class], there was an audition for *The Nutcracker*. It was a major thing, and my dance teacher said, "Well, you're gonna go to this audition." I said, "Okay." My parents didn't even have a car, so we took the bus downtown. I didn't have ballet shoes or tights or anything. I remember looking at all these kids with their ballet shoes, and everybody was put together, and I said, "There's no way that I'm gonna go in and do this thing." I said, "I'm not prepared. I don't have anything." I was gonna walk out on it, and [my family] said, "Well, we're here. We've come all this way. You're gonna audition." I auditioned and got the part of *The Nutcracker* Prince. Not only did I get in, I was the main role.

I was ten then. That started my dance career. I was the first African American to ever play the role of *The Nutcracker* Prince.

Philip's experience as an African American with few economic resources raises the issue of diversity for the profession and points out the importance of public arts schools for those with few economic resources. Even if he had seen a *Nutcracker* performance twenty years ago, in all likelihood, he would not have seen other African Americans.

It is a challenge for the profession to train sufficient numbers of young men. Whereas by age ten many young girls are ready to dance Clara, it is rare for boys to have dance training. But, because young men have greater opportunities to dance, like Philip, their small numbers create other challenges. Male high school students occasionally are paid to dance *Nutcracker*, giving them an early taste of the professional life. But academic schools may not support them as Carson found:

> Probably about thirteen or fourteen, I started taking ballet pretty heavily. We were not a ballet school. We were a very general, local dance studio. We had a very strong ballet teacher. I went to public school. I actually got a job in a ballet company when I was fifteen. I think they needed boys to dance in [a small] ballet's *Nutcracker*. They hired me and a couple boys from my studio. We got paid for it. But school wouldn't let us miss that much. I was already missing a lot because of various events or auditions that I was doing when I was a kid. I was missing so much school that it was becoming a huge conflict.

Somehow, they have to fit in both dance and academic studies.

Dedication to performing is not solely embedded in a youth's excitement and thrill of dancing. Parents, teachers, and youth institutions are also involved, and sometimes they clash. Young dancers are learning to become dedicated professionals very early, but most are concerned with academics too. The competing demands of school and performing are particularly difficult in *Nutcracker* season. Jonah danced many roles and said he was still a good student:

> I would do performances, but some things would overlap and clash with rehearsals. By the time I was seventeen or eighteen, I was dancing seven days a week—rehearsals for up to six hours on Sundays,

and four or five hours on Saturdays. My senior year in high school, I had the honor of doing the Cavalier as well as—I think I did five roles in the *Nutcracker* my senior year.

Most who dance in *The Nutcracker* do not become professionals, even those who had good roles. When my ballet teacher of a class of hobbyists asked who had danced in *The Nutcracker*, almost every student raised her hand. I was in the minority. One Marie at a studio I frequented years ago was the first in that studio to dance the role on pointe, causing a sensation. But within a few years her body changed—no longer a ballet body. She went off to college. A few years later another Marie in that studio also danced on pointe. She had wonderful feet, excellent musicality, and could follow instructions seemingly without effort. At ten their dancing skills and bodies looked similar, but the second Marie became a principal dancer in a small ballet company.

The enchantment of performing *Nutcracker* stays with many professional dancers who perform in that ballet in their companies, in addition to others as guests, but income is important. Even the largest companies rarely pay more than thirty-five to forty-five weeks. That means that the corps members' starting salaries in the second decade of the twenty-first century is a little over $1,200 dollars per week; in some of the largest companies in large cities in the United States, that is barely sufficient to live. But current salaries are better than the late 1950s when a week's rehearsal salary at the New York City Ballet was less than unemployment benefits.[36] Smaller ballet or contemporary companies may have between twenty to thirty paid weeks, and principals may earn as little as several hundred dollars per week. With the exception of the few major companies, few can live solely on what they earn as performers.

Smaller companies and schools hire professionals to perform the Sugar Plum Fairy and Cavalier roles, hoping to draw a larger crowd, or invite a former student, now a professional, as it helps the school appear successful. Guesting may mean dancing a role a corps member would rarely dance in their own company. Arron Scott, a soloist at ABT wrote:

This [photo] was not my first *Nutcracker,* but it was my first time appearing as a guest artist [as Cavalier]. I'm about 18 in this picture, and I was a member of the ABT Studio [Junior] Company at the time. I had returned to my home school to appear in their *Nutcracker*.[37]

For portfolio dancers, *Nutcracker* is the most profitable season. But they dance for more than the money. For some contemporary dancers, *Nutcracker* can mean doing treasured roles from their classical ballet pasts and performing before larger audiences than they often do.

Being a guest often requires adjustments. If guests are brought in to dance the Sugar Plum Fairy and Cavalier, they may have little rehearsal time, and the others onstage may not be professionals who know how to accommodate professionals, creating problems. Some guests may bring their own costumes, but others have to wear what the school or small company has available. Georgina Pazcoguin, soloist in the NYCB, describes her excitement when buying her own tutu for guest performances.[38] Also, the music tempo may not be what the guests are accustomed to, and the stage flooring may be dangerous for dancing. Stage size makes a difference too. If, as Sugar Plum Fairy, the ballerina is doing the thirty-two *fouettés* on a small stage, she needs to be aware of the edges, as dancers tend to move slightly.[39] Learning to dance on different stages is critical.

The discipline of intensive training and challenge makes new roles possible. Men are in such short supply that Sebastian, who started dancing in college and had never performed in a *Nutcracker*, was invited to dance the Cavalier role. In this role, he danced with an experienced Sugar Plum Fairy:

It's not like a classical role that you'll see performed in New York City; it's a place where I can [appear to] be a classical dancer professionally. What they allotted for was maybe twelve hours of my own rehearsal time in New York City, where they paid for the studio space for me to rehearse.

I asked the artistic director what she was looking for [to decide on a variation]. Was she looking for a very classical version? Or was she looking for more of a neoclassical contemporary idea, which is more in the lines of what I was comfortable doing. She was like, "I'd want a lot of turns, I'd want jumps." So you want classical. We [a friend] watched a few variations on YouTube and took pieces of things that we liked and made something that worked for my body and within my capabilities. I get there a week before, and Monday to Thursday, you're with your partner, and you pray to god that you both can, somehow, magically have a connection and an ease of partnering. You're onstage for Friday, Saturday, Sunday. She [partner] was great; if things aren't going well, she was very candid about telling me, "You need to hold me here."

Nutcracker provides a way to keep the performing self alive and make some money while attending university, as Julia did. She danced a role that is usually given to someone with a different body type. And she remains excited by performing in *The Nutcracker:*

I did a lot of *Nutcracker* where we were doing thirty-five shows of the *Nutcracker* every year, which is where I would say I've got the bulk of my stage time. I'd be the Maid in the party scene. I would be a Rat. Then I would do Snow. Then I would be the Chinese soloist, and then I would also be Flowers. I actually did Arabian this year. I was astounded. It's some of the most fun I've ever had onstage. Definitely from *Nutcracker* you can make a good chunk of change. As far as New York goes, gosh, it's probably less than $10,000 [earned last year from dancing]. It's not good.

The diversity of dance movements requires different preparations. Some contemporary dancers don't regularly wear pointe shoes, so they feverishly take classes in pointe shoes and work on balances and turns. Pink tights and tutus seem to show each additional pound that even shorts and a crop top do not. So it's dieting time too. *Nutcracker* pays.

Nutcracker fatigue of company members who dance many performances can contribute to boredom and injuries. In a short career, this is a constant source of problems, but the high of performing remains strong. An injury Allison suffered is named for *The Nutcracker:*

I was pretty lucky. I didn't have that many injuries in my career. I did have one major injury that was a pretty big factor [in her decision to retire]. I was doing opening night of *Nutcracker* in the Marzipan role. I took off for this jump, and I slipped, because we had a new Marley [flooring used for dancing] that year for the production, and I landed completely on the side of my ankle. I was onstage and I heard it. I had never done anything like that before. It was the most sur-

real experience, because you're mentally making a thousand evaluations. You don't know what happened. I'm like, "Should I go offstage?
Should I keep dancing? What should I do? I'm with two other people
doing a dance right now." In the meanwhile, if you're making this
mental decision, the music's still playing. This probably happens in
two seconds. I kept going, because you have so much adrenaline. I
knew something was really wrong with it, but it seemed to be all
right if I was on pointe. I couldn't really jump, so I ended up marking
the jumps and continuing for the rest—luckily *The Nutcracker* stuff
is short.

   I got offstage, and my foot was like, massive swells. Someone had
to go on and do the finale. I had broken the cuboid bone. It's funny,
because it's called a *Nutcracker* fracture. It's when your fifth meta-
tarsal and your heel compress really fast, and it cracks the cuboid
like a nut.

After a *Nutcracker* injury, it can also mean the end of a classical
ballet career, as Josie found, but that discipline and passion for dancing
remained:

   I think it was about six months after we moved here [New York City].
   I was doing a guesting spot for *Nutcracker,* which was great. I had set
   up an audition for [a major company], which was also great. Then I
   tore my Achilles tendon [during *Nutcracker*]. I was out for almost
   four years. That totally ended my career [as a classical ballet dancer].

Injuries can shape careers.

How to manage the deeply embedded identity as a dancer after performing is over is a critical process for many. For some retired performers, *Nutcracker* is a chance to get back onstage as Drosselmeyer or the
parents. Sometimes a ballet master or mistress, a teacher, or old friend
is called upon for these roles. In his sixties, James's face lit up when dis-
cussing performing in *Nutcracker:*

   I said, "How about if you list me as a character dancer?" He did. I go
   back every year and do Drosselmeyer in *Nutcracker.* I always wanted
   to find different ways of exploring dance. I just left myself open to
   everything.

Many company members dance in numerous *Nutcracker* productions each year. For the corps members in professional companies, *The
Nutcracker* involves doing many of the same dances over and over or
changing costumes several times during a performance, and for some
who have had a six-week run of *Nutcracker,* the final performances may
have become routine. But sometimes a corps dancer has an opportunity to do a soloist role towards the end of the run. This can be exciting. Courtney Nitting, an artist (corps member) with the Boston Ballet,
danced Sugar Plum Fairy, a principal role, for the first time in 2023.
Laura Di Orio interviewed her about her top personal highlight of the
year:

"[O]ne of my top favorites would be dancing the Sugar Plum Fairy.
This has been a dream of mine like many young girls since as far
back as I can remember. It was a special performance as my family
was in the audience and my debut was a school-specific show (meaning the entire audience was made up only of children). I was very
nervous backstage before my first entrance; however, this little girl
who was dancing as a tiny angel in the cast came up to me and gave
me the biggest hug under my tutu stating, 'You're the fairy today!' To
see her face light up just made my heart melt in the sweetest way. My
nerves definitely turned into excitement after that. My Cavalier for
the show was one of my dearest friends which also made the connection on stage even more genuine. After the curtain went down, the
congratulations I received from everyone, including a fellow company member who is practically like family to me, is a moment I hold
close to my heart. This was an experience in my career I will never
forget and cherish forever."[40]

Nutcracker provides an opportunity for many to fall in love with dance
and performing. It also serves as a funnel for creating and selecting a
few dancers who may become professionals and is an important source
of income for companies, schools, and dancers. But falling in love with
dance does not necessarily mean you can make a career as a dancer. A
dance career requires meeting a series of challenges with the help of
family and teachers. Parents may or may not be supportive; teachers
may or may not be good instructors and may or may not understand

the professional world of dance; and bodies may or may not conform to dancer size and movement requirements or may become seriously injured. While parents may suggest, stand back, or resist a young dancer's desires, artistic directors and their teaching teams make choices about whom to accept for their schools or summer intensives. We will next examine what it takes to create and maintain that aspiration to become a professional dancer.

CHAPTER TWO

LEARNING THE PRACTICE OF BALLET

Body and Self

[B]ut kids dropped off over the years. Especially like for *Nutcracker* you would have to give up your weekends, then my teacher would encourage us to stay and understudy. You don't see the payoff as a kid a lot of times. She sees the devotion and then she kind of started to take people under her wing. That's kind of when I started grasping—I really want to do this.

I would miss family parties. People were like, "Do you even have a daughter?" I think it was starting eleven, twelve-ish when you had to put in the hours to really show whether or not you're interested. It was about six to seven days a week starting with middle school. High school, that's when it's a do-or-die kind of thing, especially on weekends. In the evenings ballet class probably started around 6:00 and then it would go till 8:30, but then she would continue teaching so some people would stay. We would sometimes have an hour or so longer with her and that's when you got the personal attention and you really discovered the personal relationship, not just with her, but with ballet. That's what I really enjoyed.

I would say a lot of my friends were mainly at academic school. I think some of that competitiveness limits the number [in ballet]. Plus, in ballet, you really don't get to talk like you do at school. In ballet I had teachers where in between giving combinations there was not to be a sound, and if you talked, you were to leave the room.

It's trying to find that balance. Like I said, I missed some home-comings; they [friends] didn't always understand, after a while they're like, "Oh, we'd invite you but you had ballet." I was like, "Thanks for understanding" [said cynically], There were times where I had late nights with my friends.

Olivia is describing not only learning the movements but the traditions, habits, relationships, and how to deal with challenges when they become aspirational dancers. Much more is communicated in ballet class than training of the body. With increasing challenges created by dance teachers, families, peers and academic schools, young dancers develop dedication, persistence, competing gracefully, and cooperation that sustain passion over time and enable young dancers to deal with adversity.

Training takes place in organizations: in dance schools, taught by teachers who have been trained in ballet traditions and techniques, but not necessarily educational techniques. Those who continue dancing beyond eight or so begin to learn the shaping of the body for ballet: the turnout, body flexibility considered desirable, the appearance of effortlessness, moving, and remembering the steps in increasingly difficult progressions. How that body is shaped and responds to that shaping, in turn shapes careers. No one does this alone and some bodies resist, are injured, or grow away from the norms of dance and ballet, in particular.

"Talent" involves not only the shaping of the body but developing and demonstrating particular habits and relationships. Importantly, dancers learn that passion involves demonstrating dedication to the "ballet discipline" such as the no talking rule Olivia describes, being on time, looking right, and being quiet; developing and working towards an ideal self; and demonstrating deference toward teachers and tradition. How teachers communicate these ideas matters. Teachers shape not only the body but the identity as a dancer. Olivia recognizes that ballet has characteristics of getting into a special tradition or club. But parents and academic schools sometimes have different ideas and increase the challenges that young dancers must face.

Dancers often make decisions about their futures before entering high school, as Olivia did, like gymnasts. She looks back at her teenage self from her mid-twenties and sees herself as playing an active role in her decision making about dance, but not without the involvement of parents and teachers. A fantasy, fairy tale identity develops first, mostly of girls: of tutus, pointe shoes, and sequins; for many, dance ends here or they become once-a-week hobbyists. The evolution to aspirational dancer starts with multiple classes a week, summer intensives, rehearsals, and performances, like professionals. It is the beginning of career training. The freedom experienced from movement is challenged by required dedication, the working towards an imagined ideal, criticisms of body and practice, and balancing academics and dance. Most who start this process drop out along the way, finding other activities more interesting. Or their bodies don't develop as dancers' bodies. Or they don't like the discipline.

It isn't necessarily the same for men and women. Most of the women I interviewed, no matter their age now, began dancing early. The men, under forty when interviewed, often started somewhat later than the women, and some, over forty when interviewed, started much later—either in high school or college. Their stories are often different as are the identities they develop.

DOLLY DINKLE AND THE FANTASY IDENTITY

It's almost like being a unicorn. There's something special and rare about it. I think when you're a little girl, it's almost like the idea of being a fairy. It seems like something beyond human. As you get older, you realize it's as human as it can possibly be. It's just dirty and painful and raw. By that point, you've invested so much time. Nobody starts—I mean, some men do, but if you're a female, you don't start dancing when you're twenty.

As Kelly describes it, interest in dance is linked to entry into a mysterious and romantic world of ballet: tutus, pointe shoes, unicorns, and adults who are willing to explore those mysteries with a young dancer. Tutu-like dresses are popular among small girls. Fairies, ballerinas, and unicorns populate the books designed for them, and many become obsessed with ballet; they begin to invest before they realize the work of dancers. It is a fantasy identity, one that they present to others by wearing tutu-like dresses, buns, and special-colored leotards.

Adults narrated the beginnings of their passion as seeming to spring from nowhere or from seeing *The Nutcracker*. The dancers described how families located a small school—a "Dolly Dinkle" school. What was this Dolly Dinkle school I heard several dancers mention? Professional dancers used the term to refer to a studio offering several styles of movement classes. Josie describes, as do others, being "obsessed" after her first encounter with ballet:

> I started dancing when I was five. I was taking gymnastics, and my gymnastics teacher said, "Put that girl in ballet for grace and flexibility." My parents did. My mom said I said after my first class, "I'm done with everything. I just wanna be in ballet." That was it. My first class I was like obsessed, completely obsessed. My mom said that I was really mad at all the other girls because people weren't paying attention.

Young men are generally more measured. Many do not talk like Gabriel about "falling in love," but several, at young ages, followed their sisters into class, a common story expressed by Jonah and Matthew. Gabriel explained he danced around the house, but there are few books or images of little boys dancing:

> My mother was really intuitive, with all of my siblings. My brother was really into finance, and I was interested in dance. She would put on some music—not ballet music necessarily—and I'd just dance around the house. She's like, "Maybe you should be a dancer," so she put me in a jazz class at age five. Then, the prerequisite was you had to take a ballet class to do a jazz class. That's where I fell in love with ballet.

The way the body feels when dancing is part of the basis for this great interest.[1] It should not be surprising to those who love to dance at weddings or other social occasions. People take ballroom dancing classes, and tango tourism is a source of income for Buenos Aires. A New York City tango workshop I observed included participants of all ages and skill levels and lasted for four enjoyable hours on a Sunday afternoon. Athletes and fitness junkies also often describe the high from using the body.

In dance classes children run, jump, turn, bend, and straighten up—no one "wins" or "loses" or is the last one chosen for the team. Competition doesn't begin until later. Dance does mean hard work, though, as Anya describes:

> Well, I loved how hard it was and just physically. You kind of lose yourself in trying to attempt something. Also, the music; it kind of puts you in a state where you're just kind of all blissed out and totally unaware of yourself. I remember that feeling.

Part of the fantasy for girls is the first pair of pointe shoes. As Anita explains, with pointe shoes, the aspiration to become professional begins:

> I did start wearing pointe shoes at age ten because I was strong. I wasn't loosey-goosey. Oh, I was so excited. That was my dream. Then it was like, "Okay, blisters on every toe the first night I wore pointes—bruised toenail." I slept in my pointe shoes. I was obsessed with my pointe shoes.

Carrying out the fantasy comes with pain. Pointe shoes for the young girl are part of the fantasy, but it takes putting up with pain, and many lessons and work, to learn to stand "on your box." Families, teachers, and friends participate in developing the aspirational self as do the storybooks, Barbie dolls, and movies.[2] And something of that fantasy identity remains for those who become aspirational dancers when the work and discipline begins. Carla Fracci, a ballerina of international repute, reaffirms the hard work it takes: "Whoever said 'You are born to dance' was lying. Ballet dancing is nothing one is born with."[3]

ASPIRATIONAL PROFESSIONAL IDENTITIES

Young girls want to be identified as dancers. The presentation of self as dancer, particularly for girls, starts early. You are near a ballet studio when you see clusters of small girls with their hair tied back carefully (generally) in buns, wearing leotards under their jackets, and carrying sacks or backpacks that look as large as they are. In many schools, the color of leotards and tights indicates class level. Boys wear black tights and white t-shirts. It is a rare serious ballet school that permits wildly patterned or brightly colored leotards, large earrings, or hair flying. The "look" is shaped in the ballet studio. Girls want to be recognized as aspiring ballerinas, but boys rarely do, as they are often subject to teasing. In some studios now, boys are permitted to wear shorts instead of tights.

Wearing the symbols of a dance student is the easy part. Young dancers face many challenges to maintaining their passions and aspirational identities early in their lives: readying their bodies, learning to manage competition, acquiescing to ballet discipline, tough teachers with harsh criticism, and balancing academic school with dance. None of this is done without teachers, peers, and families who can be supportive of or serve as gatekeepers to advancement. The young people face many barriers to what they want, but they also learn much that will help them later, no matter what they do.

The Challenge of Ballet Discipline

How teachers teach is linked to how they were taught. It is a culture that is tied to the past and explicitly asymmetrical with deference owed teachers regardless of their behavior. Some are trained now in newer educational techniques. "Ballet discipline" has a reasonably specific meaning, even if some might argue about its exact content. It is about conventions that ballet teachers learned from their experiences in class; it is their "duty" to pass on to a new generation, just as older dancers pass on their dance roles to younger ones. The tradition allows teachers to discredit students when they violate the rules of conduct, execute the steps poorly, or fail to control their bodies. How teachers correct students has evolved from what is sometimes referred to as the Russian style of harsh discipline, which is questioned today by parents in the United States as it sometimes involves physical and emotional violence and explicit classroom hierarchy. Strict rules of "comportment," a word that my grandmother used, are emphasized, and rituals of avoidance, such as not touching others, are violated by teachers as they correct students in ballet class. In the United States today, some teachers still jerk legs upward, push to straighten backs or to place feet into more perfect first or fifth positions, and bend fingers into the requisite positions.

Ballet discipline is organized around deference to ballet tradition and teachers who evaluate students' obedience to the expectations of ballet class: silence, attire, promptness, striving for an unreachable ideal by constant improvement in body movement and flexibility, and keeping the body at a ballet weight. Ballet schools often remain concerned with the presentation of self that has little to do with dancing skills, including dress and hair. Individualized clothing in the studio generally represents professional status. Professional company classes look extravagant: colorful sweaters, shorts, and layers of leg warmers.

Traditions developed more than a century ago have evolved slowly. Deference flows only toward the teacher, silence and obedience are expected, and teachers traditionally react harshly to violations. Ruth Page, who directed the Chicago Opera Ballet, writes about a London ballet class, probably before 1920. "He [Cecchetti] always seemed to be bending over and looking down, but he never missed a trick; if you did anything incorrectly, he would throw his stick at you."[4]

Barbara Milberg Fisher, a NYCB dancer in the late 1940s and 1950s who rose to soloist, has a mixed interpretation of her teachers' actions at the School of American Ballet (SAB):

Anatole Oboukhov was our dread but beloved taskmaster. He was gaunt, angular, and short, and he terrified us. . . . [H]e was instructed not to use a cane in class to correct the students; parents had lodged a complaint. . . . If you missed a step . . . you'd hear a scornful "Ha!! Oho!!" Of course, he was the one who gave us the stamina we needed for performances. And he sometimes had a twinkle in his dark Russian eyes.[5]

As a student in a major company school, Remy in her early fifties when interviewed, had teachers who reacted strongly if students were not sufficiently disciplined. Touch is part of teaching:

They'd come over; fix your fingers or your feet, or the *posée*. Some of them, yes, very strict Russians, especially with the younger divisions. When I was ten, she was seventy years old, and she even had a stick. She was very, very tough. For the most part, she was quiet, but when she got angry, she would just explode. She could be terrifying. The other teachers were strict, but they didn't yell as much. She came from that Russian background. Even though you're a dancer, you're still a little girl. The whole expectation is you're going after a career.

Mikayla's experiences in eastern Europe in the twenty-first century exemplified the very tough approach. She left dance at sixteen; she saw little future in it, felt abused, and disliked performing:

> [T]hey would always get opportunities for you to perform, so that you right away get into a habit. It's a job since you were nine years old. If you would laugh in class because of a weird touch, that would not even be allowed. When I was sixteen I said, "I wanna stop. I can't do this anymore." They wouldn't let me go. I remember teachers were talking to me, telling me that there's nothing else I can do with my life.
>
> You're told you're not good enough. Even if you have the perfect body, doesn't mean that they're not gonna criticize your body, your personality. I always had the perfect body. I never had the passion or the expression onstage. I don't like performing. I love the classes and the routine. If you're for six years being told that you're not good enough, of course, you don't have any self-esteem. It totally broke me.
>
> She [mother] was saying, "Why do you treat students like this?" They said, "Well, this is part of the profession. You have to break the spirit of the child first, so you can mold them into a dancer." My mother responded, "Well, no wonder she has no self-esteem and is not talking back."
>
> They would establish that hierarchy within the class right away. They say, "You're the one who we're gonna push." It was very clear their project was with me. She would always pull me to the side and say, "You know we have a lot of hope in you. If you don't have expression, if you don't make that effort we're just gonna have to push you more." Now in retrospect, I would say almost abusive behavior, emotionally abusive. Because she would be really, really nice, then the next day you never knew what hit you.

What she is talking about is extreme, but often criticism is directed toward the students whom the teachers evaluated as having the most potential: you deserve criticism—it is your reward from the perspective of the staff. But it is not always how the student sees it.

Today, how teachers communicate with their students is more varied, but it also retains some of the past. Most of the younger dancers had teachers whom they thought were overly focused on discipline and others whom they respected and liked very much. Looking back, they thought they understood the line between strict and abusive. Allison, now in her early thirties, reflected on her summer intensive teachers. She excused their harsh discipline and required deference as she considered them excellent teachers of ballet technique and interpreted their harshness as passion:

> It was awesome. They were at that time all Russian teachers. They are very strict. I grew up with a Russian technique. Nice terminology, although my teachers were American. She liked the Russian style, so that's what she taught in. It wasn't so unfamiliar to me, but the way you interact with the teachers is very different. Even if you see them in the hallway, you have to curtsy to them, even if you're not in ballet class, especially if it's the director of the school. It was a lot of respect. They're very harsh in class. They yell. Well, so when I was in high school, I had a Russian teacher. She was amazing. She was one of the best teachers I ever had. She would have a pencil, and if you weren't pulled up in the back of your leg, she would poke you. I think they're very passionate. She would come over, and if your *arabesque* needed to be higher, she would take your leg and pull it up and pull your back up. A lot of tears and stuff like that.

While Allison saw her teacher as challenging her to do more, Greta experienced the requirements as going too far. She chose to leave the studio and left dance:

> She [her mother was working] hired the cleaning lady to drive me. I think that's where my anxiety about time comes from. It was very strict that we had to be there on time. If we weren't, we had to sit out and watch. It was pretty rigorous. It got to a point when I was fifteen that I decided to actually leave that school. He [teacher] became very controlling. Not necessarily in a verbal way. We had a uniform and we had to wear specific things in our hair.

Teachers demand deference and obedience to the rules. Despite the harshness of many in their actions, some still interpreted them as passionate.

Some ballet teachers today think students are not sufficiently disciplined. An artistic director of a small classical company and school told me she has arguments with parents when she tells students they are not allowed to wear big earrings or brightly colored leotards. Another teacher of children—Miranda, in her sixties, who danced with a major company—explained her technique for dealing with students as "ballet discipline." If the students stayed, they learned to be on time and wear the required clothing:

> My sense of discipline comes from the ballet discipline. If you have not been brought up in the ballet discipline, it's very hard to understand it. Even now when I teach its steps, they [parents] think that you're treating the children badly. I have never yelled at a child. I have never insulted anybody. Most good teachers never have, but if you're late, I say, "Honey, you're late." Oh, that embarrasses them. "Why are you late?" I always calm myself. I need to have the other students know that she didn't get away with it. You take them aside when they're adults, but when they're children, they have to understand that somebody brought the red leotard instead of the pink one. They have to understand that she didn't get away with it. I say, "I will let you take class today, but remember not next time," and I give them warning. Without discipline you have nothing.

Wandering into class late isn't tolerated.[6] It is partially ceremonial and partially substantive; to miss the *pliés* that begin most classes is harmful to the body but also demonstrates lack of deference for the teacher and the art. Most learn to start warming up before class, in the hall, if another class is in the studio.

Teachers continue to correct students' presentation of self harshly, including hair and outfits. Natalia, in her late twenties, remembers a ballet teacher who was very critical of her bun:

> I was a teenager, and I was dealing with all sort of things—like trying to become a person myself and wanting to be accepted. I couldn't quite understand what I needed to do to impress this woman. Everybody had to have their hair parted on this side, which is why it's on this side [points to her hair]; the bun needed to be very small, and my bun was huge. She had a specific image in her head of what a dancer should look like, and I didn't fit that image, which is silly.

Also, talk by students during ballet class is frowned upon; students become quiet as soon as the teacher enters the room. Many teachers don't talk much and demonstrate what they want using their bodies. But talk provides the name of the steps in the combination, instructions to improve, and sometimes images to explain. When the class moves from the barre to center floor, everyone learns early how to line up for the combinations.

As they get older, students may be punished when they fail to demonstrate that they put ballet ahead of other activities and defer to the teacher's schedule. Morgan balanced ballet training, cheerleading, and an A average:

> It was my junior prom, and I had missed a rehearsal to go [to prom]. I was told that I was going to pay. It truly happened when I was given a role they knew I didn't deserve [a role that was less than she deserved], and I was very disappointed and upset. I fulfilled the role just because I wanted the performance opportunity, but at the same time, I knew it was not based on talent. It was like a punishment.

Ballet needed to be a passion, the central activity, and a lifestyle.

Deference to teachers, accompanists, and ballet traditions are also enacted ceremonially in the choreographed *réverénce* (bow or curtsy) to both the teacher and pianist at the end of class. The silence expected and deference to authority demanded are not what is generally taught at home to middle-class young people. At home, they are generally more outspoken and allowed to express their opinions.[7] But ballet discipline often follows them into the profession.

The Challenge of Shaping Bodies

A major challenge in the aspirational trajectory of a young dancer is that of disciplining the body. The body is on display in the ballet classroom in a way that voice may not be in an academic classroom. If a student doesn't talk in class and is not called on by the teacher, others have difficulty assessing intelligence. But facing a wall of mirrors in dance class, each can see the others. Many young ballet students do not have, nor will they ever develop, the body for dance. Love of dance and moving well are insufficient to dance at a professional level. The norms of size,

movement, and flexibility for professionals have traditionally been assessed at a very young age. No one can control height, proportions, or
bone size. Most ballet companies take women between about five foot
three inches and five foot eight, though there are exceptions. To partner, generally men need to be at least as tall as their partners without
their pointe shoes. If a woman is either much taller or shorter than
her male partner, it is difficult for him to lift her by holding her waist.
Each company appears to have its own standards and balance between
shorter and taller dancers. Portfolio dancers are more varied in height
and weight.

Thus, the shape of a career is related to having a body that is "right,"
as defined by others, and by teaching the body to do what the standards
infer.[8] Whether it should or should not be this way is an important question, but to be chosen by gatekeepers to attend the best intensives and
schools or join a classical ballet company means one must have a certain
look and be able to move in particular ways.

Shaping bodies doesn't just happen. Try standing on one leg, body
erect, and the second leg held straight up from the side with toes pointed
directly toward the ceiling; then look as though your leg is rippling as
Taylor Stanley, principal dancer with the New York City Ballet, does in
Kyle Abraham's *The Runaway*. I saw him do it twice and never saw his
body quiver. Or watch Jérôme Bel's video of the retiring Paris Opera
dancer Dominique, as she demonstrates how the swan corps in *Swan
Lake* has to stay still for long periods, then turn and stand still again; the
dancer's body can't stretch before dancing again. You feel the strength
of her body. It isn't like basketball players who stretch and realign the
body before taking a free throw. Swans are playing a role, performing
for an audience.

While work can give you strength and technique, the body is only
malleable to a certain point. Teachers can communicate what the body
should look like, but how they do so matters also. Some girls learn when
they are very young that their bodies are not right. Taller and bigger
boned than ballet dancers, Briena became a portfolio dancer:

> I knew from a young age I wouldn't be a ballerina. I knew I didn't
> have the body type for it. I think with ballet, it always felt like,
> like wanting something so desperately that would inevitably never

happen. Mostly, it was from external [cues]—people saying things. I knew my feet weren't incredibly flexible. My teachers always made comments to all of us of like, about our bodies, and not being the right type.

Weight continues to be an issue for dancers. Not only is there a push toward dancers being what most would consider skinny, but how weight is dealt with matters. In some schools being "overweight" was something that young people could and needed to control, as Casey explains:

> There were some other weird things where they would tell people that they needed to lose weight and comment on peoples' bodies that I just didn't think was okay. There was a weird stress. It wasn't the worst, but sometimes they would just say things to us that—we were like fourteen and they'd be like, "It looks like you've been having too many hamburgers," to someone that was really not out of shape at all, that looked great. I would just be like, "You shouldn't say that."

But she didn't—and most don't say anything. It should not be surprising that some young women and men develop eating disorders. Several mentioned in my interviews that they had conquered these disorders. According to the data, Melissa Klapper argues eating disorders are found more among student dancers than professionals, and the rates may be lower than they were years ago with the increased knowledge available.[9] But teachers are often critical of students' bodies and weed out bodies that don't reflect the prevailing conventions, as Eva experienced:

> I do remember wanting to get more parts or wanting to get the opportunity to do more duets, but I was the girl that struggled with the body. I remember wanting certain parts, but then coming to this conclusion where it's like, she got a duet because she's like a stick, and he can throw her around like nothing. That's also why I think I didn't put too much effort into trying to continue.

Much more than the "right" body shape is necessary. Formal steps and movements are taught in all ballet classes. Although there are variations in the way steps are done or positions held depending on different schools of ballet, teachers insist that they be done precisely as taught in their classrooms. Details are critical. Each finger, arm, hand, leg, foot, and head must be perfectly placed with no room for interpretation. Although schools have style variations, a first or fifth position is the same around the world. Some teachers may rarely do a *grand plié* in fourth position or have different ways to teach *épaulement*, but experienced ballet dancers can drop into a ballet class anywhere and follow along without understanding the local language. But companies have different styles; watching one dance by several different companies, it is possible to see differences.[10]

Dancers must learn to perform long combinations of steps or movements quickly, to "get it in their body." Concentrated observation is necessary. Learning movements quickly starts early with increasingly difficult combinations in class and rehearsals. They learn to trace the movements using their hands before doing them. Some have the skill to easily imitate the teacher as they gracefully move across the floor in a complicated series of steps, but for others it takes longer. Philip said his body memory developed early:

> My learning disability worked out splendidly for dance because I'm the type of dancer who can stand in the back of the room and watch somebody do a combination, and it's in my body just from seeing them. Remembering choreography and details and things like that is so easy for me.

Teachers as gatekeepers to the profession place fast learners, a necessary skill, in classroom positions that communicate they are favored; they receive the most corrections and get the best performance opportunities. Selection and rewards start early.

The Challenge of Time and Cost

The practice of dance—several classes a week, rehearsals, and performance—often starts at age eight to ten, especially for girls, and requires dedication, discipline and parents' help through finances, time, and emotional support. Regular class attendance and being on time require the time and money of parents as does locating a professionally oriented studio. Looking back, mothers are often seen as heroes. I had no narratives of "stage mothers" pushing children. Sons had fewer stories of assistance from parents as many were older when they started to dance and many received scholarships. Most of the women's narratives involved parents driving them back and forth daily over substantial distances until they were able to drive. Those with available public transportation learned to use it early.

Several classes a week is expensive; pointe shoes (starting between ten to twelve years of age) wear out quickly and can cost about a hundred dollars per pair.[11] Girls try different brands and, later as professionals, find individual makers, as they have to fit just right. Pointe shoes that become too pliable with use become dangerous and can lead to injuries. Each dancer learns how to break them in and how long to wear them safely. All have stories of their first pairs. It is part of the enchantment of ballet.

Even more costly are summer intensives, often in distant cities, where much of the training occurs, especially for those from small studios. Again, boys are more likely to receive scholarships. Dancers talk about parents' financial responsibilities for costumes for *Nutcracker*, competitions, and recitals and the contributions of families and community volunteers to create performances.

Not all parents can commit the time or have sufficient financial resources.[12] The mother of one young woman, Chantel, could not take her regularly to class, so families from her church arranged to drive her. More common was Morgan's story:

My mom. She was always there. My dad did the weekend driving. She was totally committed to it—if my grades had started to suffer, then she would have been like, "Okay, we need to nix this cheerleading." Nothing suffered, so she was ready and willing to pick me up at points A, B, and C. Without my parents, I obviously couldn't have done it. When I turned sixteen, I got a car.

Many of the young dancers, even the men, talked about mothers' encouragement. Matthew's dedication to dancing and his identity as a dancer organized his life with his mother's support:

There was certain point where—I think, somewhere between the middle of ninth grade—I knew that this was what I had to do. I almost felt pain—I can't explain it, but I felt this ache. How to explain it best: desire. None of my friends were dancing, and I guess I wanted to participate in the more common sports. My mom put her foot down, "No. You're gonna keep going. We'll reassess things in a year or two." I'm really glad she did.

Unlike the young women, the young men often did not have peer support, either in ballet or academic classes. This was one of the only instances I heard talk about being strongly encouraged to continue by parents. More common narratives involved the young people urging their parents to allow them to continue their aspirational careers.

Most of the parents of the dancers I spoke with were not in the arts and, from the young people's perspective, needed to learn to accept their child's early passion and commitment. As Julia states, she had a different view than her parents:

> When I was eight, they actually moved me into the professional division. I firmly declared to my parents that I would be a professional ballet dancer one day. They decided that they would support whatever I wanted. They respected it, but probably were like, "Okay. She's eight." I never once wavered.

Like most upper-middle-class parents, they listened to what their children wanted. By high school, many young dancers drift away. But for those who continue, they become involved intensively in the practice of dance—the development of the body, the daily class, the expected behaviors, and new relationships. Their passion or love of dance is central, and the support from parents and teachers begins to provide them with rewards.[13]

The Challenge of Competition

Competition is endemic to dance, as it is to acting, music, or sports. Relationships among peers are often competitive—there are few important roles, few slots in the best summer intensives, and a growing number of dance competitions. While sometimes friendships mitigate competition, some teachers also emphasize classroom competition. A second form of competition is with one's ideal—that is, self-competition—working to achieve what the dancer sees as the best professional dancers on film or in live performance. Although this has a positive side of minimizing competition with peers, it can also lead to striving for perfection and potentially a negative self-image.

Much of the competition is with one's ideal self. Adji Cissoko of the Alonzo King LINES Ballet told *Dance Magazine:*

> My parents questioned why on earth I wanted to spend all my free time being yelled at, but I didn't see it that way. I found pleasure in the hard work. I loved when my teachers lifted my leg up all the way to my ear, only to let go a second later and yell at me as it dropped down rapidly. I learned quickly that once you achieve your goals you set new ones even higher. Sometimes I feel like the older I get, the more I find to work on.[14]

She learned to challenge herself continuously. I suspect she saw the attention she received as indicating potential and had an image of what it was possible to achieve—an ideal self that she wanted to reach. This is different than comparing what one does to peers or having a teacher pick "the best."

Learning what is possible and working to achieve that allows students to minimize competition in the classroom. Miranda started dancing in a performing arts high school and viewed competition as self-competition. Her comments also show the importance of the public nature of the class. Explicit peer comparisons happen sometimes. Miranda provides us with a definition of self-competition, a challenge to improve:

> These girls were all trained, studying at least four or five years, and I had to just watch and observe. I must say I was lucky. I had a good body. I was very flexible. I had good feet, perfect turnout, which I didn't learn to hold, and I just liked to move. I had a lot of advantages. It was late, but nobody ever said that to me. This is a good thing. Nobody ever said, "Oh, you have to work hard because you're behind." I knew it. All I had to do was look.
>
> You don't say, "Oh, that's wrong. Do it this way." Or, "Why don't you do that?" because they are ahead of you. No, I never felt that. *The competition was with myself.* I really think it was, and I tell my students, "There are always gonna be people better than you and worse than you." You compete with yourself. I wanna do it better, and I love to repeat the exercise in the back. I worked very hard, but so did the other girls.

Self-competition involves persisting in efforts to achieve an ideal.

Some saw classmates as competition, which is sometimes emphasized by teachers who rank students by placement at the barre or position them in the front for center floor combinations. Others experienced
summer intensives as a challenge to improve, working toward that ideal
self. Although Allison uses the word "competition," she regarded the
older students as her ideal that summer; she persisted:

> It was really fun. I loved those summer programs because you got to
> meet girls from all over the country who were the top of their game,
> the best in their class, so you could see what they were learning. It
> was competitive, but I loved that kind of competition because it made
> me step it up a little bit, and it was really fun. I was eleven. That was
> the first time that I was really exposed to a broader ballet world. I
> had never seen dancers that talented before. I got to see people that
> were older than me, professionally trained dancers. I think from that
> summer, I had this spark. "Oh, this is what I wanna do." I quickly re-
> alized that while I was lucky to have had a good teacher in my home-
> town, it was just not gonna be what I needed to pursue a professional
> career. In hindsight, it's like one of those things you wonder how you
> would have the foresight to see that when you're in sixth grade.

Many enjoyed being exposed to well-trained dancers in a top summer
intensive like Allison. She saw what was possible.

Wanting to achieve her ideal made Daniella persist in pushing ahead,
though she suffered:

> I wanted it so much. I mean, you cry and then—it was just a lot more
> every day. My feet hurt a lot, and I was constantly confronted with
> things that I couldn't do. I just pushed and pushed, and I did it. It's
> not that I ended up being able to do everything, but I got a lot further
> than I had been.

Again, she saw the training as a challenge and inched toward her ideal.

The ballet mirror can be a source of self-challenge. How can I make
my body look better—whether that means thinner or straighter legs
or arms better placed in fifth position above my head? The competition is not with others; the competition is with that unobtainable ideal.
Dancers want to see what they are accomplishing and not rely solely on
teachers' evaluations. Importantly, when dancers can see what they are

doing, they learn to feel what it is like to do it correctly. They become so accustomed to the mirror that two corps members looked at the mirror to talk to each other while seated side by side on the floor during rehearsal. Justin Peck, choreographer for the New York City Ballet, explained the problems of choreographing without a mirror:

I hadn't realized how much we really use the mirrors as a tool to study movement, especially as it's being generated. I would demonstrate something, and it was difficult for Anthony [principal dancer] to see what the full movement was. I would have to show a step multiple times, facing him and then facing away, so that he could study and familiarize [himself] with what it is and how it looks, and then translate that visual onto his own facility.[15]

By seeing how the body is positioned, the mirror provides a means to learn independently and more rapidly.

But wanting the ideal and having so much love of dance also encourages destructive behavior in some; even without telling dancers to lose weight, looking at the body in the mirror may lead to eating problems.[16] With the aid of the ever-present mirror, how do you achieve the "right" proportions? Remy, now teaching dance, reflected on her youth in a major company training center. The "perfection" she discusses is how the ideal self can be debilitating, particularly when teachers encourage weight loss to achieve it:

You're so focused on yourself at such an early age, this whole idea of perfection; it's so unhealthy. You're a human being, but suddenly, you're being held to these standards of perfection, and that can be a really dangerous road. You have to be able to gain perspective. I can remember when we all hit twelve: puberty. All the girls' bodies started to change. The school was like, "You have to lose weight." There's a lot of pressure. It was heartbreaking, because they were doing almost anything to lose the weight, and these are twelve-year-old girls. There was bulimia; there were some really ugly things I saw. They would do almost anything to stay in the program. You lose perspective, and if you don't maintain weight, then you're out.

Some situations require competition with others; auditions for roles, summer intensives, and company schools.[17] Additionally, summer intensives often rank attendees for class placement. The most competitive intensives bring together dancers, each of whom was Clara in the local *Nutcracker*. Auditions for intensives give students an idea of the national competition, as Julia remembers. Competition creates winners and losers:

> It must be perfect. I would go with my mom to Chicago to do all the auditions. It was always stress. I must get into a good summer program and get a scholarship. The summer intensives were the most exciting part of my year. The process of getting into them was the most stressful thing ever.

These programs often emphasize hierarchy and competition as Morgan explains, but friendships can mitigate some of the competition:

> At home, it's friendly competition because they're generally your friends. You're inviting each other over to each other's houses, but when you leave to go away for the summer intensives, you don't know anyone. It's like the first day you have these classes. It's so that they can place you in various levels. Right off the bat, day one: red, yellow, blue, green, violet. You learn what's the lowest, the highest, even before you take the class. I don't know how that stuff gets out. Competition is starting day one because nobody wants to be in the lowest level. Everyone wants to be in the highest.

For the ambitious young dancer at a summer intensive of a major school, being assessed as one of a handful of the best can lead to admission to the year-round program—a major decision for young dancers and families, typically requiring a move away from home, as Justine explains. A student does not have the authority to question staff; but Justine questioned the rules, speaking up and claiming a place in a year-round program, supported by her parents:

> When I came to [a major company] for their summer course, I was thirteen, and they were like, if you're fourteen and older and interested in being considered to stay for the year-round program, please let us know. Well, I'm not about to wait another year. I marched right into the office. "I'm very interested in being considered." They knew my age and asked me to stay. I worked very hard. I had so much sup-

port from my family. I think that combination of those things with timing, [the] stars aligned really beautifully throughout my whole training and career.

Competition pits one student against another and is built into the performing arts. But some teaching strategies encourage students to compete for corrections. Those placed at the front of the class (or those who maneuver their way there) receive corrections; they are worthy of criticism, though peers may see them as pushy. Acting competitively is encouraged, as Dylan recalls. Criticism becomes a reward:

It was the first time I had a teacher say "Why are you hiding in the back of the classroom? Don't you want attention?" Or we were doing a combination in center and I was standing, ready to go, and I started to go and no one else was going with me, and so I just stopped. The teacher was like "Why wouldn't you want to solo? What are you thinking? You could get so much help with everything." I got to take that home with me. My attitude changed that year.

[At his home school students said], "You're being so aggressive." "Well, that's what I got taught in the summer." I got constructive criticism for sure, but I got more attention from the teachers after that.

Dylan was not the only one who was encouraged to compete in training classes. Standing in the front, if you learn more slowly, it is a problem for those behind you. In the end you may do the movement well, but those in front, who learn fast, are favored with criticisms. When some teachers repeat a series of movements, they have the students in the back move to the front to give slower learners a chance to receive criticisms and improve. Like Dylan, the men talked much more about peer competition than the women, but it isn't clear whether that means they were more competitive, or that they experienced more behavior as competitive, or that they talked about it more.

Most dancers had friends who were dancing, which helped moderate the interpersonal competition; but sometimes competition in the dance classroom made friendships difficult. Most made good friends in high school too, but that was difficult with of the frequency of dance requirements as Olivia explained in the beginning of the chapter. Learning to

compete is necessary to audition, but Olivia realizes developing friendships and a sense of the collective mitigate the competition:

> I think that [major company intensive] definitely opened my eyes.
> Sometimes it's hard too, because you're like she is so good and I'm—
> but it's a little balancing act in some ways. Then you're like, she's my
> age and she's in Level 7 and I'm just in Level 3. Then in other ways
> you're like "we're all in this together." The girls in your class become
> close.

Morgan also argues that dance friendships are important in dealing
with competition:

> Everyone's really sweet and we love each other, but at the end of the
> day, everyone wants the lead role over the next person. I was lucky
> enough that I was—I would say I was pretty good growing up. There
> was a core group of us who alternated lead roles. There are tons of
> corps roles, but nobody wants them. Oftentimes, I was given soloist
> roles, which was truly amazing. My best friend was often given the
> lead role. We had friendly competition, but I was always genuinely
> very happy for her. I think because we were so close, it was okay if
> one of us got the role.

Despite sometimes hurtful competition, the love of dance keeps dancers
dancing.

The Challenge of Balancing Academics and Dance

Young dancers who continue in high school must meet the challenge of
organizing their lives. While their identities are becoming tightly linked
to their dancing bodies, most did not give up on academics. Many, with
the encouragement of parents, thought academics were of equal importance to dancing. Some parents communicated that, if they didn't do
well academically, they could not dance.

Convinced that succeeding in both was important, dancers met the
challenge of multitasking. Most of those I interviewed not only danced
six days a week but took Advanced Placement (AP) classes and maintained A averages. Although a few seemed to have different styles of
academic learning that made academics difficult, all learned how to or-

ganize their time to dance, do their homework, and participate in some high school activities with friends. Attending arts schools made it easier for some of the young men who were teased or harassed in traditional schools, as well as for those who danced professionally or those whose parents did not have the financial resources for them to train in private studios. All managed complicated, busy lives.

Kendell, whose parents insisted on prioritizing education, led one of the busiest, well-organized lives with dance, academics, a boyfriend, and "nerdy" clubs:

I got it all done. Looking back, some of the things I did were crazy. My parents wanted to support me as much as possible in my wanting to dance. They were also, "Your first priority is school, and dance comes second." I maintained a 4.0, and I was taking Advanced Placement classes—and scoring 5's and 4's on those tests. I was also taking college courses at the community college. They thought that if dance didn't work out, I needed to be ready—for me it was chemical engineering.

I took it very seriously. I was valedictorian. In high school I distinctly remember waking up at 6 am, going to the college, then going and taking company class, then going back to high school, and then going back to ballet to dance for four hours. That didn't get me home until 9 pm. Homework was between the minute I walked in the door and 1 in the morning. To be honest, I fell asleep behind the wheel.

I knew I really wanted to dance. I also understood where my parents were coming from. "I have to make this work." I don't know how I did it. Then when I got to conservatory, people were like, "This is the hardest thing ever." I'm like, "Are you kidding?"

Some parents insisted on putting academics first. Kendell was not the only dancer with excellent organizing skills. Morgan managed multiple activities:

I worked very hard to be good at everything that I did. I think because of the ballet, I was able to really focus on multitasking. While I knew dance was something that I really cared about and loved genuinely, I also had my dad on the other side of the fence who was like, "Education is very important." I was never one of those students who put education by the wayside. I would put in the all-nighters if I had to. It was really important for me to maintain honor roll status, straight A's, and then, also be one of the best in the ballet studio. Surprisingly, I managed to do cheerleading. I'd go from school to the ballet studio and then, rush to the high school, cheer at the game, get home around 9:30, 10:00, and then, hit the books.

Academics were second to dance, according to the narratives of Jonah and Kelly, but not by much. Jonah talked about balance:

I tried to sustain a balance. Not to be boastful, but I think I'm a bright person, so it wasn't hard for me to balance the two. I think at times, definitely my academic education lost a bit, because I was focusing a little bit more on dance. I think that was also because I liked dance more. It was more tangible; I could understand it. I thought I was learning more from going to those dance classes every single day than I was in an academic setting. I was able to go to school and not fall asleep, do my homework.

Whereas Jonah felt like he didn't give up anything, Kelly remembers her mother's strong opinion that she do well academically. She sacrificed some school social activities, though she acted in several school productions:

The deal was if my grades slipped, I had to give up dance. It was Monday through Friday. Then on the weekends there were extra rehearsals for *The Nutcracker* or I did some plays. I made videos. I remember hanging out with my friends, but I remember missing a lot of stuff. I missed parties. I was an excellent student. I feel like most dancers are. You're told what to do. You wanna make people proud. You wanna impress people. You wanna do your best; very focused, very motivated. I did International Baccalaureate.

Balancing so many activities contributes to organizational skills, but the rewards and passion are linked to dance. But focusing, following the rules, and working hard allow them to accomplish more than many young people. Families insist on it.

Although Kendell, Morgan, Jonah, and many others were able to successfully balance public school and dance, others have a more difficult time. For Carson, taking a paying performing job of dancing in an out-of-state *Nutcracker* created problems for him in a public school as they would not permit him to miss that many days of school. "They were threatening to expel us," he told me. His family's solution was home-schooling. There was no arts school near his home that might have understood missing school for performance days.

Sometimes an arts-oriented school provides a haven for those who travel for performing, those who have problems at school because they are teased, often because they are gay, or those who do not have the economic resources to train in private studios.

Chantel, like Carson, needed a school that understood her performance schedule and a place to train for no additional money. An arts school worked well for her:

> It was really cool, but it was hard because I would do school every day, and then I would perform every night my whole junior year. Then on the weekends, I would have two shows, so it's almost like I got a taste of Broadway when I was in high school. I got really sick, too; I was doing that every day, so it was crazy. We only got paid—I don't even think it was $400.

Young boys taking ballet don't have many storybooks about boys who dance. In many communities, boys don't dance; they play sports. Unlike the girls, boys rarely received respect from school peers for dancing and were the subject of bullying, according to Albert when he was in school in the 1960s:

> I couldn't get my classes in the public school system. I was in the advanced level [dance], which meant I needed an early dismissal. Dance became my PE credit. My French teacher objected to me leaving. She was right; I fell behind, I was on a seven-day schedule.
>
> My answer to the bullying was partially successful: to perform at lunch assemblies. I just put myself in their face. It didn't abate the

teasing, but the girls really liked it. I won the election for student council president. I had over half the vote probably. Then I had the closet boys. I mean the closet voters, I'll call them, who whispered to me that they voted for me, but they would never say that in front of other boys. I really appreciated the whispers. I embraced my difference. [It helps] when your name and photo appear in the newspaper for local productions.

Some still experience bullying today. Jordan, a much younger generation than Albert, transferred to an arts school to escape harassment with the help of his mother, but arts schools often focus on contemporary dance, so he also trained daily in a ballet studio:

I wanted to have the academics, too, so I went to the arts magnet school. Basically, there was a time I was getting bullied. The arts magnet school was more open; I graduated at sixteen. I don't know [how long I was bullied]. There were only a few little things that happened. As a kid, you blow it up. I wasn't constantly bullied, but in a few instances it was just not where I wanted to be. I knew I wanted to go to the arts magnet anyway. It was like, "Let's just skip ahead." I ended up graduating with AP credits.

Arts schools also provide opportunities to try dance. Graham, a musician, had not danced before he transferred to an arts school:

It was a charter performing arts high school serving kids who were interested in the arts and also kids who just couldn't cut it in public school. It ended up being this motley crew of trans and goth kids and kids who were flunking out of school, and kids who were into the arts. I feel very fortunate. It was a hippie school. I finished after my third year. I was a nerdy, artsy kid, so I wasn't sure if I wanted to go the academic route or go the conservatory route.

Elementary arts schools can be essential and inspirational, especially if a student has a different learning style. Philip told the most dramatic story. He was placed in an arts elementary school by a foster care worker after being disruptive in local schools:

I started dancing at ten. I'm thirty-seven now. I say dance found me and saved my life, so it's been a pretty important part of my life.

My first seven years, I was in an orphanage and went from home to home, so it was a lot of school changing. I also had a severe learning disability, which I didn't know. School was just a difficult place for me. I acted out, so I was deemed this bad child. I had a young lady who became a godmother of mine, who worked for the state, who decided [I should attend] the performing arts [elementary] school. You got to pick what you wanted to do. I'd never seen anything in the arts. I got put into band, which was nice. I went around to all of the other concentrations; everybody was full.

I went to the dance teacher. That was the last place because boys didn't dance at that time. That was weird. I said, "I need to be in your class," and she said, "My class is full; unfortunately, no." I said, "This is the last place I can go to. Just let me dance for you."

This is how the story went, so my first dance teacher tells it. Evidently, I just went to the stage, and I started dancing around, and she saw me and said, "You're in." That's how I started dance. I happened to be good at it. I happened to actually have a talent for it. This was like nothing on my radar. It really just kind of fell into my lap by default.

The challenge of balancing academic schools and dance is managed very well by young dancers, but some of the male dancers found academic schools to be challenging—not because of academic skills but because of how they were treated by fellow students. Male dancers are absent from childhood books, and families lack imagination about putting their sons in dance, instead choosing soccer or tennis. It doesn't appear to be a man's profession, despite the success of Baryshnikov (*The Turning Point* or *White Nights*), Ethan Stiefel and Sascha Radetsky (both dancers with ABT and both in *Center Stage*, with Stiefel on a motorcycle), or Aran Bell (*First Position*, appointed the youngest principal dancer of ABT).

The Challenge of Late Entry for Men

The smaller number of male dancers and lower financial costs of men's entry, allowed by scholarships and no need for pointe shoes, partly accounts for what appears to be male dancers' greater economic and racial diversity. Men also do not necessarily have to achieve the flexibility and turnout that women do at as early an age. Several male dancers whom

I interviewed did not dance until high school or college and had performing careers. With a smaller pool, the men face less competition for
training slots and jobs, but increasingly, young men are training earlier
and at major ballet centers, like the women.

The stories of young women's first involvement are so similar, it
becomes like a learned tale. The men, however, have more varied narratives about their first class. Some wandered by a ballet classroom in
college, joined a folk dance group, or participated in gymnastics before
finding dance by chance. Most men who start after age fifteen or sixteen
generally do not join major ballet companies but become contemporary
dancers. Because they are less socialized in deferring to authority, more
speak up.

The older men I interviewed came from varied backgrounds and
took different paths. One man started dancing after he finished dental
school, danced professionally as a portfolio dancer, quit for several
years, returned to teach at several different schools, and practices den-
tistry part-time. Most develop portfolios, but at least one, twenty years
ago, joined a major ballet company. Some found dance by chance in high
school but thought their families would be upset when they discovered
their interest, as Lars told me:

> My school schedule changed drastically. I couldn't attend my gym-
> nastics training. I had to decide if I wanted to go to a good high school
> or do gymnastics. Gymnastics wasn't really satisfying any more.
> I just decided I would do high school [chemistry, math, and com-
> puter science]. There was this dance studio randomly on my way
> somewhere. I took a dance class; it just clicked. I started off in that
> random hip-hop class, and teachers noticed, "Oh, you seem like you
> might be talented. You should go take a ballet class to get some re-
> fined training." I started taking ballet and modern classes.
>
> I was hiding it at first. Once I really got into it, I felt like this was
> something I really love and enjoy; my mom was totally fine with
> that. I remember I was afraid to talk to her. I wanted to ask her to
> pay for a workshop. I wrote her a letter because I was afraid to talk
> to her. She said, "Of course." That was more of an issue for other
> members of my family.

I remember at one point—I got into *So You Think You Can Dance*. They had to release me from school for pretty much the whole semester. I was seventeen. I had zero dance experience. I barely started training. It was my first or second year of taking ballet classes. Because I was physically capable of doing things after gymnastics, I looked like I could do things, and I remember choreography. I had no training in anything. I thought I was really strong, and technical. It felt amazing. I learned a lot. I grew a lot. I met a lot of choreographers and people that I ended up working with later. Because I ended up second place in the show, I was able to save enough money to go to school in New York.

Some discovered dance in college, as Sebastian did, while majoring in philosophy and political science. Although men can start later, the body is generally unable to achieve what is necessary for ballet. Sebastian discusses his late start:

Philosophy is super important to me, because it really taught me how to think critically and think like a human being. I knew I wasn't going to be a philosophy professor. I ended up taking the LSAT.

Starting late definitely gave me some perspective and life experience that has been really motivating and integral to the way I train, and the way I take class now. If I had been a young person training the way I was training as a gymnast under the scrutiny of a coach all the time, I probably would've been burnt out, and I probably wouldn't have enjoyed it. I really love it now.

Gymnastics training, flexibility, balance, and remembering movement allowed both Sebastian and Lars to train their bodies for dance, making it easier to begin late.

A few begin even later. James started dancing after graduating from college and had a long portfolio career:

He [partner] came home one time and said, "I signed you up for dance class." I said, "I'm not going." I ended up going, and it was a modern dance class. The instructor said you should go to [local ballet]. I'm sure they'll give you a scholarship. He said "You have all the facility." Well, I took my first class when I was twenty-three. I was late. I had no exposure to dance.

These men all had identities and lives that reached beyond dance before
they started. It doesn't mean they are or were less dedicated to dance,
but they were less deferential. Their period as aspirational dancers was
much shorter than for women. They were less shaped by ballet discipline.

PERFORMING AND COOPERATION AS EXPRESSIONS OF PASSION

Passion—the love of dance—is tightly linked to performing, which
provides social and emotional rewards to young dancers. It is a "professional" experience that typically begins long before they become
professionals and one that engages their emotions.[18] Doctors or lawyers
can't practice surgery or argue a case until they have completed medical
school or law school and received their license to practice or been admitted to the bar. But aspirational dancers perform several times a year
from the time they are small. In Ratmansky's *The Seasons* at American
Ballet Theatre, six small girls dance gracefully on pointe in beautiful
tutus and are lifted high off the ground by the men in the corps. For
all these young dancers, performance is special, whether or not they
become professionals. While the excitement is palpable, they also begin
to learn that performance requires the cooperation of many; their parents and communities are necessarily involved, and all have to enter the
stage on cue and move as directed, together. What is more difficult to
learn is true collaboration: a dancer may be Clara, a star role, but seeing
the performance as a collaborative experience all working together for
a great performance is also important. That is a tension in the world of
classical ballet as it is the principals who are likely to receive most of
the public notice. How do you make the performance into a collaborative effort rather than just people agreeing to help the others out—to
cooperate?

Performance is the emotional expression of passion and provides
social rewards. Over and over I heard similar things to what Lynn told
me: "I loved getting a costume at the end of the year and performing.
Performing is the thing. That was why I kept going back, because I just
liked dressing up and being onstage." It also involves applause and flowers from proud parents. And provides social rewards of wonderful memories, such as Tre's:

By the age of fifteen, I was chosen with eight other boys from schools around the world to go to Tokyo to do the gala anniversary, their seventy-fifth [Royal Academy of Dance]. They were from everywhere. We were eight boys from all the schools that pick their best boys, and they created a little company in Tokyo, and I was there for two months—no parents.

Performing, Philip argues dramatically, saved his life, providing him with rewards he did not experience elsewhere:

The stage was my home. Yes, that's just where I thrived. I loved doin' it, but performing was something completely different for me. When I say dance saved my life, there were a lot of other things going on in my life, and dance was the one stable thing that was good for me, where I was getting positive recognition and reinforcement, as opposed to, let's say school, where it was a miserable experience for me.

Preparation and performance with the freedom to express emotions through movement is the dream of many young dancers, as it was for Julia. The fantasy remains of princesses in beautiful tutus and pointe shoes dancing across the stage. Julia expresses her passion through movement:

I really love performing. I think now I really appreciate the process. I was never that kid who just wanted to get to the performance. I loved moving, and I loved rehearsing. I loved the structure of it. There was something about performing. I remember from age ten I was a little ham onstage. Many little girls have that dream of being the princess ballerina. You're totally living your dream when you're onstage.

I'm a very emotional person. Sometimes I feel that the best way to express the extent of the emotions that I'm feeling is just through movement because sometimes words really just don't capture the extent of an emotion. I think that's probably ultimately what drew me to it. My dad actually makes fun of me for being dramatic. He's like, "I've always said that you're best when you're onstage, that's where the drama just works."

Performance also reinforces the need to face challenges. Eva was not the only one who performed in adverse situations and managed to triumph. Many have stories about slipping or suffering an injury onstage. Figuring out what to do is important, as Eva recalls:

> For as long as I can remember I've had teachers tell me, "Doesn't matter what happens if you're honest. Something goes wrong, just keep dancing." My music stopped. I was moving a little slower. In my mind I was like, "Holy shit, what is going on here. Let's just keep doing this"—just as they were telling me over the microphone, "Sorry, we're gonna ask you to stop here and we're gonna try it again." It felt like I was going in slow motion, but I just did a perfectly straight triple [*pirouette*]. Turned out wonderful, clean landing, and I was like, "Okay, thanks, bye." I feel it must have left an impression on the judges, having not just the clean triple, but being a good sport about it.

She received a reward; she won the competition.

Opportunities to perform can reinforce the hard work toward the ideal self, as Lisha found. She saw the opportunity to perform as a challenge to work even harder demonstrating persistence and dedication; she was awarded the part:

> I was fourteen and I was cast as an understudy for *Swan Lake pas de trois*; you get the partnering, you get the solo, I didn't have the lines. Technically, I could do it better than the person I was understudying, but they didn't wanna cast me until one month before the performance. People knew I was getting better than she, and then hearing that from other people made me fight even more. If I didn't think I had a chance, maybe I wouldn't have fought that hard. They had a second audition and I was like, "This is it."

Dancers rarely talked about collaboration at this age, that is, working together to achieve a collective goal: they were more concerned with entering on time with the others and not bumping into others onstage. If they don't enjoy performing; they leave, like Mikayla. Those who continue towards a goal of professional dancer love getting ready and performing, despite nerves. Performing becomes its own reward.

THIS IS WHO I AM

You have to love dancing to stick to it. It gives you nothing back, no
manuscripts to store away, no paintings to show on the walls and maybe
hang in museums, no poems to be printed and sold, nothing but that single
fleeting moment when you feel alive.
    —MERCE CUNNINGHAM[19]

But dance and dance training does leave people with social habits that
enable them to do other activities. With few exceptions, no one really
expressed doubt that they wanted to perform professionally before
faced with college/company decisions. They knew they were dancers
by the time they were in high school; their aspirational identity had
become central to their sense of self—so much of their time, relationships, and activities were organized around dance. That self was expressed "in their bodies" in class, in rehearsal, and during performance.

    Reflecting on her youth from her thirties, Audrey explains how she
thought about her performing self. It wasn't just the act of dancing; it
was organizing life around dancing. It is difficult to know when this
critical aspect of self was recognized, but I suspect it was in her teens.
Audrey recalls:

    People are like, "Can you hang out?" I'm like, "No, I have practice.
    I have to go to rehearsal," and so, just having class after school has
    been my whole life. Thinking about wanting to be a dancer, I think
    I always assumed it was going to be part of my life, not like, "This is
    my goal," but it was just kind of, "This is who I am."

Casey's narrative confirms Audrey's:

    I don't know. It wasn't like a thought. It was just like, "This is what
    I'm gonna do. This is who I am."

The aspirational identity as a professional dancer becomes the critical aspect of self. Not only is performance an expression of passion for
dance, but the dancers receive rewards for it from family, teachers, and
audiences.

    By the time they have to make critical decisions on school and train-
ing, they have already developed habits—dedication to the work of ballet
and its expectations, persistence in working to improve toward their

ideal, deferring to those in authority, and seeing the world as setting up challenges for them—whether it is training their bodies or organizing their lives with competing demands. Collaboration comes with more performing opportunities; for now, they have learned to cooperate.

Most of these young people had parents who paid for classes, summer intensives, and shoes and had the time to cart them around. Their parents encouraged or at least negotiated with them about dancing. But they don't all receive the same supports for the different pathways at fifteen or eighteen and, for some, their bodies failed them. Some decide to attend and are admitted to company training programs while in high school, and others audition for conservatory or college dance programs at eighteen. Both move closer to "professional dancer." Some begin a move away from aspirational dancer to attend college in a non-dance program and struggle to put their passion and aspirational self in memory. Others take more convoluted paths.

No matter which path they take, dancers' bodies identify them as dancers. Something about their backs and feet remain long after they stop performing. When a retired performer, in his late fifties, arrived sweating, he reported he had ridden a city bike. "At least we can still do it," he said. I was not sure whether the "we" included me or he was referring to mature dancers. I sat up straighter.

CHAPTER THREE

CAREER DECISION CHALLENGES

Aspirations and a Sticky Self

For those who remain as aspiring professionals through high school, the deeply embodied self as an aspirational dancer takes on the challenges of career decisions at a very young age, some before they graduate from high school. But these decisions are not made without family support and the decisions of the gatekeepers at dance training centers and colleges or conservatories. The decisions are consequential; most who make it to major companies and many smaller ballet companies train at schools away from home at sixteen. These training centers are either affiliated with major companies or with a few select boarding schools.

Early decisions involve not only the challenge of independence, but also challenges to the body and self. In the dancers' narratives, some parents readily facilitated that move, while others needed to be persuaded by the young dancers. Many, after training, auditioned for ballet companies, only some successfully. Those who chose to try a second pathway, majoring in dance in college or conservatory, had to first audition for admission and then face the challenges of learning new dance styles, getting performance time, and minimizing the importance of classical ballet as their main dance focus. Most don't know much about what awaits them after graduation. A third pathway involves opting out of aspiring to become professional and attending college without majoring in dance, sometimes after studying at a major training center. These individuals face challenges about what to do with their passion. Others changed course several times. Careers involve a number of steps, barriers, challenges, and necessary supports.[1]

Allison matriculated in a ballet boarding school at thirteen with family support. Her choice fit the first pathway:

> I was really focused on that I needed to go to a professional school and study full-time. Luckily, it was only an hour and a half away. I lived in the dorms, but I was able to go home quite a lot, especially the first year. My parents would come up, and I feel that it was a little bit the best of both worlds, because I was able to really have an amazing experience there, but not really have to sacrifice too much with my parents and brother.
>
> It's such a good question [How do you know when you're twelve?] that is what you wanna do, because it's something that I felt such a strong singular drive towards this thing. I knew it, and I had on these blinders. I only realize now what a huge sacrifice it was for my family to say, "We're gonna trust you and send you to live in this dorm when you're thirteen." Now that I'm older, I realize what a big deal that was, but at the time, I just was so focused on the fact that that's what I needed to do, it just seemed right. I do think it was helpful I had really supportive parents; they didn't have a background in ballet. They were always very much, "We're gonna be here for you, but if you don't like it—if it doesn't turn out the way you think it is, come home tomorrow." I think that was super helpful in letting me feel comfortable to go down this path.

Strongly encouraged by her family to take the college route of a major ballet program, Lara found the competition and perceived unfairness of faculty decisions difficult and gravitated away from ballet to develop another passion. She fit the reversal pattern. Difficult interactions, lack of social rewards, and alternative passions may encourage some to step away from dance. Looking back from her forties, she argues she was beginning to reject the "tool" image of the ballerina. Lara saw her parents as gatekeepers and then interpreted signs from faculty as barriers and changed course:

I started studying privately. She [teacher] was really encouraging me. I decided I really wanted to make this a career. It wasn't really a choice with my family whether I was gonna go to college. I was gonna go to college. Suddenly, I was a small fish in a big pond. There wasn't a transition period. I was joining a company. There was a hierarchy with principals. We were the apprentices. People got parts in the shows, "They're not that good. Why?"

I never felt I really clicked with the directors. I need to feel that personal connection. I think if I would have been more patient—I only lasted a year and a half. During freshman year, you're exposed to so many things that you never really knew about. I had always had a love for costuming. When I was a senior in high school, I was choreographing. I organized costumes. I sewed. I was really interested in seeing the whole thing as a concept. Not just being a dancer, but also creating. Any dancer who joins a company—you become a tool for someone else to work with, and there wasn't really any place for input or personal opinion.

Lara experienced another possible passion and became a clothing designer.[2] "Choice" is a process shaped by others: family and gatekeepers, the dancers' interpretations of experience, and the body.

The emotional, physical (body), and social challenges of early career decisions by aspirational dancers involve parents and dance personnel. Sometimes experiences lead to changing directions, as Lara did. Sometimes passion weakens, while for others, it reveals itself by the absence of dance. Some receive fewer or more rewards than anticipated. Arriving at "professional dancer" generally involves a series of decisions by self and others as responses to particular situations; it is a process. Each pathway has different challenges of "how can I do that?" And each path involves new movement, more independence, harsher criticism, fewer roles than expected, and fierce competition. Some are rejected by gatekeepers or grow to see the career and experiences as risky, not as challenges.

TRAINING CENTERS

Obtaining a spot in the bigger classical ballet companies generally requires intense training prior to finishing high school in established
company or boarding schools known to produce dancers for major companies. This may mean moving at fourteen or fifteen to a large city,
sometimes in Europe or Russia, and completing high school online.
These decisions are not made without parental support—financial,
social, and emotional.

The Challenge of Moving Away from Home

Some young dancers say they had family support to move, while others
needed to persuade their parents. The sense of self that they were dancers was strong enough to allow overcoming the challenge of leaving home
early: independence, tough criticism of body and movement, competition, and continued balancing of academics and training. The financial,
emotional, and social costs of moving are high, and few had an easy time.
Striving for their ideal and their passion pushed them to dedicate themselves to training and allowed some not to be derailed by gatekeepers or
peers.

A few traveled as far as Russia at sixteen. The dancers pushed for it,
but it was the parents who permitted and paid for the experience. Anya
trained in a major company school and then in Russia at sixteen for two
years:

> I went by myself. I was really interested. I read in *Dance Magazine*
> that you could; they were accepting foreigners. I made that like my
> goal. It was really interesting and difficult. My dad thought it was a
> really exciting and interesting idea. He was in science himself. The
> idea of exploring and trying things—he's a little idealistic in that
> way. That probably was a good thing. My mom, I think, was terrified.
> I was like so stubborn and passionate about it, so no one would stop
> me. He wanted his kids to just go for broke.

John, with his teacher's encouragement, moved across the country
to a major company school that allowed him to study with other boys.[3]
But sometimes chance and a parent's reluctance allow young dancers
to make good decisions, possibly waiting to move to a major city to

train. Alicia took a summer intensive at fifteen, but her parents in-sisted she wait for year-round training, protecting her from what they saw as risk. When she moved across the country at seventeen, she was promoted rapidly to the preprofessional, then the junior group, and finally, the major ballet company. In addition to her dance skills, Alicia used her observational skills to make decisions to push herself more, demonstrating dedication and persistence; rewards started coming to her:

I was really looking forward to going. I was really just heartbroken about that. It was for the best, because I wasn't mature yet. I knew that I loved it. I didn't know that I was going to make a career out of it. Even when I came to New York, I took it from the feedback that they liked me. I must be good enough. I just took it one step fur-ther, and further. When I realized what my competition was, I got a little bit more competitive. Everything came to me, the roles. I didn't know how serious and competitive it was until I came.

The actual amazing part about it is that when I was at public school, I hated [it]. I refused to do my homework. I had terrible grades. When I transferred, I loved the school. I loved the academics, and my grades went straight up because I was happy.

She no longer saw academic school as competing with ballet; she could multitask and received emotional and social rewards from each.

Although some parents resisted their children's desire to move before high school graduation, Daniella's mother encouraged her to enroll in a major company school for better training when she graduated from high school a year early. Daniella recalls:

I guess my mother really pushed a lot. I think she understood in a way I didn't that I needed real professional training—I knew that I wanted to be professional. I don't think I would have advocated for it if I'd been left alone. I appreciate she did that. She wasn't like a stage mom. I think she just had a more practical understanding of what was necessary. I think I stood out enough that I was invited to come back as a year-round student.

Daniella wasn't sure about the challenge of moving without her parents' assistance, and she worked hard to get her body ready for professional companies in a summer intensive. She received a reward: the offer for year-round training.

The Challenge of the Ideal Self and Competition

Male and female dancers talked differently about their experiences with competition. Both acknowledged the striving for the ideal self, but the men talked a lot about interpersonal competition. Major training centers, away from parents, allow young people such as Jordan to see the "best dancers," setting the bar high, an ideal self. This can be experienced as a challenge or a risk of failure. Jordan recalls:

> Also, it made the idea of quality pretty obvious; that's what you aim for. People say, "Oh, you're a perfectionist, or you have a very high standard." I think it's to do with education. I don't think I have high standards. I think I know what's possible. I've seen it. Naturally, you want to go there.

Seeing "what is possible" can lead to frustration or determination to improve. The decision to attend a ballet training program away from home means, for many, prioritizing ballet, their passion, over school, as Justine did:

> School has always come naturally to me. A lot of dancers are type A and OCD; we're perfectionists. School for me was one of those things that I was never passionate about. I was passionate about ballet. I felt like I didn't move away from my family to go to high school. I moved here to pursue a career in dance. That's where my priorities were. I still did very well in school, but it just wasn't where my heart was.

All spoke about the competition among students, but the men talked about it in stronger terms. John did not like the competitive atmosphere in a major company school where he trained away from home starting about age twelve with other boys. He, as did several other men, talked about problems with authority or not showing the expected deference in the context of talking about competition:

> It was competitive and crazy. It was weird. I enjoyed being away from home, and dancing; but the regimented stuff and the authority I had an issue with, and the discipline. I'm kind of ambivalent about

dancing. I like the idea of it, and I like certain experiences I've had, but largely, I find most of the environments that that occurs in to be stressful, weird, you know, like competitive.

Gabriel experienced the competition as "cutthroat" in a major company school:

Well, when I first came [major summer intensive], I was eleven and twelve. I just remember crying a lot because I was suddenly within a class full of twenty kids, who were really good. They all wanted the same thing, and there's only a handful of jobs out there, in [major companies]. You're crawling, every class. By the time I got to fourteen, fifteen, and stayed the winter term, it was ruthless. It was cutthroat. You fought your way to the front, every single day.

Few women talked about authority or competition as John and Gabriel did. The female dancers talked about friends at school and their love of performing.

Dylan's narrative, however, described being unsupported by and angry at the major company training program; he saw the program as setting up barriers to his progress. But he explained his exit as feeling less passion for ballet signaled by fewer rewards and encouraged by his college acceptance:

That was the first time I took step back, and I was like "You know, that's weird. I'm almost eighteen and I'm not getting cast." I had applied to college and started to think, "Well, how much am I going to get out of another year, if my penultimate year ended as an understudy?" I became really disillusioned with dance and realized that I think I had been kind of just doing it for a long time because I was already doing it. There's a meeting [an evaluation] in the fall, but it's so generic. My meeting had been overwhelmingly positive.

I was accepted [college] while we were on a five-minute break in a rehearsal for the thing that I hadn't been cast in. I just left. I didn't even tell the choreographer. But the only reason I had anywhere to go after dance was because she [mother] forced me to do it [apply to college]. I mean, "Thanks mom." That's the ultimate "I told you so."

The competition worked differently for men and women, but not all achieved their dreams of getting into a ballet company, including men.

The Challenge of Competing for a Company Position

With every company audition comes the possibility of failure. Few find positions in major companies, even when trained at the best company schools, as only about ten ballet companies with seasons of about forty weeks each hire, at most, a handful of dancers a year. Smaller ballet companies, often with shorter seasons, dot the landscape and hire a small number too. Many don't succeed, but the situation is different for men and women.

The audition process is arduous, involving travel and expenses, competition, and little feedback by the gatekeepers of companies.[4] Sometimes no positions exist, although they audition many. Allison got a contract. Her words raise issues about the lack of transparency and deference expected of dancers; dancers do not question the process. She doesn't understand what artistic directors mean when they don't communicate—is it that they don't know how many dancers will be leaving, a lack of funding, or are auditions simply an assertion of power over current dancers by surveilling the new dancers to see if those already employed should be replaced? That is not supposed to happen in union companies. Allison explains:

> I did a bunch of auditions. It's really crazy your senior year of high school. You have to just go every single weekend and do an audition. I remember I had done so many—and made it through the end of all the auditions. They ultimately tell you, "We really like you, but we don't know how many contracts we have, so we'll have to get back to you."
>
> I was discouraged by the whole process, because I had just been getting a lot of half answers. I remember being really torn about whether I should go to New York. I ultimately decided to go to [major company], even though I went into it thinking that it was the wrong decision, especially once I got there and saw so many people. I made it through the end again, and the director called me into his office as soon as it was over and offered me a second company contract. I was just so taken aback, because—it was my first direct offer.

Her entrance to a ballet career was more straightforward than most.

Men have an easier time finding work, particularly in the 1980s. Few men waited in the wings looking for work. Theo joined a major company at eighteen:

They had me working right away; other people started inviting me to participate in things. One of my first professional experiences was for an opera company. We were hired from New York. Of course, there were ample opportunities for young men throughout the city to do all kinds of performing. It was handed to me. I didn't know what auditioning meant, which is rather pathetic, but it's just the privileged position of men in ballet. It just had its own momentum.

Male dancers are less socialized to be deferential than female dancers. Matthew, for instance, had a complex start to his career in a major company. He had more leeway than most women to follow his interests. His dance career illustrates some of the tensions between ambitions and deference expectations. Matthew signed a contract with a small ballet company but broke it when he was offered a scholarship to a major training center that had inspired him to dance. In his narrative, he doesn't defer to authority easily and also sees risk in situations:

I'm more controversial than a lot of other dancers. I'm ambitious. My ambition has been one of my best qualities, and one of my worst qualities. I'm not going to throw anybody under the bus, but at times, looking back, certain actions could have been and have been detrimental to parts of my career; but I would never be where I am today. [After the training year] I took the job [apprentice, major company]. What happened was you're apprenticed. The [major] ballet contract [American Guild of Musical Artists, AGMA] stated that you could only be an apprentice for one year. You are either promoted to corps or you had to be let go. What they [artistic director] did every year was they fired all the apprentices, "non-reengaged."

Then, as they find the money for corps contracts [they start re-engaging]. I was non-reengaged, like all the other apprentices, but I had a really weird season. The first half, he [artistic director] was testing me out. Then, all of a sudden, the second half, I was just understudying. Looking back, I see he was testing people. He wanted to give everybody a fair shot. I felt like, "Oh, he didn't like what I was doing." I was fearful, so I started auditioning other places. He wasn't communicating.

Seeing his situation as risky led him away from a job possibility. But as a man, he was able to join another major company for seven years. Matthew, like Allison, points out the problems of lack of communication by gatekeepers and the dilemmas faced by the ambitious.

Despite the challenges of what he saw as toxic competition in his training program and problems organizing academics and dance, Gabriel dealt with the school and work situation by refusing to defer to his school's wishes. He attended a second major company's summer intensive at sixteen:

They [training program] wanted me to stay another year. They basically hinted to me that I was gonna get into the company. I couldn't bear doing another year. That's how hard it was because you were dancing all day. We had to go to high school. I took five classes. I taught myself three. It [training] was really very, very difficult, on top of feeling like you need to push yourself and be in the front. They were like, "Oh, we don't want you to go to [another major company's] summer intensive." That was their way of keeping you. I auditioned for the [other company's] summer intensive. I got in, scholarship, and the next day, my future boss walks in, hires me, and puts me in the company.

Even those who graduate from the very best training programs do not necessarily find work in ballet companies and, in times of economic downturn, even fewer (especially women) do. Allison was one of the few in her class to get a job with a major company. Justine and Daniella tried European companies at eighteen. Justine, when it seemed like no one would be hired from her company school, took the challenge and organized a European tour with her family. From this, she learned not to be discouraged by what she saw as the uncaring actions of the artistic director where she trained:

I came back to [major company school] after that week [in Europe] and I had four corps de ballet contracts.

    I had a choice, and it was luxurious. It was so surreal. That was like a total career highlight. I said I would love to speak with [artistic director of her school's company], because if I have an opportunity with his company, I wanna take it, but I have these four people that I need to get back to. The response was, "They're very proud and excited but you don't just talk to him."

I was like, I'm sorry. I thought he was a human being. Call me crazy. They're like, "We'll talk to him." I had been a favorite dancer, so I was quite hopeful of an opportunity. I had performed with the company [as a student]. I didn't get to speak with him personally. They were like, "At this point he doesn't know if he's going to have in his budget to hire apprentices. While he loves your dancing, he doesn't want to make you miss out on four great opportunities without a guaranteed contract. We would encourage you to fly free." It was heartbreaking. I was like, I couldn't have a better alternative. Totally crushing—but freeing at the same time. Then I had a decision to make, and I spoke with all these directors. I ended up starting with [major European Ballet] a week later. I didn't even finish my year.

She made every effort to make a reasoned decision with support from her mother who had taken time off work to go to Europe with her and paid for it. Her experience with the artistic director allowed her to see how he could insulate himself from others and, from her perspective, how little he cared about his dancers.

COLLEGE OR CONSERVATORY DANCE MAJOR

Matthew Bourne, the British artistic director and choreographer of contemporary versions of traditional ballet stories, states: "I like the idea that people don't go into training too early. I like dancers who've got other interests, who've seen other things, experienced life a bit more."[5] Ballet companies tend to hire dancers who are sixteen to nineteen years old who have spent most of their lives training. More contemporary companies prefer older dancers who have experiences and a broader sense of self.

Many of the students who ultimately settle on dance programs struggle with themselves and their parents on whether to attend a college without a dance major or one with a strong dance program or a conservatory. Some got into all three. College and conservatory dance programs tend to be somewhat more realistic about portfolio employment today and teach a diversity of dance styles and choreography that can be challenging but prepare students for approaching the portfolio dance market with its diversity of styles of movement.[6] Students begin to think about the meaning of the different styles of dance and what suits them. They learn to think more critically about what they are communicating with their movements and to ask questions of faculty.

The Challenge of Auditions and Making Decisions

College liberal arts admissions require grades, letters, SATs, and essays. And, as in the much of the dance world, dance programs have gatekeepers who create the competition for admissions: auditions are "win or lose," based on a panel's assessment of bodies, movement skills, and ability to learn. Several of the dancers I interviewed applied to colleges without dance majors and colleges with dance programs or conservatories, and then they had difficulty choosing after acceptance in several. Dance majors in college or conservatory spend the majority of time in the studio—not writing papers, critically evaluating ideas, and reading. Some dancers told me in their interviews that they struggled with their parents over this decision.

Anthony, who followed his performing career with a top contemporary ballet company with a master's in arts administration, narrated his understanding of the conservatory audition process. He made a difficult decision between a conservatory and an Ivy League non-dance education without parental interference:

> You do a ballet class and then a very simple modern class. From there, they do a cut from eighty to fourteen. You do a solo for a panel of fifteen faculty. That was a very intense experience. I choreographed my own solo. It was well-received. They cut the fourteen to eight to do a coaching session to see if you can learn. In the first group of eighty, they're testing to see, "Do you shine? Do you care? Do you love it?" If they can pick you out of a crowd, then you make it to the next one. Then in the solo, it's like, "Okay. Can you perform?" The next one is, "Can you learn?" The last one actually is the most

important, the coaching part, because they want to see, "If you do it twice and we give you notes, can you change?"

Found out about two weeks later that I got in. The [Ivy dance teachers] asked how much I was dancing. I said, "Well, I do ballet six hours a day." They're like, "Are you happy?" I'm like, "I love it. It's my favorite thing." They said, "Well, we all went to conservatory, and we made it to Ivy [as teachers]." Then I went to [conservatory] and had a similar conversation. One faculty member said, "Congratulations. I understand you're weighing this. I just wanted to let you know, you can always be an academic, but you can't always be a dancer." That was a pretty easy decision to make. I don't regret it for a single second.

Some decide whether to pursue dance before applying to college, but not all. This is a more critical decision for a future path than choosing between English and sociology. Anthony and Kendell knew they were dancers, firmly committed to becoming professionals. Kendell, like Anthony, had to decide between an academic track and a conservatory. But Kendell had to struggle with her parents to attend an expensive conservatory rather than accept a full scholarship to an academic program. Kendell recalls:

I think because it [conservatory] was the last audition of the season, I just really didn't think I stood a chance. I just had a blast. I was like, "I'm just gonna have fun and no pressure because I'm not expecting anything, honestly." Then for university—this is what was so hard for my parents. It would've been a full ride through graduate school.

Several considered a more academic track but decided to prioritize dance before applying. Chantel explains her balance of performance and academic education. She sees arts education in her future, after performing, so she was delighted with her conservatory acceptance:

My aunt is an artist. My grandma was like straight education and kind of the same with my mom. My grandma always pushed education, and it wasn't until right before she passed away she was like, "Okay, she's serious, so I'm okay." That was one thing that always stuck with me is education; I want to be an educated artist. Then

I'll have so much more to offer if I really study my craft, not only to offer to the audiences, but then I'll be able to have schools where I'll be able to offer it to children around the world. I just saw the importance in education. Pointblank, period, I was like, "I'm going to college [conservatory]."

Chantel was one of the few interviewees who, in her early twenties, expressed an idea of a future beyond performer.

Financial issues encouraged some choices. Kelly knew her dance school did not develop her technique sufficiently, but her body is a dancer's body. She understood she needed additional training to become a ballerina so, encouraged by her mother and an academic scholarship, she decided on a top college ballet program. But she really wanted to attend a conservatory:

I think I had good performance quality, and it fostered creativity. The technique level, I was far below what I should have been. How did I know that? Because in high school, every time I would go to a summer program, I'd be put in the lowest level. I think the only reason I got into their ballet program was because my body was very right.

Actually, I wanted to go to [conservatory]. I auditioned and got an acceptance letter. I showed it to my mom, and she said, "Congratulations." Then she tore it up because I got in with no scholarship and it was $32,000 a year. My mom said, "If you're gonna be a dancer, you're never gonna make that back." My next choice was the university. When I graduated, I owed $5,000 and paid it off in a year.

Others make decisions based on risk assessment rather than passion. While Kelly attended a ballet program and also completed a social science major, Jonah attended a contemporary college program with only a ballet background. He explains the college decision as his failing to ask for admission to a company training program and his family's financial position. Instead of viewing asking for admission as a challenge, he saw it as a risk to his self—he might not get it. Seeing risk rather than challenge affected his career direction. His family's financial situation mattered too. Jonah recalls:

Senior year, I think that there was some push for me to [attend college]. We were very ballet-driven, and, therefore, the company route was the obvious next step. The summer before university, I did another ballet intensive—very instrumental in my development. That's also why I think it's somewhat abnormal that I didn't attempt or more force myself to try and get into one of those programs for the year instead of staying with my home studio—because of money and I was never openly accepted to come into it.

With that being said, they had an application process that I just didn't do. I never put my name on the list; if they want you, they won't hesitate to tell you. That never happened for me, and I didn't push, either. They're very expensive, and it's also a lot to leave your home at age sixteen, seventeen and go live in another state.

All of these dancers expressed the idea that they considered options and made a choice to study dance. For some, the choice of how to make the career decision was linked to how they saw themselves and their futures, while others were also influenced by finances and risk aversion, like Jonah. Many started college and conservatory programs as classically trained dancers, but most programs require students to learn a variety of movement styles and encourage a shift away from aspirations to be classical ballet dancers.

The Challenge of New Dance Styles

Most conservatory and college dance programs teach a variety of contemporary dance styles in addition to ballet. Contemporary choreography requires new challenges.[7] Daring movements are often required, such as leaps into the arms of another. A contemporary choreographer integrated a new male dancer into a newly formed group of portfolio dancers. They tried on scanty costumes, and the choreography required one to launch himself through the air onto the arms of three men. When I asked one of the men (a "catcher") about the risks of the costumes (very revealing) and the airborne jumps, his response was, "You trust the choreographer to choose trustworthy dancers and his artistic vision." Thus, it was a challenge, not a risk. He did not calculate the probability of failure.

Some moves are seen as challenges by some and as risky by others, explained one dancer after the Scottish National Ballet performed Angelin Preljoçaj's *MC 14/22* on March 11, 2020, at the Joyce Theater. Several men hurled themselves from a platform that looked to be about fifteen feet off the ground into the arms of others, and also threw one another around. The director said several had to be persuaded to do it because they saw it as risky. Challenges sometimes mean daring to use their bodies in a different way, learning new styles of dance, and adapting one's self-image away from the "ballerina" or the "stand on the numbers" dancer.

Some dancers relish the diversity, but it can be difficult to move among different genres: classical ballet, contemporary ballet, and more contemporary (no pointe shoes but a broad range of movement variation), and modern or post-modern dance). Graham, Limón, and Cunningham each have specific movement vocabularies, though most tell you what their best range is. Eileen explained her progression through different techniques:

> Having that foundation of Cunningham technique every single day to wake up to, it's so intense on your body, but it makes you very disciplined as a dancer. You show up, you do the work, and you do it well. That's something that I really enjoyed from her. Then, other teachers are out there, "Feel your body. Feel your bones." I don't know what that means. It was good to have an open mindset and learn; it's what I needed as a young dancer still discovering what true ballet is. I'm so grateful for the ballet technique I learned at that school because it has been the foundation of my career.

Some developed an understanding of the diversity slowly. Chantel fell in love with a different dance style every year and thought critically about the meaning of each technique. Each extended her in more than a physical way; each increased her self-expression and self-confidence:

> I definitely liked ballet. I feel like I was the representation of modern. All the other girls in my class were the representation of ballet. They were just stunning, so I won't say ballet was my favorite. Probably, Graham. I always tell my story, and they're like an emotional type of dancer. They were grounded, so it was just the

technique that I felt the most connection with. That was my favorite class freshman year.

Then every year a transition. I used to hate Cunningham, but then when I went to the Cunningham intensive, it was like, "Wow, I love this." You just feel so strong. You're doing something way beyond your limits, and I liked how it made me feel invincible as a dancer.

I hated Limón freshman year. We [the teacher and I] bumped heads, but then she saw something in me in sophomore year when she asked me to be in one of his most famous pieces. I had another chance to see it. When I had rehearsals with her, things she would say to me and the connection we made, it really stuck with me, and then I had a whole new outlook for Limón and her as a person. "Oh, wow. I'm happy that I had this because I didn't get it all at first, but now I see the beauty in this." That was one of the most special experiences.

In my senior year, I guess ballet was probably one of my favorite classes.

Every year, it was something different. I was bringing something more, something different each year, and the experience I was having throughout college, the different teachers I would have, some were negative, some were really positive. Some may discourage students, but then some encouraged us to see it in a more beautiful way, and so it would open your mind.

Some had complicated processes of finding their identities—more than just a diversity of dance styles. For Carson, the challenges of new dance styles, finances, and reorienting his sexuality made the transition to conservatory difficult. Unlike many, he told a story of his "chance" acceptance at a major conservatory without parental support. He had little experience with concert dance but met the challenge of new dance styles. His narrative is about chance, challenge, deference to others' views, and opportunity:

I've been really very fortunate and lucky. I didn't wanna go to college. I had a job offer at Tokyo Disney. I happened to be doing a ballet competition the weekend of a [conservatory] audition. My dance teacher was like, "Audition for everything." Lesson in life: go to everything. Then I went; she told me to. I got in. At that point, you're like, you have to go. How do you not go? That was a huge fork in the road for me. The same way I got into dance was all just a big fluke that proved to be really beneficial. I hadn't even been in New York. I had never taken a modern class in my life. I had never seen a concert dance company. I had only seen national tours, Broadway stuff. I'd never seen Ailey.

My first year was really hard. I had a hard time adjusting. I probably rarely had a thought creatively or independently at that time. I was just a musical theater [dancer]: "stand on number two" [routine dancing]. Your first year, it takes a lot to acclimate yourself. I can't say I enjoyed it until about my third year. A little bit of that is the program, and a little bit of it was me, just needing to adjust and grow up a little bit. I also was still straight. I had a hard time coming out with my sexuality. I worked [in the summer]. I had to pay my way and am continuing to pay for it. My parents sacrificed a lot for me to be there. A lot of people went and did summer programs. I just went home and taught at local studios so I could have a little money to come back.

Colleges and conservatories provided students with diverse styles of dance that stretched them both artistically and in their body development. Diversity is practical for a portfolio career. Bodies have to be adaptable to a range of movement techniques, as is learning to deal with difficult situations as challenges, not risks.

Chantel and, after struggling, Carson, thrived on the variety, but not everyone deals well or wants to be trained in multiple styles. Sofia did not adapt well and saw the variety as a risk to her ballerina body and identity:

When I graduated, I felt like I needed a break. I was used to training my body specifically in ballet. The performance experiences were not in the ballet genre—because I could see how Graham technique was changing me in good ways, but also in ways that I didn't necessarily want. Same with Horton technique. I couldn't necessarily focus on tiny little aspects of things that I could focus on in a ballet class. I think when I graduated, it was confusing. I took a year to sort of regroup. I went back to my teacher at home. I just wasn't really in the mental state to even want to go to a dance class. I loved dancing, but I think, unfortunately, the experience was so negative for me and so many of my classmates that I needed a break.

Sofia did not receive positive messages, as she was rarely cast, but she did not distance herself from her identity as a ballerina as others, like Kendell, did. Sofia regrouped, continuing to perform in a project ballet group, and she taught ballet to children. Her love of ballet remained strong. Many colleges and conservatories reshape the bodies of dancers as they learn the different styles of movement and the sense of self as a contemporary dancer; these dancers also see themselves as part of the creative process, not just fitting into a role created by and for others.

The Challenges of Developing Voice and Accepting Diverse Rewards

Teachers with different dance styles challenged students to develop bodies and minds that could do multiple styles, to focus on creativity through choreography, and to communicate ideas through movement. Although roles for performances mattered, alternative rewards were possible, such as teaching and choreography. Because teachers did not necessarily demand ballet discipline, student discussion was possible. Some dancers learned to stand up for themselves and others; they took some academic classes that encouraged critical thinking and verbal expression of ideas. It was more like a college environment than a ballet company, some of the time.

In my interview with Kendell, she focuses on the conservatory challenges—both the variety of dance styles and the politics of the dance world. But she found that with continuous dedication and working towards an ideal self rather than comparing herself with others, she could succeed in using her voice and maintaining her passion. She had a difficult time, but through reengaging with tap, learning to choreograph, and teaching, Kendell developed sense of being a dancer rather than a classical ballerina:

It's healthy competition. Everybody doesn't get the soloist role. It's not the end of the career either. I think for me the most challenging part was the shock—I had been doing just ballet with a couple modern and jazz classes during the summers. It wasn't just the modern that

I had back home, but like five different kinds of modern. All these other things that just never occurred to me were also dance. Site-specific things. Like, "I didn't know about this!" I didn't know who Mark Morris was. The ballet school where I trained was very close-minded.

While I was in conservatory, I was the understudy a couple times—not always the one who got picked for projects. In other ways I think I really stood out—in non-dance ways—like in academics. I wasn't a bad dancer, but I was not usually the first pick. That was to be expected at a school where they only take twenty-four of the most amazing dancers. That was hard. I hadn't had a ton of performance opportunity, less than my classmates. Tapping just made me remember why I loved dancing again. Things kind of turned around for my third and fourth year, just falling into place. I started creating work.

In addition to her choreographic success, Kendell was a valued teacher who was sent to schools around the city. Kendell stood up for herself (and others) and relished telling me this story. She did not defer to authority:

I actually wrote a letter: "This is a school. There's supposed to be two casts. This will be my second time understudying in a rep concert—I respect the process, but if I could use this time to go choreograph my own work . . . . To be honest, I felt unworthy of being in the room. She clearly doesn't want us here." Then a day later she said, "Okay, so we're going to have two casts [both casts perform]."

Kendell succeeded through persistent hard work to gain self-confidence to dance, choreograph, teach dance, and use her voice. Performance rewards came later; importantly, she was open to a variety of styles and had begun to develop a creative self through choreographing and teaching.

The Challenge of Difficult Treatment

The students face many challenges in colleges and conservatories besides reshaping bodies, such as competition, body shaming, and politics. Kendell sought alternatives to attaining good roles in performances. Some schools give all students a chance to work with choreographers who create dances for them, while others provide limited opportunities to perform. What Olivia saw as politics drove her out of the dance major to journalism; she talked about daughters of major donors dancing the good roles, while better dancers were ignored. Others dealt with body shaming and harsh criticisms.

These dancers handled difficult college experiences in different ways. Sofia, as we saw, went home to recoup. In contrast, Eda, a recent graduate of a college dance program, argued that it was essential to have a thick skin and not let others' evaluations define her as a dancer. Regarding all classmates as strong dancers can be seen as a challenge to improve rather than competition, but dancers have to be tough. Eda recalls:

> My class also was a really incredibly strong, amazing, talented group of people. I learned so much from my peers. I could see people were struggling and weren't really connecting with the faculty. That makes for a harder experience. I found it to be great. I just put my head down and worked really hard. Because of that, I got really great performance opportunities. Probably the emotionally ready people [succeed]. It's like people would sit down with the director. She would say something, and they would start crying. I feel like I have a pretty good head on my shoulders when it comes to things like that. They have favorites or they see people doing this, but the student sees themselves doing that instead. There's politics with any department. They kind of think of you in a certain way. Or they would think, "Oh, I think if we put this person in this piece, it'll be a great challenge for them." By the end, I always had fun.

Eda saw difficult situations as challenges, providing a positive meaning to situations where others crumbled. Some schools mitigate competition by casting everyone. I watched as two different casts of about twenty dancers each performed a piece. In that dance program, all had opportunities to work with multiple choreographers.

Dancers have to develop thick skins, explained Chantel, as your body is constantly under surveillance. She loved the training but saw abuse:

> He used to be a big deal in the ballet world. He's amazing, but because he comes from such a harsh ballet background—I guess ballet's never been really like a happy technique. That energy just kind of

spread throughout the division. A lot of people just weren't happy—they would pick at us about our weight instead of telling us, like, "You need to lose weight," maybe in a constructive way. Some girls were half the size of me, and they were still thinking they were fat. One of my classmates only ate unsweetened cereal every day. Every time I went to the gym, no matter what time, I was bound to bump into her. You would see people getting sent home, losing themselves.

I'm still learning how to be a woman, but especially at that age where everybody's away from their families, away from what's familiar. It's like you're lost. You have all these people telling you how to feel, what to be, so people just lose it. They forget who they are, and that was really sad to be around every day; it's like they never know how to just be nice, just to say, "Congratulations." They always have to say something nasty.

Chantel manages also to see adversity as a challenge. And the challenges are many. Instead of rewards, some receive negative feedback, which makes it difficult not to suffer. Some drop out, and others fight back and resolve issues on their own as Kelly did. Her performance in ballet was criticized until she went outside the department and studied Alexander Technique, which helped her improve.[8] Body issues can derail a career, but Alyssa still performs in her forties and looks like a ballet dancer, even though her solution to her weight "problem"—taking drugs—could have been detrimental to her health.

COLLEGE WITH A STICKY PERFORMING SELF

The decision not to major in dance does not mean the aspiration to dance disappears; the performing self is sticky. The emotion work to create distance from it can be excruciating. Whether trained at home or at a major training center, narratives of the college, non-dance choice include parental opposition to a dance career, injury, or seeing risks in a dance career. Some talk about the decision as more of a choice than others. That may be more of a reflection of where they are now. All had to go through the process of distancing themselves from the aspiration to dance professionally. No one complained, as many college students do, of being lonely, working too hard, or disliking classes. They were successful students. The struggle was figuring out what to do with their passion—dance.

The "choice" of a non-dance major is not often seen as one. Dancers hear different messages from their parents. Several explained that parents suggested they apply, and if they were admitted to the college of their choice, they should probably go there. But other narratives claimed parental opposition to a dance career was a major factor in their college decisions. A few made the decision even though their parents would support a dance career. Rita, now in a PhD program, went abroad to study ballet against her mother's wishes, but after returning and auditioning for a major ballet company and coming close to getting a position, she acquiesced to her mother's insistence on college; she remains unsatisfied by the end of her dance career despite her academic success:

I think I was the only student hoping not to get into any college. I had a scare because I got waitlisted. My dad actually helped fight for me to go to London [to train] against my mom's wishes. I had already decided that I would be going to university [after London]. My mom was just really, really pushing me to do the right things. She would guilt-trip me, and I had made a promise to her if I didn't have a job in the industry after a year.

I was depressed at that point, because I didn't know what to do, and she was like, "Well, you know I'm not gonna continue to support you. How are you going to support yourself being eighteen years old, never having a job in your life? Are you going to wait tables?" I tried out for two companies [in the U.S.], but there weren't many auditions, so if I wanted to try out for a company I would have to knock on the door and say, "Can I audition with you?" I didn't know how to do that.

It [transition to college] was so difficult; not only had I been almost cloistered in this little ballet world for a year, but it was a reverse culture shock. I had been putting everything into this life to be a ballet dancer. Then you come into American university where students are like babies.

Despite attending a ballet boarding school, strong parental opposition to a dance career and persuasion about the merits of college meant the end of a dance career for Renée too. She placed much of the decision on her parents' shoulders, but admits she chose the college option and, in another section of the interview, focused on her small size, which would have made it difficult to secure a position in a ballet company:

> Big decision. So, I come from a family where education is one of the top priorities, and so even though I was going off to dance in high school [ballet boarding school], it was a requirement that I must apply to college. I remember sitting down with my mother saying, "Okay, you have to go through this book." "I'm not interested in anything because I'm just gonna dance." She's like, "You have to have a backup" All I knew was that I liked the idea that they were small [schools] and I like the words "liberal" and "arts." My academics were always a priority as well, partly from my family and also just I was always perfectionist, a striving student. I chose three that were in the top rankings because that's just sort of what I was taught. I got into every single one of them, and I cried when I found out because I was so upset. That's not what I wanted. And relatives said, "I heard you got in. This is so amazing." But I want the ballet career!

Rita and Renée loved performing and received rewards for their dancing, but, without parental support for dance careers, the challenge of going ahead was too great. Following one's passion takes support.

Although Eva's parents left it up to her to decide, her body size provoked a reconsideration of career options. Eva was rarely picked to be partnered as she was bigger than others. She also had another partly developed interest:

> I mean I took AP literature and physics. I took a photography elective for fun. I kept going with it as a hobby. "Maybe you should think about art school." I was like, "I don't know, I like dancing." I was all sorts of confused. My parents never told me what to do or not to do. Everyone was so responsible in my family. My sister went for computer engineering, my brother went into aerospace engineering, and then came the artsy child. I was like, "I don't know what to do." I thought that maybe I would want to own my own studio. I went into a state college half-assed picked business school and didn't like it. I went to art school. I stuck to photography.

Her description of what was "responsible" in their family entered her decision making. Those who choose to attend college often acknowledged that their family experience enabled them to see alternatives to dance, unlike many of those who auditioned for ballet companies who grew up in similar families.

Challenges can become risks; some young people calculated the risks of a dance career. Greta's parents encouraged a dance career, but she thought about a healthcare profession, articulating her need for the safe choice. It didn't make leaving a ballet career easier. In her late twenties, she talked about worrying about her future, but she also did not want to be known forever for her body:

On a whim I took a tour of [a liberal arts college]. It seemed like it had a cool vibe. I met a girl who took me on a tour and introduced me to a professor who ran a dance medicine clinic; I always felt like if I did the BFA route, it was just prolonging my disappointment in not being able to dance.

All my teachers were 100 percent behind me to dance. My mom, I remember her coming to me because I was so upset, torn about what I was going to do. She said, "If you don't want to get a degree in dance that's okay. If you just want to move to New York and be a dancer, we will support you. We will help you find an apartment." I just remember being 100 percent torn between what I thought was what was going to set me up for long-term career-wise versus I know I could probably get away with mucking around for ten years as a dancer. Then what? My thought process was pessimistic, which is indicative of who I am. I can always have dance in my life if I want to—*it was the safe decision*. It was the decision to basically not follow through on something that I was so passionate about for so long. I regretted it.

I had a very hard freshman year. I cried all the time. I thought I had made the absolute wrong decision. Then it turned around. It [physical therapy] just became a new passion. I could work for a dance company and not have the stress of "what if I'm not good enough" or "what if I'm not pretty enough." I remember an application [conservatory] because I did not apply. I remember standing in the kitchen with my mother, and I got to the question that said what

color are your eyes. I remember thinking I don't want to be judged on
something that I can't change. I said to my mom, I said, "I don't think
I want to do this [dance]." She was like, "If you don't do this you're
going to regret not knowing if you could do it." I'll never forget that
because I do kind of wonder what I could have done.

Focusing on risks and the future scuttled the career she loved so
much. It takes work to distance one's self from a performing self. Few
gave up performing entirely; the self is too sticky. No matter whether
parents encouraged or discouraged dance, their bodies weren't right,
they received few rewards, or they saw too much risk, they all had much
work to do to shape and adapt a self and suffered in the process.

The Challenge of Adapting a Self

College students often spend several years trying on and shedding identities. Central identities are more difficult to construct or shed. Dance is
"in the body" and the most important aspect of self for aspiring dancers,
and few can just put it behind them easily. All had excellent academic
records, but the student identity does not easily replace a performer
identity, central to one's self. It takes work to find a place for the embodied self as performer in memory rather than as critical to what one
does and who one is. Erin Cech argues that passion is a cultural schema
that "elevates self-expression and fulfilment," but for dancers it can be
something more.[9] Among dancers, it is who they are and is embedded in
their bodies. Finding something else to do is easier than finding a new
passion and adapting a self.

Leaving behind a dance career to attend college was difficult for
Renée. She discusses the emotional and social challenges of adapting
herself:

My very last soloist performance was the last time I ever wore my
pointe shoes. It was cold turkey. It was a period of mourning, but I
wasn't really grieving yet. I didn't know how to. Like all of a sudden,
something that you've dedicated your life to, considered your entire
identity, that's all you cared about and loved was gone. It really is
mourning, but without having any sort of tools or support for that;
it was very hard. I didn't know what to do with all these emotions.

Continuing to perform in college is one way to manage the transition while working toward something else, and another is to work to distance the self from dance while trying out new identities. These are not mutually exclusive strategies.

Renée hid her one college dance performance, distancing herself from performing. She describes how much she worked to bury dance but missed the art and collaboration of the dance community:

> I couldn't relate to anybody. I was angry and bitter. I was still resentful about the fact that I'd quit, but I knew that I had to. It was just a whole mixture of emotions. I'd lived on my own already, and here I am with people who are crying about being homesick. I was probably kind of disdainful because I was also just angry, and I also was just lost. I was like, "What am I doing?" I felt so empty because there was this hole that I didn't know what to do with. My whole personality was wrapped up in dance, and I didn't know what to do with the void.
>
> I missed the art itself. I missed the community of people who were all so passionate about the same thing. Even though there were plenty of people that I didn't like, I missed the sacrifice, and there was something really lovely about knowing that you're not just like the community of, say, a company or school. It's you're all working together--it's competitive, but at the end of the day, it's not really competitive because you all depend on one another for a great performance. I loved the movement. I loved the artistry. I loved just ballet itself. You would think [I would seek art in college]. I did and I didn't. I think I probably took two ballet classes there, but it wasn't the same, and I started getting into video. The video I submitted had some dance in it, but with obscured lighting so that you couldn't see it was me.

This was almost twenty years ago. Reflecting back, Renée can see the good and bad of the dance world. She worked very hard to distance herself from dance and the body entirely. It took her ten years to come to terms with her body and develop a new, exciting profession related to the body.

The suffering that Renée experienced as she adapted herself wasn't unique, but others have different solutions. Morgan attended a uni-

versity without a dance major after several summer intensives with a
major company. Even though her knee gave her problems, she suffered
before finding a way to distance herself from her performing self by
challenging herself with performing in the college group and organizing
a full schedule:

> I had gotten into my first-choice college. I couldn't have been hap-
> pier. Long and short, my knee had continued to give me problems,
> and so I decided to go to college instead [of auditioning]. When I got
> to college, I would take class in my pointe shoes. The teacher's like,
> "Oh, do you mind not maybe wearing your pointe shoes?" I was a bit
> disenchanted, and I was thinking about my girlfriends who went to
> school for dance. I constantly had thoughts of, "Well, maybe next
> year." I just wasn't happy with what college was offering me as far
> as dance. I just kept on the academic path and stopped taking dance.
>
> I was totally lost, had no idea what to do with myself. I had spent
> all day, almost every day in the studio, and I had nothing to fill that
> void. It all seemed okay, but it was a very depressing time in my life.
> Toward the end of my sophomore year, I decided to audition for the
> dance ensemble. "I need to do something. I'm killing myself. I'm not
> nearly as productive or constructive as I can be." I'm so used to just
> a full agenda. I auditioned for the dance ensemble, and the director
> was like, "I was waiting for you."
>
> I stayed with the ensemble until I graduated. He catered it a bit
> for me. He worked very hard to break me out of that rigid frame
> and start to really move and bend. "This is different, and it's fun, it
> still incorporates some of the ballet." It took me out of my comfort
> zone completely and ended up being a really great thing. I became
> his lead dancer. I felt like I was really getting my performance time
> in. He was appreciating my technique. It actually turned out to be a
> wonderful thing.

Morgan enjoyed being busy, and the competition and challenge. Greta
did not, though they used a similar process to move away from their
sticky ballet self by dancing with the college group. For Morgan, an academic major did not fill her time and was not a sufficient self-investment.
She needed and loved challenge and performance. For many it is a slow
progression away, but dance remains important in the transition away

from aspirational professionalism. It isn't just finding something else that you want to do.

These women moved on with their lives. Greta is a physical therapist who loves working with dancers and takes ballet as a hobby. Morgan works in finance but is thinking about other careers and uses her body and competitive skills in yoga competition. The women who decided on college without a dance major found that they were miserable until they could rejoin dance on different terms. They didn't need to give up dancing, *only* the aspiration to become professionals.

CIRCUITOUS ROUTES

Knowing at eighteen what you think you want to do or should do does not always hold up over time, nor is the opportunity to follow that path necessarily available. Many take circuitous routes and make many decisions to create a place for themselves in the dance world. Passion dictates what they want to do, but it is determination, organizational skills, and meeting challenges that get them there. Sometimes parents help, but other times parents can hinder the choices. For some, first decisions are not fulfilled in the dance world because of gatekeepers' choices and poor experiences. For others their ideal self as a perfectionist trips them up; their dance skills failed in their own eyes. They chose a university path, but then dropped out to try the dance world. Some succeeded in that world, while others did not and reversed course again to return to school before making it in the portfolio market with more maturity, education, and new dance skills.

Others who trained hard and entered the ballet company labor market at eighteen didn't get satisfactory work. Julia danced with several companies in traineeships, apprenticeships, and finally in the corps of a small company. She left after some poor interactions with another dancer. But the New York City portfolio market looked more like a risk than a challenge. After a chance meeting before she arrived in the city with someone who suggested she apply to college, she moved and enrolled in college. Julia's identity as a successful student provided her with the stability she said she needed to transition to a new labor market and a more contemporary dance style:

I'm gonna move to New York and I'm gonna just try the freelancing thing. It's gonna be terrifying. Here I am at age twenty-three with an existential crisis thinking I'm going to have to retire. I'm type A, a planner, I don't like the unknown. I have massive anxiety about the future.

I knew I wanted to expand my life repertoire. I knew at some point I wanted to start teaching or go back to school. I've always had this dream of pursuing a second career in psychology. I really want to dance. By October, I had auditioned for five gigs and gotten all of them. I love school. I love it.

She completed her degree and won a thesis award. Despite an articulated potential future self outside of dance and some non-performing employment as a research assistant, she continued to perform during and after college in the portfolio world. She used college to maintain some stability, think about a future self, and learn new dance techniques, and she remains committed to performance, with a foot in the academic world.

Others started college but dropped out to dance. Katie took an even more circuitous route. Her ideal self (perfectionist) moved her away from a dance career at eighteen. She was a top academic student, so she headed to college but dropped out freshman year to dance. She found her lack of reasonable dance employment frustrating and did not know how to organize a portfolio career or dance in a more contemporary style, so she returned to college, graduating *summa cum laude*. She was still not ready to give up her passion and performing self and developed a portfolio, dancing and choreographing during and after college:

Maybe I'm like a lot of dancers. I'm a bit of a perfectionist. I would do really well in school (academic) and was always number one in my class. Not being number one in dance made me feel like I must've been doomed. I still loved it so much and kept on doing it. Of course, I had all the lead parts. My teacher there loved me, but I didn't trust her.

I got there [college] and wasn't that happy. I was in this thing called the women's leadership program. That was really cool. I just knew something was wrong. I started missing dance immediately. "I can't not be dancing." I auditioned for their summer program [major contemporary company]. It felt like I was a new person. I asked myself, "Can I really do this? Could this be my life?" The answer to that was, "Yes." I auditioned for their year-round program and didn't get in. I was really devastated. I stayed in New York. I was clueless. I got a job as a waitress at nineteen. I would take two, often three classes a day, a lot of ballet, but then I would also do some contemporary classes. I exposed myself to this different world. I really grew to like contemporary. Then I got a traineeship with [a small ballet company]. The dancing was okay. As trainees, we did not do a lot. I did yoga teacher training there.

I didn't do [university] straight. I did three courses. I got offered this contract by this company in Germany. I was like, "Great. My life is finally going to begin." Then it just fell through. I've taken a break from planning in my life because I just wanted to let myself live and just do what I'm doing right now—teaching Gyrotonic and doing the freelance thing. I have to be honest with myself about the possibilities now because I'm thirty in a month. I realize that I still want to be dancing. I used to always think that I would have my dance career and then I would go do something else. It's taken a more circuitous route.

Despite her excellent academic record, Katie "has" to continue to perform professionally. Katie's self is still anchored in performing, but she has already looked at it from the outside and has a broader sense of self, having balanced the worlds of contemporary dance, portfolio building, and academics. Her identity is broader, but her passion remains strong.

Isabel, like Katie, made commitments to a non-dance college major but reversed course too. Looking back on her career as a dancer and as she completed her master's degree, Isabel narrated her Ivy start and her leave-taking in her first year as embedded in being self-critical about her dancing (as Katie did), seeing auditioning as a risk and having many interests. But Isabel "had to dance":

I was very focused and good at time management. I took AP classes. I would change in the car while my mom [drove]—take class and spend two or three hours rehearsing with that company. Six days a week, I'd get up at 6 am to finish my homework; I was completely obsessed with doing it—happy to do it. I wasn't sure. I loved doing it, but I also had other interests. But I never stopped training. It wasn't until I had gone through high school and danced in productions that I decided that I was going to college, because I didn't think that I could make it.

I had seen what the competition looked like. I think, also, my personality was very self-critical: "Well, I love it, and I'm good, but I don't know if—" I was very practical. My family was very academically oriented, so no one said, "Go for it." The natural progression was college. I thought I'd try dancing while I was in college. But it became pretty clear quickly that that was not a path to dancing. I realized that I wanted to do it after I had left it.

She saw what she loved after leaving it; she took the challenge of leaving college to join a major ballet company.

Entering the portfolio market at eighteen is socially difficult. Chloe feels her voice is unexplored in classical ballet, but her identity as a professional dancer is only sporadically affirmed in the chaotic world of portfolio development, and she misses the academic environment during her struggles:

I had auditioned for a full-time dance company. I didn't get it. I was like, "I need to be back in school. This is too unreliable and inconsistent." In the freelance world it's like you'll have a million jobs happening at once. You don't know how you're gonna manage. Then they all end, and there's nothing. I'm bored with myself. I miss learning and being in that environment and just being stimulated in that way. Planned to go back that fall and booked *The Nutcracker*; it conflicted with school. I deferred that semester.

Dancer can be part of who one is, one very important identity of several incorporated in the self. Despite Chloe's educational success, her performing self remains salient and leads to scheduling conflicts, even while she invests in her academic identity.

This is now coming up on another conflict. They're hiring women right now. I'm fully set to study abroad next semester. I would love to work for them. I knew I wanted to commit to school. I'm in a no man's land place. This makes it really hard because I'm trying to stay in shape so that I can audition. I'm just trying to do side projects. I'm trying to get a full-time degree.

While Chloe seeks opportunities to affirm her identity as a dancer and holds onto her performing self, she remains heavily invested in her intellectual development and traveled to Europe to write her thesis. She saw herself as betwixt and between. To afford this transitional phase, she lived at home and then worked in a dorm. After graduation she continued to develop her dance portfolio, performing with a project-based contemporary group and several small companies.

All career pathways have exceptions. Most of Jenna's fellow ballet corps members auditioned for companies at eighteen after training. Instead, she chose a university with a ballet major before joining. She described her early life in a similar manner to most who danced in major companies except she stayed at home training rather than attending a company school. Jenna argues that she had a broader sense of self than many others who joined companies at eighteen and began to see herself as a potential professional only when her university ballet teacher confirmed the possibility. Her first decision was between a university ballet program and an academic scholarship to a college:

I was left with this decision to make at the age of eighteen: do I want ballet to be my central focus, with academics on the side, or do I want academics [to be] my focus with ballet as, sort of, my after-school activity? I trained really hard [university ballet], and, at a certain turning point, I ended up saying, "Wait a minute. If I really keep working, I could be a professional dancer." Mostly my teacher [well-known ballerina] took me aside and said, "I really see something in you." That little bit of encouragement from the outside world was enough for me to think I had something special. I started to get cast in more things, worked really hard. I must have gone to seven or eight auditions. I ended up at a major company's cattle call, taking a really beautiful recommendation letter from her, and I got a job in the corps.

Jenna's path was an exception. College and conservatory dancers may look like they are taking fewer risks than those who move away from home at fifteen, but most, if they perform, must develop portfolios of work, which is a life filled with uncertainties.

Jamie was a different exception; she attended university majoring in Spanish and sociology, following her parent's wishes, but maintained her body by performing, like Greta and Morgan, in the student group. And the self as a performer remained sticky even after working for several years in arts administration after college:

> Moving here [New York City] on my own was gonna be hard, so I'll move here with the security of a school and start to make connections. I danced through college. But I didn't major in dance. I had to have an identity outside of it. I'm gonna still dance because I have to. I don't feel myself if I don't, but I'm also interested in other things.

As Jamie reflects on how she made her decision, it was partially family, partially a broader sense of self, and partially the calculated risk of moving to New York on her own at eighteen. When I emailed Jamie a year after we spoke, she said her dream had come true; she was leaving for Europe to dance.

The performing self is sticky; Isabel took the challenge to leave university and succeeded with a major ballet company before returning after ten years, while Jamie waited for an opportunity to join a company. All continued to perform. Passion and the sticky self remain strong. But these dancers have also gained other identities and skills.

WHO KNOWS THE FUTURE?

Decisions don't always work out as planned, especially those made before eighteen. Some who trained in major company schools decided on college, strongly encouraged by their parents or discouraged by injury, or didn't get reasonable positions with companies. They weren't among those chosen by artistic directors. Some who started out in college or conservatory majoring in dance changed majors. Personal experiences may limit passions, or they may not receive enough rewards or develop other passions; or challenges may become risks. Others overcame obstacles of different dance techniques and limited rewards to complete college and conservatory programs. Some who attended college and didn't major in dance ended up dancing professionally; career choices were not set in stone. But leaving performing for non-dance majors requires figuring out what to do with your relationship to your body, the major focus of self since childhood. There must be a period of distancing to redefine it.

That requires time, as Dylan's experience confirms. A year after giving up his aspiration to become a professional ballet dancer and leaving a company school, he is still adjusting:

My friend keeps saying, "Oh, I was just like you when I first quit dance too." I have taken two classes since I stopped dancing last June. "You'll eventually come back to it. Now I take jazz and I love it. You'll do it too," but I really don't think he's right. It's just, for me—having been at such a high caliber school, to then go to pretty much anywhere else and not only see people dancing in a way that I'm not used to, but also to see myself dancing—because after a year, I'm not gonna look the same, not even close. I feel like after having been around such talented and motivated people who were dancing so well and doing that myself, then taking classes with beginners, it's just not gonna be fun. I run.

Neither he, nor his friend can predict where he will be in several years.[10] He is just beginning the process of distancing himself from his aspirations and developing an identity as a math major who runs for exercise—adjusting his self. He could return to performing.

Renée suggests what dancers give up when leaving dance for college and a non-dance major: body experiences, collaboration, and collective challenges:

The experience of moving and being with your body, it's intoxicating. It really is. But I think there's a shared collective that was the thing I really loved. But also even to this day talking to people who were dancers--it's like you've gone through boot camp with somebody or the army, and you get each other because you went through a lot of real, rigorous challenges, but also something that you believed in so wholeheartedly like as a patriot, so to speak.

Although both Dylan and Renée left dance, they took with them the work ethic, dedication, body knowledge, and skills for competing. For some, the next stage is as a professional dancer, but which labor market they enter depends on their training, the gatekeepers, and their choices.

CHAPTER FOUR

COMPANIES

Corporate Bodies/Human Bodies

Biographies, autobiographies, books, and films about dance in the twentieth century tend to construct an image of ballet companies as restrictive institutions and dancers as miserable or as willingly bending to the authority of an artistic director in hardworking but benevolent organizations. Are dancers as miserable as Suzanne Gordon argues in *Off Balance: The Real World of Ballet* in the 1980s? Are the agonies of training, the injuries, and the difficult relationships with artistic directors as bad as she presents them? Do the dancers just "put up with it?"

> Somehow, in the course of their training and their career, these men and women lose part of themselves. . . . [T]he ABT lockout does not fully allow them to reclaim their sense of self. . . . I learned that dancers must sacrifice any semblance of social and emotional life if they are to advance in a fiercely competitive and overcrowded field; injured from pressure to perform, anorexia. . . . And I found that dancers have terrible difficulty facing the real world once they leave the world of dance. I discovered that there was as much anguish as art in ballet, and that the anguish was created by the dance establishment; it was not inherent in the art. . . . [W]hat has been stolen from them is not only their power but their enjoyment of their art. . . . "How do

you find the world?" asks Michelle Benash of ABT. "How you main-tain that incredible dedication to dance, a dedication you can't do without, and yet still build friendships, have love relationships, not wrap yourself in the tight little cocoon of ballet?"[1]

An alternative image of life in a ballet company is described by some famous ballet dancers with storybook careers whose autobiographies are filled with the joy of dance and their wonderful partners. But often the men worried about money, and Gelsey Kirkland of ABT presented a miserable story.

It is problematic to reanalyze the past, but I found that the current situation for corps members appears to be more measured than either image; both the beauty and the agony were part of their lives. Problems such as body shaming, injuries, poor communications with the artistic director, and lack of promotion and creative outlets make life difficult, but few of the corps dancers I spoke with, either currently in larger companies or recently retired, seemed miserable. Most love perform-ing and have strong company friendships, although they are challenged by the precariousness of their labor, fighting with their bodies, holding on to their desire for success while remaining in the corps, and find-ing ways to express their individuality and creativity. Companies make more extensive demands on workers than a typical worksite, but each company has different leadership, which is important to the experience. Although companies encourage loyalty of those the artistic director chooses, they often have problems with dancers voicing their opinions or desires. The staff's efforts to surveil and control dancers in the or-ganization are often countered by friendships both inside and outside the company and activities other than dance. Most of all, they love to perform.

GREEDY ORGANIZATIONS

Some institutions have been characterized as greedy, such as some uto-pian communities, the Catholic priesthood, and families in the 1950s. To what extent are dance companies "greedy institutions," as Anna Aalten proposes?[2] Greedy institutions make more demands on the in-dividual than most institutions. People are elected for membership for their special skills or knowledge and personal qualities, and here the gatekeepers who elect dancers are artistic directors, sometimes choreographers or artistic staff. The greedy organization's authorities don't want members to have competing interests; they want exclusive and undivided loyalty from their dancers and pressure them not to participate in other organizations or outside relationships. Do dancers have relationships and activities outside of their companies? Although there is no physical separation or external coercion (like a jail or a mental hospital) enforcing compliance, greedy organizations depend on voluntary acquiescence activated by loyalty and a desirable lifestyle or work so that members don't want to leave.[3] Who develops and what activates the mechanisms to ensure loyalty? Here, it is the artistic director and staff, but also peers, identity repair narratives, the family trope, and performances.

Dance companies change as societies change. That the situations of dancers today are different and companies less greedy than in the previous century should not be surprising. Dance companies and dancers are connected to the social world around them; the role of women, gender and sexual identity, racial inequalities, the distribution of wealth and income, the general level of education, and medical knowledge have evolved. In the late twentieth century, ballet companies may have been more isolated from the rest of society and distinguished by their own social norms, as Toni Bentley remembers under Balanchine, an especially charismatic and talented choreographer and director of the New York City Ballet (NYCB) from 1946 (when it was Ballet Society) until 1983. Bentley remembers a purity, vocation, and complete dedication to Balanchine. "Dancing is a commitment that refutes real life" is a valid feeling and may have been an accurate description of dancers then.[4] Balanchine did not approve of ballerinas who married and had children. Merrill Ashley's autobiography is titled *Dancing for Balanchine*. The title raises the issue: are dancers purely instruments of choreographers and artistic directors? Bentley's 2018 editorial in the *New York Times* describes the sexual misconduct of three dancers as the "fall of the NYCB."[5] It was bad behavior, as reported in the press, but not very different from what was happening in theater, business, medicine, and academia.

Dancers who performed in the twentieth century can recognize changes today, especially the weakening of company constraints. Marcia Haydée, who retired as principal dancer of the Stuttgart Ballet in 1976 after fifteen years of performing and served as director for twenty years, saw change between 1975 and 1987. In 1975 she said:

> I have never had a change of heart about becoming a dancer. Never. Of course, I soon learned there were many things I would never be able to do, like going to parties, drinking, smoking—all those things a normal person enjoys. But when you are in it—really in the dance—then nothing seems to be a sacrifice.[6]

But in 1987 Haydée saw a change in dancers:

> I gave myself to Cranko almost like a virgin: fresh, unformed. Now dancers want to be great in their own right and for their own persona. They don't want to lend themselves as creative vehicles, or be molded by another's inspiration.[7]

Merrill Ashley, principal dancer with the NYCB, also noted change. In a 1982 interview she said: "A professional company is comparable to a monastery, in terms of the dedication and single-mindedness it demands from its members . . . their devotion to the art must come before everything else."[8] But in 2014 she remarked, "When I was in the company your career was everything. You weren't worried about school. About boyfriends, about your social life. . . . That is not the case now. Everyone has a boyfriend, everyone's going to school."[9] The more one is isolated in the world of dance, the fewer the opportunities to develop important identities beyond as a company dancer.

Some dancers in the late 1950s were not entirely embedded in the ballet world. Sharon, who spent eleven years with a major international company and rose through the ranks, looked back on fifty years of her career. She lived around the world, taught dance and performed, and wrote and starred in a one-woman play. While she was still performing, she met a doctor at another dancer's wedding; they married and had children. Though passionate about her dancing career, she had other interests too:

> I didn't have any downtime, so to speak. I was in love with languages, as well as dance music. My goal was to be an interpreter at the UN.

I got all my requirements to go to study modern languages and literature at the university. Then I joined that company. I was multilingual. I just ended up living in various parts of the world.

Oh, yes [I was paid at seventeen]. It was heaven. On one hand, I was really old, and on the other hand, I was really young—it comes out in my play. I was very sheltered—closeted, you might say, growing up, and didn't have many friends. There was this family all of a sudden; all of them dancing together. The woman who ran it was just a great organizer and great getting people to work together. Not that there weren't huge fights and drama. We all loved it. We all helped each other onstage if something went wrong. It was a dream come true.

The world continues shifting in the twenty-first century. Dance itself evolves. Runners run the mile faster, and dancers *sauté* higher and turn more revolutions without stopping, ending slowly in a closed fifth position. Alexei Ratmansky recreated a fascinating *Sleeping Beauty* for ABT according to how it was danced in the nineteenth century—on demi-pointe; some dancers looked as though they were weighed down by their costumes. Today more dancers marry and have children while performing, and, like many other busy professionals, some do marry those with whom they work. A COVID-19 Guggenheim Works & Process video showed Troy Schumacher and Ashley Laracey, soloists with the NYCB, practicing dance moves while caring for their twins in their New York City apartment. And many marry outside of the dance world. Lucy Gray's *Balancing Acts* describes three San Francisco Ballet principal ballerinas with children, none of whom married dancers.[10]

While claims of separateness with an alternative all-encompassing lifestyle have some validity, other professions appear similar: many occupational groups socialize and have strong investments in their professional identity. Some of my university colleagues are in relationships with other academics, talk to other academics, are thoroughly involved in being academics, and have spent years in training. It describes much of the modern world. Most of us live in small fragments of the social world and only sometimes cross the boundaries into different ones. But many dancers now have long-term relationships with someone outside the world of dance.

With the growing need for both men and women to complete a college education for employment, some companies have developed relationships with universities and have arranged scholarship money for
dancers. The busy performing season when the institution becomes
greedier with daily class, rehearsals, and performances does not last the
entire year. That leaves time for other activities. Gia Kourlas's article in
the *New York Times* describes the college graduation ceremony of seven
New York City Ballet dancers; one will start law school, and another is
planning to attend medical school.[11] It is difficult to imagine these dancers' identities subsumed completely within the world of dance. Matthew attended college while dancing, and Allison and Justine started
immediately afterwards. Paula completed college, and Jenna finished a
master's degree and had children while dancing. Melissa was studying
acting and making films, and Gabriel painted and worked on his college
degree. Are ballet companies so encompassing that one's self becomes
immersed in the company to the exclusion of everything else? This does
not appear to be the case. These changes do not necessarily mean dancers no longer have a passion and do not push themselves continuously to
improve technique and artistry.

Greedy Organizations as Precarious Labor

In the United States, companies can't depend on regular government
support for schools, a grand theater, orchestras, costumes, behind the
scenes artists and workers, and dancers as they can in much of Europe.
Unions (American Guild of Musical Artists, AGMA) may negotiate salaries and benefits of the unionized companies, but someone has to raise
the money to pay for them, and that can be difficult. When city residents support an opera, symphony, and art museum, dance companies
must compete for resources. Funders may want to see classics requiring
many dancers; hence, I suspect, in some smaller companies, trainees
or apprentices may fill in the corps roles and be paid little or no salary.
They rarely are promoted into the company. Funding and boards do
play a role in shaping the companies and dancers, particularly in the
choice of a new director who shapes the repertory.

Several characteristics of dance companies make labor especially
precarious. First, artistic directors decide what is to be danced and who
to hire, non-renew, promote, and cast. Nevertheless, they use this power

differently. Some directors appear to like keeping people on their toes by letting a few corps members go every year; others keep dancers for extensive periods. Some choreographers have their own ideas about whom should dance in their works and may influence decisions. Second, companies have needs for particular styles of dancers or a balance in partners' heights, particularly in companies that dance the classics. If all tall male corps members retire or are injured and can't be replaced by tall men, taller women may be let go. Companies also have different ideas about how thin dancers should be. Third, many well-trained dancers are waiting for a position, especially women. Fourth, injuries may sideline dancers for a significant period, or frequent injuries may make dancers vulnerable to non-renewal. Fifth, unions affect company life in the twenty-eight (in 2023) unionized companies. Contracts have restrictions on the number of hours worked, breaks, extra pay for dancing roles designated above the dancer's position in the hierarchy, pay when traveling, length of the season, and pay for the corps and soloists. Dancers can't be fired without cause, but they can be non-renewed at the end of the year. Dancers may guess the reasons for non-renewal, but they are rarely provided with reasons. These factors make labor precarious and enable artistic directors to exert control over the lives of dancers.

An artistic director's decisions about the type of repertory contribute both to the precarity of labor and who dances. The vision of the artistic director, often chosen by the board for that vision, is critical. At Atlanta Ballet, the board's selection of an artistic director from the San Francisco Ballet over an in-house dancer led to a change in the mix of dances performed—from more contemporary to classics. Several dancers rebelled and left to form a new company; they found space and donors:

> Atlanta Ballet announced that John McFall was leaving. . . . Lee, Clark, Gill and Van Buskirk were selected by their peers to be on a dancer search committee to vet the three finalists. . . .
>
> The dancers' unanimous choice for the position was Welker, who had aspired to replace McFall and prepared himself by founding Wabi Sabi—Atlanta Ballet's popular summer troupe that performed modern works outdoors—and by pursuing a degree in dance . . . followed by a master's degree in business. The dancers felt in tune with

Welker, who is beloved among the Atlanta Ballet company. . . . Early in the process, however, they had a growing belief that it was a done deal to bring in Gennadi Nedvigin, a retiring principal dancer . . . who is steeped in traditional classical ballet from his training at Russia's Bolshoi Ballet School.[12]

When a new director is appointed, dancers may not remain long if the new director wants to clean house and/or changes the repertory requiring a different style of movement or skills. Anthony found that, with three years as a dancer in a unionized contemporary ballet company, he had the longest tenure of any male:

They [dancers] were faced with challenges that were not in their skill set—therefore, not challenges they wanted to tackle. I think different directors could have picked different rep to fit the dancers he inherited. He chose to pick rep that he thought important. If the dancers didn't fit it, then it was trial by error, and they learned the hard way—either I can't do this or I'm going to refuse to do this and create a problem, which then leads to their termination.

Everyone, Anthony said, acted professionally, but they kept silent while dancers were pushed out, as did Alicia when a new artistic director provoked a similar change-over in a major ballet company:

The dancers that were there saw their peers get fired through this new director, I think there was a little animosity; he was changing things up, bringing the classics back. He needed strong pointe work dancers. It's a highly competitive industry. You feel like if you speak up, you're replaceable. They can always find somebody younger and cheaper to come in.

Whether a small or large company, a change in artistic director can change the shape of the company and affects dancers' lives. The control over programing, hiring, contracts, roles, and promotion provides artistic directors with power over dancers, but that doesn't tell us how they use that power. Nevertheless, the labor of dancers is precarious.

Greedy Organizations as Family

A word constantly bandied about in many companies is "family." I regularly heard company dancers using the trope, "It's a family." What does that mean?

"Family" is a broad term that is used differently both in terms of referents and tone. It can be used to describe poor relations (conflicts) and also to describe the close ties that develop among dancers, many of which last a lifetime. "Family" can be used cynically or with affection. For dancers it can mean a way to express their affection for peers, put up with squabbles, be touched and touch others regularly, but it can also make it difficult to deal with unwanted behavior or complain about non-promotion. Family members don't voice their criticisms of poor working conditions, salaries, or the poor behavior of staff and peers. It isn't all love and affection.

Is it a way to let everyone feel as though they are members of the company rather than employees? How do dancers interpret what staff mean when they use the term? To what extent is the trope linked to loyalty? What keeps corps members in a company, if they are unhappy with their treatment as corps members and when success means promotion? Most don't leave a major company, as Gavin Larson did to become a principal dancer in a smaller company.[13]

SURVEILLING THE BODY AND THE BALLET COMPANY IDEAL

Dance companies need bodies to dance, and those bodies need to look and move in particular ways depending on the repertory and artistic visions of directors and choreographers. The body is the means of communication in dance, but it takes a mind and determination to push the body to do what a dancer wants. As greedy institutions, companies are concerned with what dancers do with their bodies both inside and outside the company.

To maintain the shape, strength, and flexibility of the body, ballet class is a year-round activity. Although dancers are not paid after the season, they can't stop taking classes. Unless someone volunteers to teach, they may have to pay. Many dancers were laid off or furloughed during the COVID-19 shutdown, but all needed to take daily class. How the artistic director and staff evaluate bodies—both the movement and look—is expressed in their choices for roles, promotion, and yearly contract renewal.

Staff communicates differently about body issues. But deference is often the response to the artistic director's views of the body; self-discipline can contribute to eating disorders. Sometimes dancers are reprimanded or pushed out for gaining weight, but dancers may provide excuses to explain away the director's harsh actions.[14] Casey joined an important small company at sixteen. The regulation of the body went beyond dancing skills and stage presentation, but she was, many years later, still unwilling to be too critical and provided an excuse for the behavior of the artistic director who appeared concerned not only with weight, but with what dancers wore in class. Casey recalls:

> We were really isolated there so I didn't have a sense of the world outside of that. We had it really good aside from the emotional abuse. Well, I was very anorexic. That was the one thing I could control. People were told to lose weight. I was never told to lose weight. I could at least have that. It's like I'll beat you with this cane if you don't point your foot kind of stuff. They're not actually gonna whack you really hard. It was all with love. It was all with a twinkle in the eye—one dancer got caught looking at the clock in class and then was made to stand and stare at the clock for the rest of class. If a girl was wearing lipstick, he would untuck his shirt and wipe it off. If their nails were too done, he'd send them out. It was old school.

Isabel who danced with a major company about twenty years ago and directs a preprofessional program with various size dancers, talked about her company's focus on weight:

> Yes, it was more eclectic in the look, but everybody had to be skinny. It was the skinny years. Oh, my god, yes [Did they criticize bodies?]. "Ten pounds. You, ten pounds." The ones that were emaciated, "Five pounds. You, five pounds."

Body size is used by some artistic directors to justify decisions for roles and promotions. Some dancers challenge "body explanations," especially if an artistic director focuses on unchangeable characteristics, such as height. Importantly, Justine with several experiences of success, saw possible options to pursue:

I danced principal roles from the beginning and throughout my entire career there [major European company]. No promotion. That was one of the driving forces for me to leave. I basically went in and was like, I didn't move this far from my family to be thrown carrots and then not see progression in my career. I had a very curious conversation with my director. Even he was basically like, "I totally see where you're coming from. I totally respect your confusion, but I'm at a time where I just don't have enough short girls in the corps de ballet. I just can't afford to move you out." I was just like, alright. "I see more for myself than that. I know you do too." I auditioned for [major U.S. company] on forty-eight hours off. I went there during *Nutcracker,* took a warm-up class onstage before the matinee show, and got offered a job.

Justine challenged the director, auditioned, and exited. Others say they see through the body criticisms. The body does age, but the artistic director's claim about being too old for a role was not credible to Jenna. She experienced what she saw as ageism, rejecting the artistic director's account, but saw no options to respond directly. With a performing career of more than ten years, a husband, child, and a master's degree, Jenna obtained an excellent job in the dance world, explaining that she wanted to leave before non-renewal:

> I guess, at certain points, some of the dancers are taken aside and said, "You're a little bit mature for these roles," but others continue to do them. That's happened within our company. A couple of people have been told they're too old. I was told I was too old to do a part this past year, which was ridiculous. It was just a silly thing. Then, somebody older than me was cast in it. It's just an excuse.

These women could do little about age or height, yet these reasons were consequential in their experiences. "Too old" or "needing a short dancer" may have been a way of "cooling the mark out": a way of encouraging people to leave without the artistic director having to non-renew, especially dancers who have played important roles in the company and were "family members."[15]

Men, always in short supply, particularly twenty years ago, had more leeway to deviate from body standards. Steven started dancing in college and joined a major ballet company, but his body had several weaknesses. The artistic director still tried to persuade him to stay after he decided to leave. "I had horrible feet. I had no turnout. I had no extension. I really took to partnering. It felt natural to me. I quickly understood, that's my thing."

Dancers are often typecast or criticized because of the director's view of particular body skills or type of movement.[16] It is a challenge to get beyond that, and dancers often must work on their own to fix "deficiencies." Again, it is difficult to respond except to work even harder to demonstrate change. Michael shows deference by providing the artistic director with an excuse of "lack of time" to show dancers how to correct deficiencies and worked hard to improve his skills:

> If you're seen right away as somebody that picks up contemporary stuff well, you get called for all that stuff. If it's not something you were good at, but you've slowly gotten better at, you may not get as many opportunities to do it. The director did not see me as a good partner right away, and that definitely slowed my progress down of getting to do certain roles. I really had to work and prove change to him. It probably wasn't my strong suit, but also, when you're not given chances to work on those things, you don't get to improve. He only has a limited amount of time to teach people things, so it's hard to say what's right.

Dancers know they likely will be injured.[17] It is part of the job. Injuries can mean a fast change of dancers, dancing while injured, time off from dancing, or the end of a career for the individual—and, for the company, a scheduling headache. Dancers struggle with these issues; their bodies are what matter both to them and the companies. But expectation of deference to authority makes speaking up about an injury difficult when dancers are treated as bodies without opinions. It was particularly galling when medical personnel didn't listen to Jordan's complaint:

> Had a stress fracture in my metatarsal. I had issues with authority in the company. "I think it's a fracture. Can you please give me a bone scan?" They wouldn't do it. They kept working on it. Then I'd keep dancing. It was trying to dance through major pain. I did have a bone scan, and it was broken. Then the physical therapists were

apologetic-ish. It was a whole stressed out, awful scenario where it was like these physical therapists don't have my well-being at the top of their list. It's about making me dance. Getting me to dance is their number one goal. That soured me a little bit to ballet companies. You just feel like this commodity that's being used. They're not listening to you. They think you're stupid.

Both injury and focus on weight without help to change diet are difficult to manage for many young people. Despite her passion for dance, with all the pressures to lose weight and without a voice, Ariel felt her only option was exit. Promoted from their school to the major company at sixteen, she danced important roles immediately. But the assault on her body and person overwhelmed her passion for performing:

I look back on it now; it's way too young. Your body's not ready. Your mind is not ready for that kind of pressure. I was super-thrilled to be invited, but just being propelled into that kind of schedule was absolutely grueling—you're dancing from 10:30 in the morning until 10:00 or 11:00 at night and rehearsing all day, so it can be eight to twelve hours of dancing, and my body was definitely not ready, and my head either, and you're dancing with your idols, people that you've grown up admiring and loving, and it's very nerve-wracking.

When it's such an honor to even get in, you don't wanna be sitting on the sidelines. I became very unhappy because of my body; I had been told to lose weight probably five or six times. I didn't know how to maintain the grueling schedule with proper nutrition. Every day was like, "How am I gonna get through this day?" I'm amazed that I was able to stay there as long as I did. Finally, when I was twenty-one, "I can't take it." I just couldn't even look at myself in the mirror. I hated looking at a pair of tights. I was really suffering; "Nobody knows how I feel. I have to get out of here."

I finally got the gumption to march into the artistic director's office. Best decision I ever made. I think he was shocked. He was like, "When does this take effect?" and I was like, "Today. I'm done today." He was like, "Well, we're really sorry to see you go, but you seem like you've struggled a little bit. Our doors are always open if you leave and you decide you wanna come back in the future. *We're a family.* Of course, *providing you're still in shape,* we'll see."

I knew I would never go back, but he was actually the nicest to me when I was quitting. Just even artistically, he felt that he couldn't get from me what he wanted, that I had my own philosophies about movement, and that he didn't see me as a fit for that company. It was the right move for me. I felt like I was getting out of jail.

Ariel suffered before using her voice to exit. Had she felt able to speak up before then or been encouraged to see a dietician, perhaps her company career might have been saved. The artistic director's response appears to rebuke her for not bending to his view, implying that she was not meeting body and movement standards. It was a "family" so she might be able to return ... *but.* She read his statement as cynical.

Dancers don't have many strategies to deal with challenges to their bodies (age, style of performance, size) or their injuries. They can work harder, "dance through it" (perform while injured), diet more, or leave, but they rarely question the staff. Sometimes they excuse the behavior of the artistic director or the body criticisms of the ballet master even when they know how unfair the behavior is. It is through the assessment of the body—based on perhaps taste, social skills, or "need"—that promotion decisions are made. How can a dancer achieve affirmation of success, if not promoted?

REMAINING IN THE CORPS

It is the work of the corps de ballet which ... reflects the artistic stature and spirit of the company as a whole. It expresses the creative vision and direction of the management, in management's willingness to spend the time and money on lengthy rehearsals needed for fine corps work. ... [I]t expresses the morale, the communal feeling of the company, the ability of dancers and staff to work together for a common vision. ... The corps is the core, the heart of the company, and its strongest expression of community.[18]

The tension, between community or collaboration and success for the individual dancer is palpable as Deborah Bull, former principal dancer with the Royal Ballet, explains:

Despite the individual ambition to dance alone—an ambition most dancers harbor . . . the challenge and the skill here is to dance as one: to stay directly in line; to mirror the shape, line, and angles of the dancer ahead; to replicate exactly her timing and musicality; to lift legs, arms, or eye line only to the height the dancer at the front dictates. . . . You learn quickly to have eyes everywhere; you learn to restrict your exceptional jump or your outstanding *arabesque*.[19]

Most ballet companies are organized as hierarchies; dancers are ranked as principals, soloists, and corps members. Rank today doesn't determine who gets what role, but ranks are influential as roles are designated by rank. The shape of the hierarchy of American Ballet Theatre in the spring 2019 program was sixteen principals (including one injured out, one on maternity leave, one guest, and one retiring that season), thirteen soloists, sixty-seven corps members, and six apprentices. Some companies hire principals from outside the company. Thus, competition for promotion is significant.

A number of mechanisms keep corps dancers loyal. First, repair identity narratives allow corps members to continue to view themselves as successful. Second, soloist and principal roles provide opportunities to express some individuality. And third, they occasionally can use their voices to ask for promotion or roles. But individual corps members still have a difficult time establishing themselves independently of their social identity as corps members. They are treated differently than principals; and, from Paula's perspective, a corps member of a major company for a decade, corps status makes a difference in their daily lives:

Scheduling priorities, just considerations throughout the day of, like—if a rehearsal was canceled—everybody would be tripping over themselves to let the principals know, and then the corps de ballet members maybe wouldn't know. The corps seems to be left in a state of ambiguity a lot, and that's also true for casting. The principals, most of the time, would have a better idea of what they would be performing, and then the corps was constantly made to feel like everything is constantly and perpetually up for grabs.

Most ballet dancers remain in the corps throughout their careers, as was the case with most of the ballet company dancers I interviewed. "You've no chance to communicate and know you are being successful," Toni Bentley complains.[20]

Corps members often dance in large groups with wigs or hair pieces making them all look the same. Corps synchronization is easier for some than others, according to Melissa, but differences in treatment —such as whether the costume is made for you or you have to fit into someone else's costume—matter too. Melissa explains:

In the corps, learning how to stand in line, it's really hard for a lot of people. For really flexible people I think it's harder because their natural feeling is way higher. Then, if you're not flexible, then it's really hard to just try to get to that equal level. But I think for most people it's, "Okay, good, I can do that." If you're first cast, you have a fitting. Sometimes second cast, if it's a new ballet or if they're making it on you, you have a lot of fittings. But if you're an alternate, you just have to wear what your first cast wore [costumes have multiple rows of hooks to allow for different size dancers].

Dancers' careers are heavily dependent on the assessments and decisions of the artistic directors, no matter how benevolent. Dancers often look forward to perceived choices by stagers who set older dances, and to choreographers, who are creating new dances. Like Bentley, few want to remain in the corps; thus, they are competing with peers for roles or promotion. Many could exit to soloist or principal jobs in smaller companies, but few do. So we need to understand what mechanisms companies have to instill loyalty.

Identity Repair Narratives

Remaining in the corps and reasonably satisfied with one's career requires identity repairs to continue to view oneself as successful. It takes work. Embodied deference to teachers and directors is reflected in resigned acceptance of the artistic director's authority. The hierarchy can't be ignored entirely.

The "gray area" of personal artistic choices and judgments is one narrative. Other repair narratives focus on the company's financial limitations or blame the director's efforts to control them as political. Some compare the difficulty of corps to easier soloist roles, or dancers deny the importance of promotion, claiming reasons for promotion are unclear, and say life is more important. All explanations have some truth to them, but what is important is that we all have to make sense of our lives and narrow the gap between what we believe should have happened and what did happen. All deflect attention from dance skills and focus on factors external to the individual.

The artistic "gray area" is a powerful narrative. Unlike athletics, there are no statistics in dance on which to make assessments: height jumped, baskets made, tackles accomplished. One could assess dance by the number of turns completed, but that is too far from art. Gabriel narrows the gap between staying in the corps and promotion by explaining non-promotion as a matter of the director's taste:

> The director; he's up here, and you're down here. He's the boss. I don't know why it's that way. No, actually, I do. This is my theory. We're artists, and art is not objective. There's an enormous gray area. Everybody wants something. When you're in that position, I think, of being a director, if you open that door, what's going to happen? All these people are going to question every judgment you make. Then, there's the other side, too. Maybe he's afraid of being questioned about his decisions because it is, again, a gray area. We differ on the way we like dance to be danced. That's where I think it comes from, I guess, an insecure place. Well, yes, I like it that way, but yes, it could be this way. Sure, definitely [I didn't get parts I thought I should have]. I think that's where the gray area happens.

The gray area isn't a far-fetched narrative. Dance is a visual art; bodies have to be able to achieve the movement and have the right presence and artistic skills to suit someone's vision of the particular dance. The choreographer, stager, or artistic director has a view of how something should be danced and who has the look they think is best for the role: tall or short, muscular or dainty, long-legged or long-necked, able to *penché arabesque* with legs at a 200-degree angle, have acting skills, or skilled in contemporary work. Do you want elegance or dynamism? If the principals are short, do you pick short corps members? These are the types of issues choreographers, *répétiteurs*, and directors argue about, as Allison recounts below. Who is a "better" dancer or "better" for a particular role?

Helgi Tomasson, artistic director of the San Francisco Ballet (1985–2022), illuminates the gray area from the staff perspective:

> There is no set formula. The way they dance or what I think can be done with their talent . . . need taller . . . work with another dancer, way move in class, hold themselves . . . form of approach, feel there is something beneath. . . . What is fair to one is not to another.[21]

Gabriel's thoughts about the gray area are confirmed by Tomasson's remarks. Gabriel eventually left the company and used his new situation to invalidate partially his prior concern with promotion. He develops a new repair narrative:

> When I left, I said to myself I've been so driven to do one thing, to be a principal dancer. I did that for a long time. I think it was unhealthy. Being a principal dancer is fantastic. It's a great accomplishment. At the end of the day, it's not the biggest deal. There's a lot more to life than being that. I think when you're in that environment, that's all you think about. We always talked about it [promotion]. Again, you never know the rhyme or reason behind things sometimes. In fact, there's that gray area.
>
> I auditioned for a couple [other major companies]. I didn't wanna leave and uproot my entire life I had built here, my community, my friends—I guess I love ballet, but I don't love ballet that much, to where I have to feel like I have to go and fight for it that way.
>
> I'm sensitive about that. I'm just like nine times out of ten, you're not gonna get the job, no matter how good you are, because you have red hair. It's so subjective. You can't take it personally.

Several years after leaving his company after more than a decade, Gabriel still performs and teaches. His passion for dance remains, but he is developing additional passions (teaching and painting) and receives rewards from them, weakening his performing self. He excitedly told me when he very successfully completed his college degree.

Some give credit to the artistic director for insight and perhaps taste as Melissa, a corps member of a major company for five years, argues. But she also sees some decisions as a matter of finance, which deflects attention from skill:

> Promotion's a weird thing—mainly because it takes so long, or sometimes it doesn't, and you never really know what he is thinking. There's been some really surprising promotions since I've been there, but after a bit of time, "That makes a lot of sense." But when it's first announced, people are, "What? Why?" Not to say that they didn't believe in that person, but just this person that wasn't even on anyone's radar suddenly is a soloist. You're, "Oh, why?" But it happens for various reasons. Sometimes it is very much a financial reason. If someone's in the corps and they're doing a lot of solo or principal parts. Instead of giving them step-up pay, you should just give them a soloist salary, because they'll actually make less.

Other narratives focus on artistic directors' efforts to control dancers by generating competition for the possibility of promotion and contract renewal. Allison saw her artistic director's choices as pressuring dancers to work for that slight promotion possibility. She tries hard not to self-blame for remaining in the corps:

> Our director at least, despite whether the company was doing good, bad, or the same financially, always fires somebody. There's usually more than one person let go every year. I think that he has this fixation on new. It does create this perception you need to always be on your game, because if you are complacent, he's gonna get rid of you. If you're not excited about the organization, if you're not doing new things, constantly growing, they do get rid of you. If you're there long enough, you see how it happens. You can almost predict who's gonna be *fired*. Sometimes it's surprising.
>
> There're all kinds of, I think, political things that go into keeping someone or not. If you have a director who's not around very much, they can see you one time, and then make an assumption about the way you are, which is not necessarily true. I saw that happen a few times. I always found that a disappointing thing that even if the company is doing really well, even if you had a really strong group, but his feeling that he needed to constantly keep people on their toes. He

liked to create this—and I think this is a very American way—create a sense of constant possibility of upward movement, whether or not it was actually true, whether or not it was in the cards for you to be a soloist or a principal. There was always this sentiment conveyed that it's in your hands and that if you try hard enough and that if you are committed and focused and always going the extra mile, you can create progress for yourself. That's not always the case. That's certainly the feeling they like to create, because then they have a bunch of people that are working their butts off.

In Allison's view, the director is trying to pressure dancers into working even harder, an unjust system that blames the "victims" for non-promotion or non-renewal. She uses "fire," though in union terms, it is non-renewal.

In any work world, politics are part of promotion. Philip's narrative focuses on politics too: donor requests, audience reactions, and the physical attributes of the dancer, not dance skills. Dance skills remain intact:

> Sometimes, it doesn't even come down to who's the better dancer. It comes down to, okay, well, this person is pretty, and I know that this donor's gonna like seeing this person in this role, or this person brings in more of the audience so then, they're gonna be onstage. The politics is dirty.

Not all repair narratives focus on the artistic director's actions. Comparing the difficulty of soloist and corps work repairs the self by narrowing the skill gap between where you are and where you would like to be. Sometimes corps work means standing completely still and then moving fast, as Gabriel describes. He asks if this is any less difficult than doing a solo:

> Ladies in *Swan Lake*, don't talk to them the whole week, because they'll cut your head off they're in so much pain. There's a section in *La Bayadère*, you do a dance, and then you stand forever. There are six men. You're just standing there for ten minutes. Standing in parallel, after dancing a couple minutes, your calves are just on fire. It is painful. We're all trying not to look like we're shifting. I don't know what's harder or easier, being a principal or being in the corps.

Every corps member has probably danced these or similar roles. Standing absolutely still after dancing is painful and makes starting difficult.

These narratives make staying in the corps more acceptable; efforts to repair one's identity as a skillful dancer matter. The dancers need to make sense of why they are not moving up the ranks in order to see themselves as successful.

Soloist Roles: Establishing Loyalty

Companies need to ensure the loyalty of some dancers; they need senior corps both for the traditional corps work, to assist in the training of new dancers, and to fill in as soloists or even principals when companies have too few soloists or principals or have a need for a different style of dancer. The importance of being thought of as meriting soloist roles contributes to the loyalty of corps members, especially for those who remain five or more years. These dancers see such roles as allowing them to put their personal stamp on a performance and as a reward for skill. Dancing these roles provides pleasure, excitement, and a new challenge. But it isn't promotion.

Dancing soloist and sometimes principal roles increases loyalty. Michael, a long-term corps member of a major company, explains he is satisfied to remain there. He finds performing exciting, dances many soloist and principal roles, and may earn as much money as a soloist with the fee for dancing soloist or principal roles as a corps member:

> I've done many of my dream roles, and there still are new things once in a while, so I'm pretty satisfied with my career, even if I didn't get promoted. My season, I typically only have one or two corps parts, and the rest are solos and principal stuff, so I feel like I'm dancing a lot of nice things that I enjoy. It's literally just the director's taste. I saw the director promote people, soloists, then treat them like garbage.

The artistic director may need them to fill in, but being selected for soloist roles involves the perceived need to please artistic directors and staff by deferring to them and disciplining one's body to achieve an ideal while competing with peers.

Some may be given a chance for a soloist role by choreographers after being overlooked by staff, according to Paula. The choreographers or stagers have various levels of independence. For instance, a young choreographer with little company experience said she was happy when the artistic director pointed out whom she should choose. But an experienced choreographer explained that, although some artistic directors encouraged her to choose, one told her, after she named particular dancers, that she should pick others. She stayed with her choices. Paula explained this process from the dancers' perspective:

> There's this undercurrent of performing like every day is a performance, every moment is a competition. There's opportunity and failure at every step. It just makes for a heightened kind of stress. I mean everyone's always competing for parts—everyone's dancing, learning steps, like a cattle call. Artistic staff will present suggestions and recommendations, with a varying degree of aggressiveness, but the choreographer has ultimate say most of the time. There was another thing that I loved about dancing was that I very often danced soloist roles. The director loves giving people opportunity. If I were just doing corps roles, I would have had a big problem.

Choreographers add a different voice to the evaluation of dancers; many have their own ideas, and some pay less attention to rank, giving corps members dream roles. This affirmation of success and the enjoyment and challenge of performing new roles make it easier to remain in the corps.[22]

Corps members are aware of the involvement of others though they are often unsure of the particular power balances. Allison observed negotiations among staff members and choreographers that provided corps members with opportunities:

> It's something that as a dancer, you're never really totally sure. Some choreographers are very adamant they pick. They don't want any input from artistic staff. More common is our stagers that come in when they're representing the choreographer who are, I think, generally given a preliminary casting list from artistic staff when they watch class. We usually workshop with them and learn a little bit of the piece. Theoretically, they're casting it during that time. I was there long enough to know that you don't start out with a blank slate most often. They'll be an artistic staff member sitting next to them with a list. They're pointing out people.

I think it's nice when they chose completely blind. I think that those can be really great opportunities for people to do things that they're not necessarily typecast for. Many times, you can tell there's a conflict between who the director wants and who the choreographer wants. Sometimes there's some negotiating and flip-flopping of the cast. It just depends on the choreographer and the director's dynamic, who gets the final say on it. Sometimes you see that play out, where it'll be one day someone's gonna be first cast. Next day somebody else. Then by the time you get to the show, it's settled down. I was lucky. I was in the corps my whole career. I did get the opportunity to do a lot of solo and some principal work as well. Those were great opportunities. I think that's increasingly the case. I think that the strict ranks in companies has faded somewhat.

Special skills may improve opportunities. For some, more contemporary pieces feel better on their bodies, and they are chosen by more contemporary choreographers, as Paula explains:

But I remember really loving it and loving the way it looked on my body, it felt on my body. The thing that was perfect about the company was at the time they were really excited about contemporary movement and pushing the limits and all these extremes. I was extremely flexible, so it was very exciting. I really felt like I was in the right place. I loved the rep.

Justine, recently retired and in college, talked about a public discussion of choreographers' choices:

Ratmansky [world renowned choreographer] and Justin [Peck] were talking about that exact thing. They were asked this question; both of you tend to disregard rank in a lot of your ballets. What's your motivation behind that? Now Ratmansky is from Russia. Coming from a history of strictly hierarchical culture, he was thrilled to have the agency to disregard that in his works. Being in the company [NYCB] himself [Peck, soloist], the ranks are something that you face every single day in a very real sense.

A choreographer's or stager's choice can be an important validation of success without promotion, particularly if chosen to be the dancer for whom the choreographer creates the dance (being "choreographed on"). It invigorates the life of a corps member and shows the importance of a second voice in the provision of roles. Justine had a well-known choreographer make a major evening-length ballet with her in the lead role, later performed by principal dancers. For her, it meant the life of a corps member could be special; the choreography was a collaborative effort, influenced by how it looked on her body. Justine experienced it as a creative process unlike dancing an older ballet in which former performers pass on the traditions. It also provided evidence she might be hired by another company when the director told her he needed small dancers in the corps:

That was an amazing experience. It was mind blowing. I was always the dancer that wanted to be choreographed on, which is funny because I'm very outspoken and I take charge. If I ever have a group assignment, I'm the one that ends up doing all the work, because I'm a self-initiator. I just always wanted to be the instrument. Working with choreographers that are making things on you, it's thrilling. It's a very unique experience--it's like preparing a dish together. You might have these ingredients and they have an idea, but because you're making it, it's not going to be exactly how it comes out of their mouth or their body. Then they're weaving these ideas into your body. It creates a very collaborative experience that's quite beautiful. It's unique because in classical ballet, the majority of rep has been around for hundreds of years. You can't just change something because you can't do it or it doesn't look good on you. There's a liberty and a creative agency that comes with being created on. It's very humbling, flattering, and a very unique experience.

These dancers did perform soloist roles that they truly enjoyed, permitted self-expression, and helped ensure loyalty. But they still had to deal with no promotion. Some take action and use their voices.

Developing a Voice and Taking Action

Greedy organizations work to control the voices of workers, reaffirming the deference required as children to authority, whether to raise questions or ask for something. Some use their voice and threaten exit or act as Justine did when she left her first company. Voice may be more accepted now, particularly for men. But standing up for oneself, asking for a particular role or promotion, may create an assessment as uppity. A Joffrey ballet master, Scott Bernard, said in 1982, "Some dancers have become increasingly independent. If they offer resistance, I think they may have to be let go. . . . When dancers are disciplined and have people to look after them it gives them confidence."[23] He wanted them all on the same airplane. He implies they should be treated as children. More recently, Lauren Cuthbertson, a Royal Ballet principal, appears to favor initiative: "Sometimes I feel dancers can be the most uncreative people, because they become so concentrated on doing something in the way they have been told, to please other people that they forget to breathe and to grow."[24]

To ask for roles, promotion, or different treatment, one must stand up for oneself. Men can threaten exit and possibly succeed more often than women as women are replaceable. Occasionally, it can work for promotion, but Jenna, a corps member for over a decade, didn't think it would work most of the time:

> Sometimes they'll fight for themselves. One of our dancers went in and said, "Look. I do all this work. I'm smarter than all my peers. I hold this thing together. You have to promote me." He kept being told, "Yeah. I will eventually. We'll see how you do in this next program." Finally, he was like, "Look. You have to promote me, or I'm leaving." That doesn't usually work, and it did, which is great. He got promoted to demi-soloist. It all is in how you play your cards, and no two cards are the same.

Jordan stepped up to the challenge when the lack of useful instruction by staff made improvement difficult. He succeeded in remaining with the company by seeking outside help to improve his dancing and then successfully auditioned for a soloist position with another major company and exited:

> I don't know [how people are chosen for roles]. That was always a question. I mean, it's all very subjective. My first season, I was the understudy. The soloist ended up injuring himself. I got to do that. That was a big—but I remember afterwards, the director didn't even say anything to me. I was like, "Maybe I didn't do well." The direc-

tor, right, his opinion matters most. Then I had been in the company five years, the director told me he was gonna let me go maybe, because they didn't think I was doing a good job. He just said that—I wasn't dancing with enough energy at my back. I was like, "I don't understand what that means." I went around to all the teachers that I knew. Immediately, the director noticed that I got better. They ended up giving me better roles.

It's like if someone else wants you—"Should I leave or stay?" I talked to the director about it, and he was like, "You should talk to the director there and see what you're gonna do and weigh your options. It's your decision, but this is a *family*. You can always come back." I ended up taking the job. Really didn't like it. I was struggling. I felt like I hadn't completed my work with my teacher. Called him [former director] on the phone, "If I'm not happy here, would you give me my job back?" He said he would but couldn't guarantee that he'd have a contract in a year when my contract was up and that I would have to talk to the director; back for *Nutcracker* again.

Jordan was able to return, as "family," but he was less easily replaced than the women dancers and never was promoted. Men don't always get what they want as Matthew discovered. Speaking up showed lack of deference and got him in trouble, even with the shortage of men. He exited a major company when he was not promoted after asking for it and then was not given the good roles he had danced previously. He moved to a small contemporary company where he did not get along with the artistic director, was injured, and the salary was insufficient without a second job. Matthew recalls:

I'm gonna be amazing, because I'm a contemporary specialist with one of the best companies. Contemporary work with a major ballet company is not like contemporary work with true contemporary companies. I struggled a bit. I had never been that slow before. That was a stressor. Beyond that, being in a big company they give $600 a year to use towards physical maintenance outside of the stuff they provided. I went from $60,000 a year to $20,000.

I was freaking out, "I don't know how to survive on $20,000 a year, and I don't know if I'm gonna find work outside of that." I waited to do physical therapy. "I'm gonna really show her that I can pick it up." She was so nasty to me, unlike anybody had been in a professional studio. She stops the music after half hour, and I'm in a positive frame of mind. She was like, "What are you doing?" I was like, "I'm sorry." She goes, "What's your problem?" I said, "I don't understand what you're talking about." She was like, "You know, you're really starting to piss me off. Why are you marking [walking through it]?" "What do you want from me? All last week, you were so nasty to me," which was not my crowning achievement, especially for a dancer who's supposed to be submissive no matter what.

He left. But Daniella used her voice and succeeded:

I had carved out a niche for myself in certain roles. I was a very strange dancer, or perceived that way, and would get cast in certain really bizarre, distinctive roles that I guess they felt like they didn't want someone else to do them. It doesn't usually happen like that in dance, but I struck a bargain. I'd been fighting with the director about whether I was gonna come back after I wasn't promoted. I would go in his office, and we would argue. He would tell me that I would be making a big mistake if I left. I would ruin my life. I proposed doing these two particular productions that were being reprised where I had special roles. "I'll do your Web video and I'll do these two productions." To my surprise, it was just accepted.

Some who have spoken up for themselves or others succeeded; others have felt penalized for their efforts. With voice, relationships outside the company, ideas about the future, dancers expand their selves beyond performing selves. Jenna suggests how college facilitates voice; however, she never asked to be promoted and was content with seeing nuances in roles. She turned to education and starting a family, developing her life outside the company. She gained strong identities and rewards beyond the company and performance:

We don't allow people to pipe up if something is going wrong. It starts from when we're very young. We are the students. We are meant to be quiet. We are meant to fall in line. The teacher knows everything. The teacher doesn't make mistakes. Then it goes up the chain of command. Unless somebody at the top opens the door, and allows it to change, it doesn't change. I was very fortunate to operate in two social circles. My husband is not a dancer. I very much value the opinions and point of view of people that are not in my art form. I think that a lot of the times you can get oversaturated with what you're doing and then you can't differentiate between good and poor decisions, and happiness and sadness, because it's all the same.

She chose exit but did not complain to anyone about being denied a role because of age. When the self is wrapped up in one's identity as corps member, the need to work to construct a positive self-image without promotion is strong. But acting can also matter such as seeking out another teacher or getting a counteroffer from another company.

The artistic directors have authority over dancers. Deference to authority makes criticizing an artistic director difficult when the staff behavior is detrimental to the welfare of the members of the family. That's what company unions should be able to moderate; it is a work organization too. Some dancers dared to speak up as union representatives for the collective good, but, from the representatives' perspectives, standing up to management appeared to backfire personally. Deference is preferred by management. Thus, questioning staff actions is difficult, and some artistic directors do not appear to deal well with those who do. Not only are dancers worried about creating poor relationships with those in power, but they don't have experience standing up to others. This is not new. Greg Huffman, a Joffrey dancer, told Wendy Neale in 1982:

> The companies would not want to admit it, but they can make your life very difficult. If dancers insist on the five-minute break . . . they are looked down upon by the ballet masters, management and board of directors. They may not say anything, but maybe they'll show you how they feel by not giving you a part you want. This makes the dancers feel insecure. They can't be fired, but they can be held back. . . . Many times, you feel that you are a machine—a body out there. Instead of refusing to do it, we keep going and then break down in tears, and they cannot understand what's wrong.[25]

Some spoke of being fearful of active union involvement. Jenna, a longtime corps member, believed her casting, after serving as union representative, was affected. She wasn't the only one:

The union is good, in the sense that it regulates break time and makes sure dancers aren't overworked and abused. I was union rep one year, and I remember thinking it affected my casting and then I never wanted to be a union rep again. I think that it's very hard to represent the whole where the director, it's his opinion that controls the system that creates good opportunities for people. There's a system in place to protect those dancers who were complaining, but there's no system in place to protect the representatives representing the dancers.

Dancers say it is difficult to speak up even when the company claims they can't pay what is owed, and they see expenditures on other items. Gabriel describes his failure to speak up in his company:

You were too afraid to be too active. I've gotten more involved there [a different union] because I don't feel like I'm gonna get my head chopped off. We were all very afraid. To go abroad, they had to pay us X amount of money. Well, the company would come and be like, "We don't have the money for that, so if you don't waive the fee, we're not gonna go." Everybody would waive the fee. They just spent a lot on props. Everybody was afraid: fear of losing your job, or a part, or not getting ahead, if you got too pushy with the union. I remember the artistic director saying, "You should be grateful to get the opportunity to do a solo part." Like, we shouldn't have to pay you.

But others successfully defend themselves. Chantel, a recent conservatory graduate, stepped up for herself and other performers in a Broadway show:

There were more and more people getting injured, and so they had this thing where it was gonna be internal swings, where everybody already cast would learn all the tracks, but they weren't paying us. One day, they called me in for a rehearsal, and I was like, "Well, I don't have to go to this rehearsal. I haven't signed my contract." The stage manager was like, "We've been told by management that you have." My manager actually lied. They sent over the contract, and we started getting paid that following Monday. The people bully you to make you feel like your voice doesn't matter. If you do speak up, you're gonna be blacklisted. No, that's not okay. People have to learn how to come together and speak up. Everybody's crying alone in corners instead of actually being a *real family*.

Chantel sees the power of the collective and spoke out without repercussions, but she was a member of the more powerful Broadway union. More dancers want to perform than there are reasonably full-time paid positions. With the hierarchy of big companies, all cannot be principal dancers or soloists or perform their roles. The strategies used to ensure loyalty, to keep senior corps members dancing and reasonably happy without promotion, impact on dancers' lives. Through limited communications, threatening non-renewal, expectations of deference, they keep dancers quiet and obedient. But by holding out the promotion possibility and doling out soloist and principal roles that allow self-expression and indications of success, artistic directors promote loyalty and continued work towards perfection. Disciplining the body without irritating the director by asking for roles or promotions, affects contract renewals and getting soloist roles. There are rewards that ensure loyalty: the excitement and thrills of performing, especially soloist roles; the identity repairs that allow the corps to claim to be skillful dancers; the friendships that develop; and performing.

FRIENDSHIP, COOPERATION, AND COLLABORATION

Companies are partly about relationships. Deborah Bull, Royal Ballet former principal, talks about feeling like a hamster doing *Swan Lake* over and over but seems wistful when she writes, "But what really stands out, at least for me is the sense of comradery and togetherness and I realise now more that it is this, more than anything that sets the corps de ballet years apart."[26] It is more than just the corps together that creates a good performance. It involves collaboration among all the dancers, no matter what rank, and many more offstage talents, to create an excellent performance where all are working together towards the best performance possible.[27]

Any behind the scenes competition needs to be restrained by cooperation for successful performances. The ballerina needs a partner and the performance needs swans, peasants, parents, and all the characters that fill out a cast. Competing for attention on the stage destroys the performance as children learned in *Nutcracker*. Partners who appear more concerned with the height of their leaps or the rapidity of their turns, rather than communicating to the audience that they will catch their partner flying through the air, ruin the performance. Companies are organizations with some of the constraints of most organizations—people have to work together in preparation for a successful performance: scheduling rehearsals, injuries that require enormous scheduling shifts, musicians with their own unions, all the behind the scene workers and the understudies who must remain ready to replace injured colleagues. Somehow, all need to work together, cooperate. Friendships facilitate cooperation.

Friendships and the Collectivity

Some companies have a greater sense of collectivity and friendship across ranks than others. Activities and organizational features can divide the company or bring them together. Jenna argues that some contemporary dances with no ranking bring dancers together, but dressing room divisions work to create smaller communities and to construct boundaries between ranks:

> *Artifact*, the Forsythe work; there are no principals. Everyone's a principal. Those things, I think, bring it all together in that way. It also depends on the way your structure is. The soloists and demi-soloists and principals are upstairs two floors and the corps de ballet is downstairs in the theatre. That separation just naturally happens. I think that you develop a comradery with those people in your dressing room. I witnessed, a girl got moved up to be a demi-soloist and would constantly come back to the corps dressing room just to put her makeup on because her friend base was there. This past year essentially everyone in my social circle had retired. It greatly affected my enjoyment of that space because my friends weren't there. It made getting ready for a show not a social experience. It made it a chore that I'm doing.

Sometimes barriers are overcome, and the sense of the collectivity overcomes the corps/principal divide. Paula uses the family trope to describe the smaller gap in her company:

I have such a problem with the hierarchy in the ballet world. The other thing that I loved about this company was that, at least compared to things I've heard about other companies, what we had was a very communal, *familial* sensibility throughout the company. Principals, a few of them were divas, but a lot of them had actually been corps de ballet at some point, so understood how hard it was, which was always so important when it came time to doing those big *Swan Lake* ballets, and [one principal] after her variation, when you're standing on the side as a Swan, she would do a very quick bow, "No, I know how long they've been standing there." I think internally there's never been a huge discrepancy of status. There would very often be a mix [relaxing after a performance]. When I left, I would say that the company had become a little more segregated into little nuclei of social gatherings, a lot based on age because the age seemed to be getting younger and younger.

At times and in some companies, the collectivity is stronger and more broadly inclusive than others; some share apartments across ranks. One young corps member kept referring to a principal as her "father." He helped her during their international tour, she said. Another principal showed up for a corps member's performance with a project-based group. The collective and friendships may change with new players who are organizers of social events, disruptive, or stand-offish.

But becoming part of the collective is not easy, especially for a sixteen- to eighteen-year-old. Apprenticeships or second company membership can be a way to integrate new dancers slowly; they often form lasting friendships. In some companies, union rules govern apprenticeships, and the payment schemes have improved; some receive a stipend rather than hourly pay and they must be promoted or leave after a year. Nevertheless, some of the smaller ballet companies appear to either fail to incorporate or over-use apprentices or trainees. Michael, senior member of the corps of a unionized major company, describes his apprenticeship favorably:

In a way, I was kind of lucky to slowly gather my repertoire like I did. The group that I got in with—we were all very supportive of each other. I would say in the school we were not. We definitely felt that competition, but as soon as we were out there, that felt better, and we all got along much better. I'm still close with them.

Unlike a college dorm where senior students organize activities to help freshmen learn the ropes and meet others, little is done to integrate new dancers. One company member mentioned they were starting a mentoring program. Most new dancers have to find their own way as Jenna found:

> You find the people that—for me, it was the people I lived near. Sometimes you would see people that speak the same language hanging out together. I mean, it's just the way it is when you go to school the first day. You gravitate towards people that either are in the corps with you and you share certain rehearsal times together, or you have a chemistry that is beyond the studio walls.

Even when dancers talked about the collective as weak, everyone talked about friends in the company. Spending so much time working together in classes, rehearsing, and especially during touring allows friendships to develop. Friendships need not be hurt by competition as the identity repair narratives permit dancers to see success as the taste or fault of the administration, not that others are necessarily better dancers or more deserving.

Those who stay beyond the first few years develop lifelong friendships that sustain them when times are rough and serve to maintain positive memories of performing life. Some friendships begin in the second companies. Allison already understood that they will experience successes and failures so that when a friend didn't get into the company, she could see it from the friend's perspective. Dancers understand how the others feel, and acknowledge it creates tension but hold tightly to their friends. Allison recalls:

> You get into the studio company, the three of you became fast friends, but only probably two were gonna get taken into the company. Only me. She was my roommate. She got a contract at [small ballet], so she had a great career. It was tough because we were really good friends. We both found out at the same time. It was hard. I'm sure it was much harder for her to try to put on a good face for me. I just tried to be supportive. It's something that never really goes

away because your whole career, you're constantly dealing—you're so close with the people that you work with. They're my best friends, but sometimes you're in direct competition with your best friend. I was never angry with a friend. It's something that is a tension. I had really good friends fired one year. It's completely devastating, even to you, we're so close.

They also know it could happen to them.

Friends can reinforce both good memories and memories of serious conflicts. Gabriel maintained friendships after leaving his company:

I've made a lot of great friends. Unfortunately, some companies, I think it's like a mafia family. We love you, and then turn around, stab you right in the back. It is that ruthless. Throughout the company, I've made some great, great friends that I still have. We still talk all the time. We laugh about old times. That was so much fun on this tour, can't believe that happened onstage that one night. It's always the bloopers we remember. You have to have your shield. It's not easy being a ballet dancer in a ballet company.

Smaller companies without hierarchy can provide interesting opportunities for new roles and close friendships or become a place where a few poor relationships can make the entire company miserable. Sometimes a new person can be disruptive to a tight community or, in her words, a family, as Anita found when she started with a small contemporary ballet company. She used her interactional skills and her ability to see the situation from multiple sides to smooth over what started as a difficult situation:

The directors, they handpicked the dancers they really loved. They want to help nurture them as artists. You feel it's more of a *family*. You feel cared for. Probably the first thing that I danced [was my biggest challenge], which was a *pas de deux*. I was paired up with a guy who was another dancer's boyfriend. I think she expected to dance with him. She was my understudy. That felt terrible. I'm making all my new dancer, new partnering mistakes with him. She's standing there, "Why can't she do it?" I think the [artistic director] really saw me in that role.

Closeness does not always work in organizations. Though most people using the family trope use it in a positive way to describe closeness and friendship, families are often greedy institutions too; one must subsume individual interests to the family, and some are dysfunctional.

Rehearsals, class, and touring together sometimes can strain relationships, especially when antagonists lack a way to retreat. All are in the same room and onstage. Philip argues that everyone manages, fitfully, in times of major disruption; performances do not suffer. They are professionals, but one can imagine the ceasefire might break down at any moment:

> I've never had a partner that I really disliked. That's not true. I did have a partner; we just did not get along. It was like oil and water. I dreaded going into rehearsals. That's not fun because partnering is such an intimate thing. It was blank, emotionless partnering thing, which was so unfulfilling to me. I never want to do that again, ever. No, that person did not stay in the company for very long. I don't know if I had anything to do with that. I don't think I did. It's like a *dysfunctional family*, sometimes, because we're all together. We're so close. One time something happened with one of the guys who was my really good friend, and he was married to somebody in the company, and I got in the middle of it. We didn't speak for a year and a half, but we had to dance together and be in rehearsals together. It was very uncomfortable. When we got on the stage, all that had to go away because we were professionals. Now, we're best friends again.

The use of the family trope, whether positive or dysfunctional, does reflect the feelings of many dancers about their relationships within their companies. These are the people they spend much time with in intimate situations—changing clothes in front of others in studios or wings, sweating and touching while partnering or being partnered, and being grabbed or grabbing in the wrong place while partnering. Bodies are always present and on display, often along with emotions. No private office or cubical is available for retreat. Until recently no one talked much about these issues. But working together as professionals onstage is also a resource that families don't have to smooth over conflicts or resolve disagreements, as Philip argued.

The friendship and cooperative relationships formed in most dance companies appear not to translate into strong union activity. Too many saw that union representatives were punished for speaking out. Perhaps the ABT dancers' loss of self during the strike discussed by Suzanne Gordon was in part because of union activity, but also because they could not perform for a period during their short careers. Through the pandemic, they made films of dance (outdoors and often solo) and did interviews and some choreographed. Performing is the most pleasurable activity, affirms their selves, and expresses passion, providing social and emotional rewards. During a strike, they have no performances.

Performance and Collaboration

Although rehearsals are important expressions of cooperation, the fullest manifestation of the collectivity is the performance. True collaboration is achieved when everyone works together with the same goal to make a truly wonderful performance; the corps breathing as one, repairing a mishap, or helping an understudy through a first performance by whispering counts. Watching a dress rehearsal with few flaws and then the performance with the same cast the following day revealed a difference in the level of energy, communication of emotions, and precision of everyone onstage and in the orchestra pit. The performance appeared to be a true collaboration.

Cooperation evolves into collaboration and friendships as Allison found when she was in the second company and served as an understudy in the main company:

An understudy is at all the rehearsals; you're supposed to learn it on the side and know it so you could go in if someone asked you. It's tough, because it never feels the same when you're doing it in the group as it does when you're doing it by yourself. Generally, for emergency situations, you'll go through it onstage maybe once or twice before the show, and then you'll have to go. That's why being an understudy is tough, but it's really important, because that's usually your opportunities, if you can prove yourself. That was one of the things I liked most about the company. It was an *incredibly supportive environment, well, supportive group of dancers.* All of the dancers are extremely close-knit. If there's ever a situation like that, people are always helping out, even onstage. Someone's whispering to you.

"No, five." If it's really complicated counts, they'll be counting it for you. That's really helpful. I guess I could imagine that maybe some companies, if it's super competitive, it might not be like that. That was never my experience.

The corps is collaborative; they have the same goal—a good performance—and they work together to achieve that. And Allison separates the dancers as supportive and the staff, which she infers is not.

The performance itself has a non-substitutable feeling, creating a strong reason for staying despite no promotion. Allison explains her love of performing looking back after a year in college:

> When I think of my professional career; performing is the best part—being on the stage in front of all those people. It's just this surreal life high that you can't get in any other experience. A lot of it was the beauty of the process of going in every day and working towards this thing that is—it's a perfect art form. We're imperfect human beings. It's something that you never achieve. It's a deeply gratifying feeling that you can train or encourage your body to do these things and reach new levels. Something about that is just very attractive to me. I loved that.

Gabriel's face, despite regrets about remaining in the corps, lights up when talking about performing:

> I love the thrill of being onstage. I think, for every dancer or every performer, it's a rollercoaster process. Whoever says they're not nervous before they go onstage, they're lying. You have to be nervous a little bit. Not completely petrified, but to have your wits about you; if you don't have that focus, something will go wrong. The audience is paying to see, at this level, perfection. Falling is one thing. If you do something silly, run into something.

Some say they don't remember dancing, according to Michael:

> It's so fun when you're dancing with someone you like a lot or dancing one of your favorite ballets; it's the best. Sometimes they're memorable in a way where I don't remember what just happened. I'm, like, I don't even know. I wasn't thinking, I wasn't counting—but it was fun. You get offstage, and you're just so satisfied.

Michael achieved as did Allison and Gabriel, what Mihaly Csikszentmihalyi called "flow"—feeling fully involved.[28] Flow is generally accomplished with full mastery through rehearsal and being so involved
in the dance that nothing outside or inside a person such as pulled mus-
cles or broken bones seem to matter. No room for self-scrutiny exists,
and collaboration of all the dancers is achieved—principals, soloists,
and corps—along with all the technical and musical staff. The energy
level of the best performances is different than rehearsals and is felt
by the audience. Performing can blur competition, gloss over conflicts,
and dancers love it; it allows them to express their passions through
communicating with their bodies.[29] Performing dance brings together
mind, body, and emotions in a way that few other activities do. The experience of performance is a strong basis for company loyalty.

ARE YOU "JUST" A CORPS DANCER?

Performers want identities other than corps dancers to include in their
selves. Not only do they want roles where they can bring a personal
interpretation to the role, but they want to be creative individuals with
additional relationships and activities. Toni Bentley seems to disagree.
"Our roles as dancers are to be purely instruments in an artwork . . .
learning by way of repetition. . . . For this art form, dancing, thinking
should not go beyond steps, toe shoes and ballets. It is best that way.
That is how we remember fifty to sixty ballets in the repertory in a
season."[30] As dancers begin their careers when young, they struggle to
develop a sense of self that is less tightly tied to their success as company
dancers. Alessandra Ferri, a beloved principal dancer with ABT, spoke
with John Gruen about being hurt by a bad review. While recovering
from an injury and looking at art and listening to music, she realized
what was missing:

> But it was also a life lesson. It made me realize that you can't be
> loved by everybody in the world, and also, that you don't perform to
> impress—only because you really love what you dance. . . . I had to
> be a person before being a dancer. . . . Of course, I would continue to
> dance, but I felt it didn't make any sense being in one's twenties and
> not having a life. By having a life, I mean being in love and enjoying

one's youth—doing all the things that a 24-year-old girl should be doing.[31]

Like families that have to allow their children to fly free, greedy institutions like ballet companies have increasingly allowed dancers space to develop as individuals and exert less control over their lives both inside and outside the company. But remaining in the corps means working to reconcile being a team member who is told what and how to dance, working to improve constantly, and being an individual and artist.

All dance in performances choreographed by others. Most ballet choreographers set the movements, story, and the drama of a dance. Dancers in classical companies aren't asked often to contribute to the choreography; but more corps members try choreographing today. And as Justine explained, when a choreographer creates on your body, it is partly shaped by your body; it allows her to feel part of the creative process, and the choreography expresses something of herself. Principal or soloist roles allow some interpretation; the black swan in *Swan Lake* is danced as powerful, mysterious, or sexy depending upon the ballerina's interpretation.

But it is particularly difficult for the corps members to stand out and bring something special to a role as they must dance in perfect unison for the classical story ballets. The dance may be a work of art, but to what extent is a corps member "Swan," "Wili," or "Shade" an artist? It is breathtaking to watch the symmetry when the corps achieves unison and perfect harmony with the music. The twenty-four "Shades" in *La Bayadère* slowly moving down the ramps and zig-zagging across the stage are an amazing sight as they deeply *arabesque* (thirty-nine of them for the first in line), then step bending back with the arm up and walk two steps before repeating the *arabesque* in *plié* as they descend the ramp across the back of the stage and then cross to the other side and then back again as the lines move closer to the audience. It requires dancers to concentrate, feel where they and others are, and listen carefully for musical cues. They appear ethereal but must be incredibly strong to keep going for so long (about six minutes) before they again in unison complete their dance in about eleven minutes total (with a few minutes with soloists in the middle). The corps members may do this four to eight times a week before going on to the next ballet for which they rehearse during the day. The principals may change for every performance or perform twice a week. The style of storytelling and choreography does not permit anyone in a corps role to stand out. It is a challenge to develop an individual identity within the company as a corps member without soloist roles or more contemporary, less hierarchical dances.

Whether corps work becomes too routine or one continuously finds nuances in a role varies from dancer to dancer. Some tire of the same repertory, while others say they learn new things all the time. Principals have more opportunities to experiment both inside and outside their companies with new and contemporary choreographers. Freelance choreographers creating a project get excited when a principal works with them. I watched an elegant principal dancer struggle with the contemporary movement of a choreographer creating a new dance. The others were portfolio dancers and accustomed to more contemporary movement. They worked well together, but the principal kept turning in high *relevé* while the others (as intended) were turning somewhere between skimming the floor with their heels and the high *relevé* of ballet dancers. He said he struggled but loved the opportunity to dance new movements and subject matter. Corps members have fewer such opportunities but, increasingly, more do, especially during COVID-19 when more corps/principal partnerships appeared onstage (outdoors) and corps members made films. In recent seasons, more corps members have danced solo and principal roles.

Corps members have opportunities in their companies to dance soloist roles, but few have opportunities like Justine to be choreographed on in a principal role or to contribute to a new dance being choreographed. A contemporary choreographer brought into a major company for a special project encourages the participation of dancers in the choreographic process. I watched as four young dancers and the choreographer finished a short piece. Two had done a project with her the previous year and were beginning to understand her movement vocabulary, which differs considerably from classical ballet. The choreographer was surprised with the ballet dancers' first-time engagement in her creative process, as in the past some ballet dancers appeared uninterested in doing so.

Some dancers start a second profession while continuing to perform. They find a new passion to add to performing and to fulfill it, use their voices. Michael found he enjoyed teaching and found his voice to ask for a teaching position in his company. He developed a second work identity and new passion:

> I was teaching casually and just enjoying it. They would talk to me and say, "You know, you're a good teacher. Have you thought about telling the artistic director that you teach?" I responded, "No, he's just gonna ask a principal to teach at the school." We had a meeting, and I told him, "I just want you to know I've been teaching a lot, and I like it." He said, "Oh! Very interesting; no one's ever told me they liked teaching. I always just ask people to teach. They say they never thought about it, and I then make them teach."

Michael began to receive rewards from teaching, and his relationships with non-dancers may have helped with his development of voice and other interests. He turns to his husband who works in finance when he wants to know more about the world and worries about dancers who do not branch out. After several years, he became a regular teacher in the company school.

Others are able to create opportunities to perform and to express their own ideas about the social world through their choreography. Silas Farley, in the corps of NYCB at the time, choreographed a wonderful performance for a mixed-rank group of NYCB dancers in three rooms at the Metropolitan Art Museum. Gia Kourlas writes about the performance:

> "Songs from the Spirit" also poses a question: What does freedom mean? The dance, a collaboration with the Radiotopia podcast Ear Hustle, a nuanced look at prison life, features spirituals and new music created by incarcerated men at San Quentin State Prison in California. . . . For some of the men involved, Mr. Farley was surprising. "Not too many people of color come in to San Quentin trying to help us," LeMar Harrison, known as Maverick, said. "He was the first dude who actually looked like me, and he kind of reminded me of all the kinds of things I wanted to be as a kid."[32]

They danced eight packed performances that expanded both the range of dance movement and the subjects these dancers typically perform. It looked like a true collaboration with Silas Farley's tall presence in the lead. Projects that allow dancers to choreograph are another opportunity that Melissa took in her company and Jordan took outside.

Some search for individual artistic expression or self-actualization in other arts. The ballet may be a work of art, but some see themselves more as an instrument of the choreographer and yearn for more. While performing, Gabriel worked on his college degree and began painting:

My grandmother was a painter, so she would come over and teach me. It wasn't until I was like twenty-four—and started to realize that this is a job, more or less. This is not, "Go out there and express yourself." As a ballet dancer, you have to hit a mark. You have to hit this count. I would be like I wanna just go home and express myself. That's how it [painting] started. It wasn't [enough of an art]. I think that, if you ask most dancers, they'll probably say the same thing because it is so intense. You're dancing with a group. You're not somebody who's like, "Oh, with a paint brush, I get to go, 'I feel like doing this right now.'" There are certain times that you do [feel free]. It's so great to get out there and perform. I love the thrill of being onstage.

Companies, desperate during the pandemic to remain in the public eye, provided more opportunities for dancers to expand their voices and creativity: choreographing, making short films, speaking about their lives on videos, and increasing their social media presence. Some have spoken out loudly about diversity and Ukraine. I noticed in September 2019, before rehearsals started, that several of the men sported beards and longer hair. Those were gone before the fall performances and returned during COVID-19 even during filming of performances. A mild deviation, but a statement nonetheless. Companies remain greedy institutions though less so than in the last century. The body is still surveilled. Although corps dancers maintain their identities as corps company members, they have more opportunities such as education, teaching, family, arts, writing, and choreography to develop additional identities and creativity. And they dance more interesting roles.

COMPANY VERSUS FAMILY

Companies are not families though the word is liberally employed; they are organizations with powerful leaders who hold dancers' careers in their hands. Dancers, corps members in particular, don't have much voice, and their loyalty is maintained through performing soloist roles, identity repairs, good relationships with dancers in the company, and importantly, opportunities to do what they love: perform. The belief that the company will take care of you like a family may strengthen the artistic director's influence over dancers and also excuse a director's bad behavior. Justine understands the difference between family and company employee after a year in college:

> You don't think of it like you *work for* a company. You're *in* the company. It's just the relationship from the very beginning is different. Logistically speaking, career speaking, you have to realize that. It takes away the romance of the career a bit.

Many see themselves as company members, like family, not employees. But they are employees too.

As cultural businesses artistic directors need to produce performances that donors, audiences, and critics appreciate, in addition to keeping dancers in their company who make those successful performances possible. Moreover, they need to decide which choreographers may create exciting new performances that interest dancers and audiences, which may not be the same. Loyalty of dancers is, thus, an issue, not generally in families. While corps members are replaceable, particularly women, companies need senior corps dancers who know the repertory and dance soloist roles. Artistic directors are partially dependent on carefully constructed rewards, such as solo roles, while encouraging dancers' performing skills so that they can deliver wonderful performances by relying on dancers' continued passion and work towards the ideal. But dancers owe their employment to directors who can non-renew them for any reason. Families assume loyalty and can't dismiss a child for talking back to the parents or not performing well, at least not without difficulty. But the use of the family trope can also make it more difficult for some artistic directors to non-renew a dancer who has been a cooperative "family" member; they need to "cool the mark out," with fewer solo roles to allow a voluntary, perhaps more graceful, departure. It protects dancers somewhat.

But voice may be an issue in families and companies when it comes to challenging parents or staff. Most dancers have learned to interact with great deference to their teachers, to remain obedient and silent. Speaking out is seen as troublesome, and some dancers feel they are penalized for acting as union representative or for asking for roles, without ever learning why. Families deal differently with voice. Some shut their children down, but many middle-class families accept the challenge and debate. Children are expected to state their needs, opinions, and desires. But dancers who ask for a role or promotion may lose their jobs. The steep hierarchical structure and the power of a few in ballet companies exacerbate the competition for promotion, roles, and retention, which staff can use to incite striving for the perfect performance, but also fear and suffering. While children may feel that some are loved more than others or given more resources, all the children can succeed equally, at least in theory. They are different institutions despite the importance of the trope of family for life within the companies.

Ballet companies remain greedy institutions today, but with more space for self-expression and autonomy to participate in other worlds. But dancers still need to demonstrate loyalty to the company and companies need to ensure the loyalty of dancers.[33] Traditional ballets don't often permit much space to express who the dancers think they are, their personal identities. Herman Cornejo, principal dancer of ABT, in an interview with Damian Woetzel for the Vail Dance Festival's virtual 2020 season, declared that in Jerome Robbins's *Suite of Dances,* he "moved as a human being" not as a classical dancer: "I feel myself. I felt Herman Cornejo onstage."[34] Acting with the body in classical roles, which he usually performs, may allow some individuality of interpretation, but the performances are rarely an expression of who dancers think they are—their personal identities. *Suite* allowed him to do so through dance. Few of the corps members have opportunities to speak for themselves, but they have more now; some speak out about their sexuality, explore other dance and art forms, create dances and other types of performances, attend school, and talk publicly about politics and race. Alexei Ratmansky, the world renowned choreographer, and Christine Shevchenko, principal dancer, unfurled a Ukrainian flag after an ABT performance in 2022. Companies, especially ballet, are thus partially like corporate bodies.

But, most of all, the dancers still love performing and collaborating, as Steven reminisces:

> I'm glad you asked it that way [performing] instead of the, "Did you miss dance?" I don't miss the daily grind of the class. I did miss performing. That's why I liked it. I like traveling, performing, and the community around the performing, the camaraderie about going onstage and getting a piece done and knocking it down with people that you've rehearsed with. I loved all that. I love that community that we had. I miss that. I didn't miss the grind of it. I ran it for as long as I could. I loved performing.

A ballet class.

New York City Ballet production of *The Nutcracker* with toy soldiers dragging off the giant mouse. Choreography by George Balanchine, 1980.

The corps de ballet in the New York City Ballet production of *Swan Lake*. Choreography by George Balanchine, 1959.

Étude No. 16 presented by Dance Lab New York. Choreography by Gabrielle Lamb, 2021. Dancers are Zimmi Coker (corps member of American Ballet Theatre) and Randy Castillo (portfolio and Broadway dancer).

The Carpet Series presented by Pigeonwing Dance, performed at Astor Place, New York City. Choreography by Gabrielle Lamb, 2021. Dancers (*left to right*): Victoria Sames, Gabrielle Lamb, Kailei Sin, and Giovanna Gamna.

Kwento: "We Just Seem to Be Here" presented by Konverjdans. Choreography by Jordan Miller, 2022. Dancers (*left to right*): Amy Saunder, Tiffany Mangulabnan, James Anthony, Antuan Byers, and JoVonna Parks. Lighting design by Conor Mulligan and costume design by Reshma Patel-Cline.

No Man's Land presented by Indelible Dance. Choreography and artistic direction by Robin Cantrell, 2018. The dancer, Mira Cook, was in her last trimester of pregnancy.

Flow and Diversion from *The Carpet Series* presented by Pigeonwing Dance. Choreography and artistic direction by Gabrielle Lamb, 2023. The dancers— Tiffany Mangulabnan and Blue Richardson—attracted a fascinated outdoor audience in New York City.

CHAPTER FIVE

PORTFOLIOS

Precarious Work and Creative Labor

Portfolio dancers sometimes work seven days a week, combining work in different locations and different types of work: dancing, work in the dance world, and work outside that world. Managing this life is often complicated and requires moving around the city in a single day. Then, these dancers may have no upcoming performances scheduled after a busy several months, and some will create projects for themselves and others. This blog excerpt illustrates one day in a seven-day work week.[1]

SUNDAY

6:00AM–7:00AM: Wake up and eat breakfast.

7:00AM–7:30AM: I head to the gym and do an intense workout again because I won't have a chance to take class today.

7:30AM–8:15AM: Get ready for the day and grab pre-packed meals.

8:15AM–9:00AM: Take the 4/5 to Union Square and walk to CSC.

9:00AM–12:00PM: Tech rehearsal for *A Midsummer Night's Dream*.

12:00PM–1:00PM: Eat lunch. Administrative work.

1:00PM–3:00PM: Tech rehearsal for *A Midsummer Night's Dream*.

3:00PM–3:30PM: Meet with Tyne to discuss a few things. This is the last rehearsal I can attend before opening night.

3:30PM–4:30PM: Walk to Forever 21 and Nordstrom Rack to begin shopping for a Cubicle costume. No luck.

4:30PM–5:00PM: Walk to New York University.

5:00PM–10:00PM: First Alientologists rehearsal with full cast, director, and choreographer. We do a read-through, learn more about the concepts behind the work, stumble through the scenes, and officially learn the whole dance.

10:00PM–11:00PM: Walk as quickly as possible to Whole Foods to shop for the next week before they close at 11:00pm.

11:00PM–12:15AM: Take the M14 to 8th Ave, transfer to the A to 181st Street, and then walk home.

12:15AM–12:30AM: Unpack groceries and collapse into bed. Set alarm for 6:00am.

Organization and the ability to be flexible and change locations are critical; portfolio dancers cross multiple social, geographic, and personal/professional boundaries in a day.[2]

Despite his organization and dancing skills, Carson, who showed me his color-coded chart of his week, sheepishly told me he made about $22,000 last year. A conservatory graduate, he said he was thinking about auditioning for a Broadway production as he had to make more money. Carson and the poster of the blog were able to cobble together enough performance time to affirm themselves as performers and eat without taking jobs outside the dance world. It takes constant effort; many leave. The portfolio world is precarious economically, socially, and emotionally. As few company dance positions pay for more than twenty-six weeks a year or pay enough to eat and shelter, many create dance work for themselves and others. This dance world consists of the cultural entrepreneurs who create work, running small companies or developing projects, for themselves and for others who seek work. Some do both.

Increasingly in the United States, people work as freelancers,[3] contract workers, or develop portfolios of work. In New York City, coffee shops are full of people who appear to be working. Freelancing covers everything from day laborers to software engineers who can make substantial money from their consulting or contract work, which may last for six months or even a few years.[4] Although white-collar contractors may not be fully integrated into the full-time workforce, many enjoy what they see as independence, flexibility, better lifestyles, and increased creativity. Freelance editors and proofreaders make less than software designers, but, working from home, they can make reasonable incomes. Many are paid by profitmaking organizations that claim benefits from the efficiency and lower cost of hiring for projects and not paying benefits.

Freelancing is not new for artists; people with highly specialized skills such as acting, scriptwriting, lighting, photography, or costume design are contracted for projects, often by large-scale organizations. But even New York City Ballet dancers in the 1950s to 60s needed extra work.[5] They took every opportunity to dance on television, in movies, on Broadway, or at events, as both Jacques d'Amboise and Edward Villella, among the best-known American male dancers of the 1960s and 70s, explained in their autobiographies. But no one questioned their professional status as ballet dancers, as they sometimes do with portfolio dancers.

The portfolio approach to freelancing is typical for dancers and other artists; dancers may work in several small companies with names and not-for-profit status, at anything from almost twenty-six weeks of work a year to a weekend project.[6] And they need additional work, other than performing, to eat. In this chapter, first I explore the construction of the demand side the market: the cultural entrepreneurial work of some dancers and choreographers. Someone needs to fundraise, write grants, locate venues, organize others, buy or design costumes, decide on music, design lighting, develop audiences, choreograph, and create a unity of style and vision in a short period to make a performance and collaboration possible often in spaces that contribute to the shape of a dance. Some have the savvy and luck to develop connections to establish small companies with reasonable seasons. This is a space where choreographers with small companies or projects can innovate in both movement style and dance subjects, often in collaboration with the performers. A few also adapted quickly to the constraints of COVID-19, expanding the types of venues where concert dance could be performed—parks with open spaces and sidewalks.

But what are the challenges faced by dancers looking for work? How do dancers work to construct selves as professional dancers along with social and financial lives? How do they deal with challenges to their identities as professionals?[7] Company dancers may be all-consumed by identities as corps members of a specific company; their struggle is to develop identities apart from their company and to find ways to achieve self-fulfillment. Portfolio dancers must work hard to maintain a professional performing self by looking and auditioning for dance work continuously, organizing their lives, and balancing "work to eat" jobs and performance. They struggle to maintain a professional artist sense of self. The challenge is to charter their own paths; as freer agents they may avoid stagnation, but few have job security, insurance, or rights.[8] They may benefit from the rewards of innovation, collaboration, and community, but most must search for work continually and deal with periods of no performances. While passion remains, the challenges to body, self, and finances are high, and social and emotional rewards are sometimes hard to come by.

Economists might ask whether some are engaged in a labor market of professional dancers, or they are a community of people who come together to produce performances for the enjoyment of it. But most who create evenings of performance or direct small companies feel obligated to pay, even if it is a small amount for performance only, which links it to a labor market. Money, no matter how little, has become a sign of respect and professionalism, though some may work for nothing, if it is art they respect. Dancers who do not receive promised pay get angry.

BECOMING CULTURAL ENTREPRENEURS

Cultural entrepreneurs create companies and opportunities to dance—some become significant companies over time, while others are small companies with short seasons or only a few projects.[9] Here we are concerned with small cultural entrepreneurs who create companies or projects and seek venues to perform. Without them, the dance world would be very small. Many are either dancers or choreographers or both. I am not making a major distinction between small companies and project-based groups. Some have several weeks or even a few months of rehearsals and perform around the country or internationally, while others have only a few performances. Some are better known with more resources to perform in higher status venues. A hierarchy of small companies exists, but it is less obvious than the larger companies.

Constructing dance opportunities involves raising money by writing grants, locating an angel investor, creating a board to contribute money, using social media, or contributing personal money. Occasionally, a major foundation contributes as the Ford Foundation did for Tabula Rasa Dance Theater performing at the New York Live Arts theater in May 2019. Other "supporters" also helped out in that production. To rent a theater and rehearsal space costs money, as do costumes, photography, and lighting design. Even when one choreographer "won" a small major theater, she still had to pay the lighting designer, the costumer, the dancers, and rehearsal space. She sold out the performances as the dancers were from major companies but received none of the box office proceeds. Another received a grant for $500, but then had to raise money for costumes, rehearsal space, and to pay the dancers. Museums pay union wages so are good venues, and groups are hired occasionally to open a new nightclub or hotel.

Putting on a performance requires organizational skills and networks for finding suitable dancers, and knowledge of costuming, music, and lighting. Someone must be a bookkeeper and fill out tax forms. In one loft at a rehearsal, I noticed a signup sheet with arrival and departure times for the dancers next to the exit. Another choreographer had a sheet that the dancers signed before they left rehearsal. Choreographers often film their own rehearsals with cellphones for a record of their creations, but professional videographers and photographers are necessary to promote the work. Choreographers often use networks; the mother of one dancer took professional photographs during a rehearsal, and another dancer who was studying filmmaking shot another group. At a rehearsal with a third group, a young woman whom I had seen dancing entered to take photos; several appeared on Instagram the following week. She majored in dance and had taken photography courses. A professional videographer of another group filmed the performance; he was on their board. Another choreographer, dancing in parks during COVID-19, knew a photographer who used to dance who took wonderful pictures of the dancers for Instagram without charge. Several have partners who are in other arts and help. Voluntary or low-cost labor is important to the small companies and projects and in most of the arts.

People try many strategies to fundraise; some have luck. One dancer, working at a gym, trained a couple who bid on a space for an evening of dance at a fundraiser. They gave the space to the trainer/dancer/choreographer, raised additional money that allowed performances in several unconventional venues around the city, and helped her form a board. One entrepreneurial dancer, Jane, not only worked her way into curating an evening's performance in a popular outdoor venue but developed her own project-based company. She uses the money she earns from teaching and commercial work to support her dancers and choreographs pointe work performances for them, occasionally hiring other choreographers. She also dances with the group. Over the past several years she has secured performances in several festivals, held studio performances, and received small commissions. Jane explains:

> It was our idea. Sofia, was like, "We should perform in the park [formal stage in a park]." Sofia had sent materials to the curator for the modern program. They were like, "Oh, well we only do modern. This is too balletic." Sofia was like, "Fine." "I'm [Jane] gonna call the park. I'm gonna see if they have a ballet festival." I got the receptionist. I pitched her an idea. She was interested enough to say that she'd connect me to their arts coordinator. I had gone to school with her [arts coordinator's] husband. He's now in finance. What I can see in terms of curating is really based on relationships.

Jane has the audience in mind when thinking about the invited groups. The audience appeared to appreciate them as about a thousand people attended, gathered across the grass. Most of the groups were contemporary ballet. She was so successful that the following year the festival decided to invite a major classical company instead; Jane was out of a gig as were the groups she would have invited.

It takes organizational skill, effort, and luck to hold a core group together to work on a piece over a lengthy period for a few performances a year when the pay is minimal. Some of the projects are created through networks and include many of the same dancers every year, which makes it easier; they become collaborative efforts.

Space, Flooring, and Groups

Access to the major theaters and outdoor stages is rare for the smaller groups. Someone must be on the lookout for small, often unconventional spaces that cost less. Inexpensive rehearsal space is also a necessity. Space matters—size, seating, flooring (slope and cushioning), wing availability, and price, among other things. As dance is a collective art, the dancers need to be in the same space to create and perform. Choreographing a group on Zoom is possible but very difficult, and pastiche films got tiresome after the first few of the pandemic. Small companies need to adapt to unconventional spaces, including what is danced.

Zoom classes during the pandemic exposed the need for space. Everyone tried to create enough space for barre work: using the back of a chair, the desk in the bedroom, or the kitchen counter. Some bought portable barres. Most people seem positioned too close to a counter or sofa. One tall ABT dancer (Thomas Forester, promoted to principal in 2020) hit his head on his apartment ceiling in an ABT video. A few classes moved to parks in the summer, but that presents other problems—weather, gawkers, and uneven terrain. Choreographing when people are in tiny spaces or not in the same room is extremely difficult.

Space for rehearsals is at a premium; these spaces are spread around New York City, especially Manhattan and Brooklyn. Several large studio complexes have multiple rooms, but small studios are often in unlikely locations. Most rehearsal rental spaces are the studios where dancers take classes. In one such space, upon exiting the elevator and entering the "front desk" area, a computerized board lets everyone know the time of their class, audition, or rehearsal and in what room. Some rooms are well-suited for dance; others appear less so with uneven floors, columns in the middle, and are either over- or under-heated. Any group staying a minute beyond the scheduled ending is likely to experience people peaking in. In all dance spaces one sees bodies strewn everywhere in the corridors stretching, often standing with a leg high above their head pressed against the wall, warming up for class or rehearsal.

A few dance companies in New York City perform at Lincoln Center, City Center, Brooklyn Academy of Music, or the much smaller Joyce. Some use university theaters, the 92nd Street Y with its dance series, or New York Live Arts. Alvin Ailey and Baryshnikov Arts Center have nice small theaters with regular dance performances. The Guggenheim

Museum theater also hosts dance events. Churches have created spaces too, and Arts on Site has developed a black box theater. Several spaces in Brooklyn have banked seating. Others perform in studios. Rarely do these venues seat more than 200, and many seat only about 50.

Outdoor spaces can range from formal to those created by the dance group. Throughout the summer, stages are constructed in parks and along rivers; others use park open spaces and sidewalks. Central Park and Lincoln Center have outside formal venues with chairs. Bryant Park builds a stage. For Dance Theatre of Harlem in 2018 at Lincoln Center on a sultry evening, a line strung out along more than three city blocks, waiting as two security men checked each audience member and examined each bag. All seats (about 2,500) were filled. The Statue of Liberty rises behind the Battery Dance stage and boats sail past; runners jog between the stage and the audience, seemingly oblivious to the performance. In Bryant Park, people buy food from the kiosks and stop and watch from the sides, while others sit randomly on chairs or on blankets provided by the organization. My estimate is as many as a thousand people observe some of these outside performances. People amble in front and behind and sometimes through performances. These more formal outdoor venues require invitations to perform and additional funding to create, rehearse, and pay the dancers.

Interesting performance sites often have poor flooring that can cause injuries, which means the choreographer may have to adapt the flooring or change the dance to allow wearing sneakers. The museums offer venues interesting for site-specific dances and dances connected with an exhibition, but I worry about injuries with the cement or marble floors. MOMA has dance events in the Atrium on a very hard surface. Anne Teresa De Keersmaeker's group danced *Work/Travail/Arbeid* in sneakers (2017), but NYCB, for the Lincoln Kirstein exhibit, brought a Marley (flooring); the women were on pointe. One dance group initiated the opening of a new hotel's bar. A red velvet rope kept the guests in order as they checked our names off on an iPad. The group improvised on several wooden boxes, which reminded me of large coffee tables that rose about three feet off the ground, randomly moving from box to box. The cement floor on which the audience stood made my knees ache, but at least the dancers were on wood. On a beautiful early fall evening, one small dance group performed in a roof garden in the West Village around the plants and objects on the brick floor. The audience moved with the sneaker-clad dancers who appeared in and around the foliage. One of the choreographer's board members lived in the building. Repurposed factory spaces also become performance venues, but they have cement floors. One small traveling group encountered holes in the stage flooring. The local company choreographed around the holes while this group found cardboard to stuff the holes and then laid down a Marley. Flooring and space can affect the choreography, requiring pointe-shoe dancers to wear sneakers, as many of the outdoor COVID-19 films showed.

One boutique hotel lobby had marble floors, two small bars, and sofas spread about. A choreographer had persuaded the manager to allow four groups to create performances. I grabbed a seat at one of the bars so I didn't have to stand on the marble floor; no one used pointe shoes, but some did get down on the floor. The groups danced for about an hour, some with recorded music and others with live musicians. Many of the seventy-five audience members who sat on couches or stood were friends of the dancers and choreographers and were talking with them afterward. The performance was free, and the hotel sold at least seventy-five drinks.

Other spaces place further constraints on the choreography. Although some loft spaces have stage lights and projectors attached to ceiling pipes, the dancers must enter through doors (no wings) to the performance space from (more) private spaces. How do you make a dramatic entrance or exit with a graceful *grand sauté* (leap) or fast *piqué* turns when you have to open a door or move to the side to stand until your next entrance? Nor can one pant visibly after exertion while "exiting" to stand against the wall, visible to the audience. The dancer is always in performance, which requires skill and sometimes additional choreography. These spaces and parks don't permit grand entrances or exits, but they are larger than venues such as Joe's Pub at the Public Theater where perhaps three dancers can move carefully on the tiny corner stage. One move too many, and dancers will step into the front-row audience's drinks—limiting what choreographers can do.

Unconventional space and seating may change the look of a dance: something to which the choreographer has to pay attention. When the audience is seated above, or below, or at the same level as the dancers, it looks different. Some dances lose their poignancy when performed with banked rather than flat seating. At one of these performances, a dancer slowly poked her head through the arms of another and peered, eyes wide open, straight at the audience seated on the same level. The banked-seated audience saw only the top of the dancer's head. It ruined a wonderful effect. On other occasions an outdoor stage was well above the audience, making it difficult to see the dancers lying on the stage. That works better when the stage is below the audience.

The pandemic closed indoor performing spaces and the formal outdoor summer stages for 2020. Some small project-based groups wanted to perform before the winter set in, and, by June 2020, several had started performing in public outdoor spaces around the city. Finding good locations required new skills, as did the need to use social media to advertise the events. Gabrielle Lamb's group, Pigeonwing, had four dancers who wanted to perform. She found a variety of outdoor locations in Brooklyn, Queens, and Manhattan. Choreographed on Zoom, Pigeonwing used a five by eight rug to create a stage. They had to carry the rug and cushioning up and down subway stairs. Locating good spots to dance was new—it had to be public space, have some shade, preferably something to serve as a backdrop (such as a tree, statue, flowers, or wall), plenty of space to socially distance for the audience and passersby, enough foot traffic to attract an audience, and even ground. The group continued to perform *The Carpet Series* regularly twice a week through the summer of 2023. More groups performed around the city during summer 2021 with grants from the city. But it does rain and get very hot.

Despite the many constraints of creating performances, the dancers clearly get a strong emotional high from both creating and dancing in such performances, like dancers in the big ballet companies. They continue to talk about the performance afterwards and, when it has been filmed, critically focus on the details of what each of them did and how they can improve. A choreographer's self-expression does entail creating for a particular space and flooring—thus constraining what can be performed—but most portfolio dancers love to be part of the creative process.

Audiences and Odd Spaces

Audiences can affect the performing experience and what can be performed successfully. Many of the smaller performances are attended largely by people in their twenties and thirties—former performers, friends, and family—while the traditional venues in New York City are filled with mature audiences, except in the highest balcony. In one museum performance at MOMA, many gray-haired audience members sat on the floor. Not only did they look reasonably comfortable, but they rose easily. I guessed many were former performers. But sometimes audiences in museums don't know how to respond, as when the dancers used sculptures as part of a dance. After dancing for forty-five minutes around and under huge sculptures, another woman and I started clapping as the dancers trooped out of the space. No one joined us. I don't think it was the quality of the dancing; it was the unorthodox space. Some audience members thought performance belonged on a stage.

The audiences for many small companies and project-based groups are often necessarily small. In one loft space, sofas, armchairs, and dining chairs provided seating for about forty. Most of the audience appeared to be residents of the neighborhood when it was filled with artists, who were now in their seventies and eighties. But they climbed the steep steps and waited patiently until someone opened the apartment door. A few cushions made up the front row where I sat, and the latecomers, mostly dancers, sat cross-legged with straight backs on the floor at a right angle to the rest of the audience. All left small donations in the jar by the door.

Finding out about these events is not easy unless one is in the groups' networks or knows where to look on Instagram. A choreographer told me about a fascinating performance in an Airbnb studio apartment. The audience was limited to ten, and we all waited in the hall until let in for the performance. We moved aside when the residents from across the hall left their apartment. The performance involved two dancers whose relationship we followed as it evolved around the apartment. Some of the audience, leaning against the kitchen counter, had to move for the dancers who used the counter. A lighting expert hooked the ceiling lights up to a computer that changed the light intensity during the performance. The dancers exited into the bathroom and turned on the shower.

Dancers' friends attend and stay afterwards to congratulate them enthusiastically and discuss the work. In most small performances this happens. It is part of the performance experience for performers and audience. I started to stay and listen to the engaged conversations and add my own thoughts. It did contribute to feelings of audience involvement. The audience was part of the dance community, though not necessarily dancers, and influenced the experience of the evening for the dancers.

CONSTRUCTING A PERFORMING LIFE

Many portfolio dancers attended conservatory or college, but majoring in dance does not necessarily prepare students to approach the portfolio world. Acting in a professional manner— like being on time and suitably warmed up—is ingrained in their bodies. Learning different dance styles and techniques in college, everything from classical ballet to Graham to Gaga, is critical. Some feel comfortable in pointe shoes, others see their main strengths as more contemporary or experimental—sock, sneaker, or barefoot dance. Each has a comfortable range, but they have to adapt the body with every new choreographer. The social and economic life of portfolio dancers is also more difficult to construct than for those in a large company whose lives are largely structured for them; they need to seek dance work continuously to maintain identities as professional dancers, find and pay for their own classes, and develop ways to financially support themselves.

The labor market requires organizing a life that includes auditioning, developing networks, taking classes, rehearsals, performing, and working to eat. Dancers need to be outgoing in their pursuit of dance work—both performing and behind the scenes work; just waiting and being nice when so many good dancers, especially women, want the few available opportunities doesn't work. A choreographer expressed annoyance after teaching a class and seeing a young woman who picked up her movement style beautifully but who did not come up to her after class; she had to approach the dancer and hired her for a project. But the dancer had auditioned for a traveling company and, if she had gotten that job, she would not have been able to dance the choreographer's final performance. How do you find meaningful opportunities to perform to affirm yourself as a professional dancer when you have to put together your schedule and work outside of performing to eat?

What Portfolios Involve

BFA programs haven't always prepared students for developing portfolios with business and networking skills. Although some are doing a bit better today, Mila was disappointed in her program. She persevered and continues to dance in her early forties with a small contemporary company that pays reasonably well and a project-based group of more traditional ballet dancers who dance on pointe. She worked as waitstaff for about ten years and now teaches Gyrotonic. Her partner is also an arts freelancer. Mila recounts:

> I decided on a college with a strong dance program. I knew dancers didn't go to college, but I felt like I wanted those four years of transitioning into being sort of a person out of your parents' house. I figured I should be able to get auditions and jobs. They were going to help us get jobs, which is not something that's really possible, but that was sold to our parents, who don't know anything about dance and believe that they're gonna put you in this expensive college and something's gonna come out of it. None of that happened. Our parents were mad.
>
> Some got jobs teaching, but I and my friends came to New York to audition and none of them wanted to go. Most continued dancing very little after college. I just wanted to pursue it. I felt if I keep dancing and worked hard enough, something had to come of it, which is not really the case. You can't just work hard—I learned this the hardest way. Because I danced in small companies, I'm basically living like a sub-par version of the dream. It's great. It's just not the perfect ABT. That high route.

Mila holds onto her ballet company dream after dancing for almost twenty years, linking her identity to a childhood dream, minimizing what she has achieved.

Kelly also had no idea how the dance market worked; after graduating from a major university ballet program about eighteen years ago and dancing for a small ballet company where she earned almost no money, she also worked in a coffee shop. But she had little idea about the job market in New York:

> I needed to go somewhere bigger. I decided I was gonna to move to New York. I reshot all my head and body shots. I didn't have a computer so I would go to the library. I would send a cover letter. I came finally into a bunch of auditions. I got a job with [a small contemporary company]. They called and said someone was injured, could I come and start learning the work. That was great; really not a good environment. The directors are so bad. I was with them for a year. I had sent them [second small contemporary company] that video. The director was one of the people who wrote back, "Find me later." When I saw that they were having auditions, I thought, these people already showed interest; just cattle call auditions with a hundred dancers.
>
> I didn't understand the difference between a pick-up [project-based] company versus Paul Taylor [major modern dance company]. I just assumed that all companies were all the time. I didn't know there was such a thing in New York as somebody who would just do a show here and there and that you would need to be working with a lot of other people.

Her persistence paid off, and she created a career in a small contemporary company that used her dancing, choreographic, and social skills; they travel and pay the dancers/teachers a great travel per diem. For several years, she also worked intermittently with a small project-based ballet pointe shoe company but stopped when she no longer wanted to wear pointe shoes. She also dances with a group that does innovative contemporary choreography, is director/choreographer of a project-based group and has made short films—a cultural entrepreneur. She loves all the work, which she finds very creative: choreographing, performing, talking to the media, working with children, and making films.

Many of those who graduate from New York area schools know more about building portfolios today; at the very least, they know that they will have to build one, if not how. These dancers have found ways to enter the labor market and maintain their selves as professional performers over an extended period. They learned to organize complicated lives and to use their voices; their professional performing identities are still strong, but they have additional identities as teachers (Mila, Jane, and Kelly), choreographers (Kelly and Jane), and cultural entrepreneurs (Kelly and Jane) that they incorporate into their self. Kelly also points out the relational issues of some small intensive groups. Few remain portfolio dancers as long as she has. Her life, she explains, is very fulfilling.

Strategies to Protect the Self as Performer

Although dancers in big ballet companies may feel like each company class is a role audition, portfolio dancers need to find auditions, keep in touch with several networks, and locate classes that keep them fit, extend their dance skills, and put them in sight of choreographers who may be looking for dancers. Unlike the situation in other fields, no dance recruiters exist.

Dancers must work continuously to find enough opportunities to perform. Some dancers show up regularly in different performing groups over the course of the year. One woman I saw, by chance, in four different projects over the course of the year: her own group performing outdoors, a project-based company of a choreographer with several sporadic showings, a museum event over several days, and another weekend project. She works as a restaurant hostess. A second woman I saw three times in a year with three different project-based groups with different choreographers—all by chance. These dancers have opportunities to reinforce identities as professionals and have danced in more performances than I saw, but others are less successful at finding ways to affirm themselves as professional performers. All need to develop repair narratives.

Some start repair work before they enter the market; it isn't always productive. There are no organizations to help a dancer create a portfolio as there are for songwriters in Nashville to try out their songs for producers.[10] Access to a community of older portfolio dancers or creating a network takes time and perseverance. Both Zoe and Jonah, recent graduates of urban university dance programs, are unsure about how to get started in the portfolio world. Zoe thinks she won't be able to get meaningful work until she has more experience, but she distances herself from Broadway work. Notice how she slips in work outside the dance world. Two years later she works as an administrative assistant and occasionally as a performer:

> I don't think that's really going to happen, like right out of college. I need to gain more experience, I'm hoping to dance with a couple of smaller companies as well as—I'm applying for some arts administration jobs, and I'm going in for an interview to be a dog walker tomorrow. I went to an audition [Broadway], and I left before I did it because I was like, "I don't want to do this." There were just a lot of people in fishnets with really high-cut leotards, their whole butt hanging out and hair-sprayed hair, and I was like, "That's just not me."

While Kelly and Mila have enough artistic work to maintain themselves as performers, Zoe does not, but she has developed a boundary between artistic performance and other work to maintain herself as an artist: she is too inexperienced to get artistic work, and Broadway isn't really art.

Jonah doesn't express much self-confidence by anticipating failure even with the shortage of men. He develops his identity repair narrative before beginning his career. An important choreographer invited him to take classes, a sign of interest. His response was, "I won't have to pay for summer classes." It didn't go further, but I saw him by chance twice in small roles in performances around the city. If Jonah had little hope of employment, he was not putting his skills on the line, continuing his strategy of risk aversion as he did by not asking for a place in a major company training program as we saw in Chapter 3. He might fail:

> There's so much up in the air. "You're the next generation. You're gonna do this, that, and the other thing. You're gonna spice up the dance world. It's in your hands. It's so tangible." At least personally, I feel rather clueless as to where to take it. I think that just means I have to sit down and think about what I think would be best to happen next. How much can I do?

Building a portfolio for Eileen is a challenge at the start of her career, despite assisting a well-known choreographer. Connections can help, but it is a difficult challenge to locate enough work to affirm one's identity as a professional dancer:

I guess having that on my résumé, people see, "She worked with [choreographer]." They're like, "We wanna see what this girl's about." Through that, I have gotten many auditions that normally I wouldn't have been second glanced at. I'm constantly in the process of auditioning. That's just the ebb and flow of the dance world. It gets exhausting because you're constantly putting yourself out there and you're like, "Take me." It's part of the job. I auditioned for [small contemporary]. I made it through three rounds. It was very intense, and he was only looking for one girl out of 300. I've gotten lots of smaller project-based jobs that I did from January to now. It's so hard because the freelance life is you can have work for six weeks, and then, you don't have anything.

She persists with projects that protect her identity as a professional unlike Zoe and Jonah who pull back, arguing they are too inexperienced to get work and seeing audition failure as risk, thus, partially contributing to their own barriers.

To get through constant auditions and not getting jobs, those, with more experience, sometimes focus their identity repair narratives on their presentation of self to others. That may mean what you wear, presenting yourself as nice and cooperative, but also communicating you want it without appearing pushy. What companies or choreographers (gatekeepers) are looking for is rarely clear to dancers, so many worry and strategize. Rejection is part of the audition process: "my presentation didn't fit the type of person or the look they needed," which deflects from dancing skills.

Remy argues that developing the "look" is critical and different for each kind of audition, which makes moving among them difficult. Anita thinks she sees evidence of this when she auditioned for a small major contemporary ballet company wearing different outfits; the first time she looked like a classical dancer and failed to get the position; a short time later, she secured the job with her "more contemporary" attire of black, not pink, tights. Remy explains her thinking:

Your height, are you gonna fit the costume? It was always a mystery. I would get a lot of callbacks. My stomach would be in knots, because you're getting so close, and you're wondering. Then, I wouldn't get it. No, they don't tell you [why]. They just say, "Thank you very much for coming." I always wondered, "What did I do right, and what did I do wrong?" I realized, "Maybe I'm not doing anything wrong. Why am I using right and wrong?" It's just what they like. There're a million reasons why—you're never gonna know. After a while, I think I gave up. You see, you could do everything right and still not get it.

The self is continually under assault, but Remy has figured out a repair narrative: "the look" or "mystery." It focuses on characteristics other than her dancing.

Holding onto the ballerina ideal makes repair work difficult, but Jane acted; she formed a group of dancers for whom she choreographs, with whom she dances, and for whom she finds performances in small festivals and studios. Jane still works hard to make her performing career exciting, affirming her identity as a ballerina, but she does not always convince herself fully. She works hard to define a successful audition and talks about pay and contracts, and, as a ballerina, when she can wear a tutu, holding on to her ideal. She emphatically separates her ballerina (art) and commercial work; commercial dance provides income to produce her choreography and pay dancers. She wants to be a ballerina and so creates a repair narrative when she fails to get those jobs: if she feels that she had a "successful" audition, she finds it fulfilling. She does find some ballerina work:

> Some auditions I made it to the end. You feel so accomplished because there are so many people in the room. Going to an audition doesn't mean you get the job. That doesn't happen very often. The realities of the profession are very different than what you think of when you're training. Even what your professors are telling you. A successful audition is not getting the job. A successful audition is having a stress-free audition; having the résumé prepared; having the right outfit; demonstrating the material to a degree that you feel proud. Getting the job? I mean, I just feel like it's a lottery. There were a lot of auditions, but there just weren't a lot of jobs. I feel proud of every professional performance job I had. Getting a paycheck to dance is something that is like a badge of honor. Having been able to be a credentialed professional is really a treasure. I got a job with this [small ballet] company, but it has all the trappings of a professional ballet experience. You're wearing tutus. They get you shoes.

You have company class, and you get a paycheck. For me, all those things were really great to have as a freelancer.

She goes on to list several jobs she had and refers to fashion week and modeling work as "commercial-y." But she is proud of a small performance of *Sleeping Beauty,* which she refers to as a gig and good for experience. There are too many dancers for the work.

Repair narratives are not just for the presentation of self to others; dancers need to convince themselves too. It takes persistence to deal with the challenges of portfolio building and working on identity repair narratives to deal with lack of work. Sadly a "success" can turn to dust; it is precarious labor controlled by artistic directors who may treat dancers poorly. Hope feels she was treated badly when she failed to get the "regular" job with a small well-established contemporary company without learning why. She suffers as she hasn't created a convincing repair story yet:

I just walked up to him boldly, I said, "I've loved your work and I wanna dance for you." I could tell there was positive feedback. "I could see you being here." I ended up taking company class. I get a text message saying, "Hi, this is [artistic director], "Can you come in tomorrow?" In two days, I learned all the rep for the entire evening performance. Wednesday we're on a flight. Thursday was tech. Friday was the first show. We performed all weekend.

"I know this is weird, but just come to the audition." I responded, "Okay, I kinda already did the audition." It gets to the final—They don't call my name. I was like, "Oh, my gosh, that's so weird." I normally don't get too upset, but I was pretty bummed. "I just was onstage," he's like, "Had nothing to do with your dancing. We were just going for some kind of composition with the company." I didn't get what that meant. I talked to a few other people, and they had similar things. I don't know if it's one of those things where maybe down the road it'll work, but I guess it was a "look" thing. I don't know if they needed a shorter dancer, maybe more exotic looking. I have no idea to be honest.

There were some weird things. I'd come in, it seemed I was gonna be hired part-time, and then they were bringing me in to fill in again. "Oh, actually, we can't afford to pay you. But we'll pay you for the time you did." Never got paid. I was like, I'm kinda getting tired of all this. It was never like, "You're a bad dancer. You know you're not really right at this time. It has nothing to do with your dancing, it's just kind of not a fit right now." What does that mean? I think that's the frustrating part.

Hope is treated poorly, but she hasn't learned to protect her performing self or demand to be paid. Something she does not understand keeps her from becoming a company member. She has the words of repair but hasn't convinced herself it is "valid." She still thinks discovering why is possible. She needs to experience rejections not as risky to her identity as a skillful performer to stay in the portfolio world. Her experience of dealing with poor treatment by small companies is not unique, and she hasn't been in the city long enough to engage with others who can convince her that rejection must be expected.

Others understand that some artistic directors want a diversity of types and use this narrative successfully. Tara convinced herself of its validity:

> I would be performing, but I always had to have a job [to earn a living]. During rehearsals, sometimes I would not work as much, and things like that. I went to the [major small contemporary company] studio and was studying there for a while. I thought, "Well, maybe I can get in the company." I was part of company class. Then he chose a dancer for his company that was just like me. I knew that was the new me because he has one of each type—a waspy, just my body type, a modern dancer. Not a ballet dancer. He took her. I thought, "You know what? That was my spot." I left that studio and started doing all kinds of things. I danced with a number of downtown choreographers, and people you probably heard of. I never danced with someone big. We would go on tours, like with the kitchen touring program.

The professional performing self is in frequent need of protection. Tara tried out for smaller companies and made a long performing career.

The inevitable ebbs and flows of performance opportunities are difficult to manage. The affirmation of self as professional is rarely regular. When things have been going well for a while, even the more successful have to deal with periods of few performances. Career management remains difficult, even with some success. Kendell, like Eileen, found her calendar full upon conservatory graduation, but six months later had little. It picked up, but when I spoke with her, she was nervous as an injury meant no work at all. Not only did she have less income, but no way to affirm her identity as a performer. When a dancer is with a company, the dancer can still claim membership when injured. This is not necessarily so with small companies and projects. Kendell relates:

> When I graduated, I had that whole summer filled, booked a *Nutcracker*. I wasn't out of work until January. I rode on cloud nine. Come January I'm like, "Oh, so this is how this feels—not knowing what's happening next." Right. I had a couple connections from all the stuff I had done during the summer and was taking a lot of classes. I started auditioning for smaller projects. When you're in school, you really have no idea what's going on except for shows. Getting to know where the classes were and who the teachers were takes time. At some point I auditioned for his [known choreographer] company, got a callback, and wasn't hired. Then, I auditioned for [shows with him]. I started dancing in his company after; I guess that went well. We had a really busy October through August. Then we haven't had that much as a company. He's had a couple other things going on. I also got injured. This has been kind of the slowest fall that I think I've ever had. It's a little disconcerting.

She did end up performing at a good-size venue about a year later and was singled out in a major newspaper review. After theaters reopened in fall 2021, she danced again.

Carson maintained a full schedule but wasn't making enough for food and rent. At the time of the interview with me, he was dancing with a major contemporary company when they needed additional dancers:

> I got my job with [small contemporary company]; he set a piece on my class my senior year. A couple years later, he wanted to do some larger works, so he needed some men and asked me. That snowballed from there, and I joined the main company. I'm now his rehearsal director. I assist him on his outside projects. I started working with [another contemporary company] by cold audition. I only did one

season. I went to a [major contemporary company] audition. He offered gigs as they come about. He has a company of twenty people.
When they do those larger works, they hire supplemental dancers.

Carson saw his problem as his inability to make enough money to live
on, as we saw earlier; he had sufficient dance work to uphold his dance
identity. He persisted and worked his way to the top of the contemporary dance world when he joined the prestigious contemporary group as
a regular. He also began to choreograph.

Finances nearly tripped up Carson; holding on to a performing self
without enough work may become too hard. Repair narratives don't
always succeed at maintaining a performing self. Adrian described not
having the social skills to find work, which convinced him to exit:

> The other thing I would have done differently is I would have gone
> up to [director, small major contemporary] and said, "Would you
> please consider me," like other dancers were doing. I got good feed-
> back in class. I felt very good in the movement, but I didn't have
> the guts to do it. I didn't survive [auditions] very well. I took it very
> personally. That was probably why I didn't go up to him in the first
> place—I didn't want to be rejected. The chances of being rejected are
> much greater than being accepted. I hated that wait. They would call
> you if they're interested. You wait. That first day no call, the second
> day no call, and then you realize, "I'm not getting the call." It's just
> a lot of disappointment. There's despair involved. "Should I be doing
> this?" or "I'm not good enough."

Over the long-term Adrian was unable to develop a strong enough narrative to avoid thinking he was failing and left dance. He was not getting work frequently enough; auditions and dance became risky, not just
challenging.

Shaping the Body, Careful Scheduling, Being Safe

Portfolio dancers need to be in control of their own bodies—whether
weight, movement skills, or safety awareness—and in scheduling all
their different activities. Body size in contemporary groups is often
more varied than in ballet. In a project-based company, two women
were very short, a third was much taller and broader than the typical

dancer; all were excellent dancers and aesthetically they looked good together. Moreover, as a member of the audience, it was possible to discern the individual qualities of their dancing as they didn't look alike.

Keeping the body in shape is left to the individual; this means daily classes that enable dancing the movement styles of different choreographers and networking for work. As few small companies offer their own classes, most have to pay for their own. The training of ballet dancers is similar.[11] But today's contemporary choreographers each have their own movement style and only sometimes develop classes reflecting that style. I observed as a woman worked to develop a new class that would bring together classical ballet and contemporary techniques. Four professional dancers tried to follow her; one danced in a classical ballet company, had terrific feet and turnout, but his body had not yet yielded to the technique, while the others were trained in contemporary techniques. But only one truly embodied this hybrid technique. Contemporary classes vary from those that use themes and improvisation to others that choreograph barre exercises to include more upper body movement than traditional ballet—contractions or arms swinging. Natalia explained her movement style's relationship to herself, a creative stance:

It's not about the body. I think it's about what is the language that allows you to be yourself. I don't think I am fooling myself when I do strictly traditional classical ballet work. I can be more myself when I do something that allows my body to give in a little bit more, like to have a sort of movement that is more natural to me. I love to use my spine for example, they [ballet] use the spine—but it's very up all the time where I like to also do spiral-ly things. I think I was trained to be versatile, to just see what the choreographer wants and try to get the style.

But portfolio builders need to be ready not only to learn the movements required, but the way the choreographer uses the body. Natalia explained the complexities of learning a new contemporary style:

It does something interesting in my mind. I feel like my brain has to work really hard to execute her work because it's very brainy, and I think I like that because it's a challenge, not just for the body, but

also for my mind, the technique of it is very different from the classical technique that everybody's trained with. You really have to find
the physics of each movement. I know if I have to do a *pirouette* what
I need to do, but this is so different. It's a lot of stuff on the floor, and
you have to put the weight on your arms, which you don't normally
do in ballet. It's like the mechanics are so intricate too that it's like
a little machine that you have to start it right so that it can roll in.

Switching among movement styles is not easy, but it keeps dancers
engaged and experimenting. Each dancer must find classes to fit with or
extend their range of movement styles. Some portfolio dancers, when
running between groups, change from pointe shoes to socks to barefoot
in one day and, occasionally, in one evening's performance. It takes significant effort to embody the styles of different choreographers.

Scheduling classes, rehearsals, auditions, and various worksites is
daunting. As a collective art, scheduling and being on time are critical.
Occasionally, dancers don't work "professionally." Trouble in choreographing occurs when someone is late or the dancers' schedules don't
fit. It is difficult to "see" a dance on oneself or in one's head. If someone
is late, creating and rehearsing suffer—studios are rented for a specific
period. One group had the studio for an hour and a half, and one dancer
was twenty minutes late. The choreographer had planned to start with
a continuation of the duet. He went over her movements, but the lift
hadn't gone well the previous day, and the integration of the movement
was essential to progress. The choreographer stopped and threw himself on the floor and started doing pushups. He kept his cool when the
dancer walked in and said he was sorry. The choreographer gave him a
few minutes to warm up before putting him to work. On another occasion he stopped a young dancer to lecture her about taking class before
rehearsal, explaining why it was important in a quiet, yet firm, voice.
I asked another dancer how he knew she hadn't taken class; it was because she wasn't exactly where she should have been standing high on
her pointe shoes, which wasted time and could lead to injury.

Rehearsal periods are expensive (renting studios and paying dancers); thus they are short, intense, and focused. No one fools around, and
all are ready to start when the choreographer arrives. They are warmed
up, if the choreographer has not planned a class. Typical in my observa-

tions is the intense concentration demonstrated by dancers as the choreographer conducts a warm-up on the floor. When the choreographer
stops to set up the music, without a word, the women do barre together.
They then dance seriously following the choreographer—working together with assignments in different groupings, then coming together,
and the choreographer deciding with them which movements to use.
Sometimes one is not working with the others, and she goes over her
movements. No one speaks much, and the dance moves forward. Occasionally, the choreographer uses metaphors and images to underscore
what she wants, or one of the dancers asks a question. Several times,
they laugh when a movement doesn't work, or someone mistakenly
knocks into someone else. No time for gossip or fooling around; they
look focused but relaxed.

They must learn very quickly with the expensive short periods for
creation and rehearsal, explains Sebastian:

> The idea with the studios and rehearsal spaces are mind-blowing to
> me, in the sense that you've got an hour to do this. You must be very
> good at picking up steps very quickly. It's a skill you have to acquire,
> because no one has time to show it to you a thousand times. To come
> in the second rehearsal, after you learned it the previous rehearsal
> and not know your steps, that's kind of ridiculous. There's a lot of
> expectation, as a freelance dancer. When you're in school, the fac-
> ulty bring in a lot of choreographers to expose you quickly, and to
> not only give you physical tools, but to push you mentally to pick
> up movement fast. If they're looking for a new dancer to fulfill a
> role already danced, you're expected to look at it [video] before you
> come in, then the choreographer can give you real artistic detail, the
> nuance they're looking for.

I found the speed at which dancers learn astonishing. Contemporary
choreographers show movement sequences to dancers who may not
have worked with them before, and, as they have their own movement
vocabularies, remembering it takes work. It's not like classical ballet
that has steps with names even when the choreographer changes the
way a step is done.

As dancers often belong to several groups and have paying jobs,
scheduling rehearsals and performances is difficult. No one has the flex-

ible schedules that freelancers in other work worlds often valorize. All talk about having conflicts for performances and having to choose, requiring directors to bring in a new dancer at the last minute, like Hope. This creates tensions for everyone.

Moving among different groups and dance sites requires continual efforts to protect one's body: uneven or cement floors, choreography beyond the limits of one's training, and choreographers who don't seem to care about safety. Kendell has begun to calculate risks. She is very concerned about whether the choreographer is using dancers conscientiously and will take responsibility, if problems arise, especially after her injury:

> Is it good floors? If I get injured, are you gonna help pay for it? These are things I think about only because it doesn't take more than once for you to get injured in a bad space for you to begin to be really cautious of where you're dancing. Sometimes choreographers are like, "Don't do anything that hurts. I understand this is concrete. If you need to modify it, okay by me. I don't want you to get hurt." Sometimes that's not the case. That's also why it's very personal and very situational and specific.

Working with multiple groups often means dancing with unknown people. Will they be reasonable to work with, and if problems occur, will the choreographer or artistic director deal with it? How will the choreographer treat the dancers? Dancers also must look out for themselves as not all choreographers are trustworthy, as Graham found. After new dancers get together, they must trust the others immediately, by trusting that the choreographer chose good people. Touching and partnering is a challenge, and sometimes risky. Not everyone is responsible, according to Graham:

> Trust me, I get it. I would make creative choices where I wouldn't have to stand near the dancer I didn't like. I would do my best to craft the piece in a way where I didn't have to dance with the people that I didn't feel safe dancing with. Maybe that was just like a survival tactic. This particular choreographer played dumb. I think on some level he probably understood, but he wasn't willing to address it, which I think is too bad. I think it's the role of the choreographer

as the leader of an experience to take care of everybody's safety as much as they can. I feel like he shirked that responsibility. I felt it became my responsibility to watch out for my safety. Sometimes, maybe that got in the way of the creative process, but if the choreographers weren't gonna do their part, then that was what had to happen.

Sebastian agrees dancers have to trust each other quickly and accept many challenges. He lifts both men and women; some are difficult. He caught a man who had launched himself high in the air seemingly without fear. I gasped when I saw them. The group met only two days before. Sebastian explains that he saw it as a challenge:

You trust that you have all the tools you need, based on your training and your experience, to guide you through an experience, in terms of the physical aspects of what's being asked of you. You really do have to trust the other person quickly. You can't assume that they're gonna know how you breathe, and how you make contact with them, because they don't. You energetically have to be very open and available to them in this space. Because ultimately, the goal is to do the project, to perform it well. You have to relinquish your ideas and your way of doing something, if you realize it's not working with this new person. If you can do that quickly, and you can be malleable, then you're going to succeed with this new partner.

Respecting others' bodies and time are important to many choreographers and tiny companies; unreliability and unpleasantness in the studio ruin the joy of creation for some choreographers. But some choreographers are, at best, unpleasant, and in small companies, "staff" is the artistic director/choreographer; there is no place to complain. Leaving may be the only option for poor relations or treatment. Loyalty derives from positive relationships and thinking well of the choreographer, in addition to performance.

Sometimes dancers need to complain about a safety issue. Chantel described the reaction of a choreographer when she complained about a partner who didn't appear to be able or willing to catch her properly:

I think a lot of them are shocked. I think, they would expect it from an older woman because I'm only twenty-four. They're in so much shock. You have to hold yourself with respect and dignity, and so I think they're shocked to see that I hold myself with dignity at such a young age. When I tell them that, they just kind of look at me like, "Wow, nobody's ever said that to me before." You have to tell them, "That's not okay."

Despite limited options, several dancers left companies when they no longer trusted the artistic director. The challenge had turned into a risk with too few payoffs.

ART AND MONEY

Many portfolio dancers earn more money from non-dance activities than from performing. Traditional views of work don't adequately describe dancers' portfolios. Feminists have questioned the nature of work by demanding that work women do at home without pay be considered work. Economists probably don't call much of what is done in the dance portfolio world "employment" or "labor," but dancers generally insist on being paid for performing, and many choreographers/artistic directors insist on paying something. Although the pay is rarely enough to be financially rewarding, it does indicate that dancers are professionals. Portfolio dancers have complicated, varied, and changing relationships with income and how they earn it.

Reluctant to talk about it, a few get financial help from their families, often staying on family health insurance as long as they can, and others receive help from partners. Some with enough weeks of employment are eligible for unemployment. Many teach dance, manage small companies, run rehearsals, do publicity, work on costumes, or film dance. They may consider these activities as supporting their art. Others work as baristas, waitpersons, bartenders, caterers, babysitters, bookkeepers, models, models for drawing classes, trainers, or yoga or Pilates instructors, which may be seen as supporting a dance career or as necessary to eat. One more mature dancer worked for many years for a law firm, word processing at night, which paid well and included some benefits, but this became obsolete with the new generations of lawyers. She talked about it as financing her long performing career. The boundary between her performing work and her income was easy to draw as it was unconnected to dance. Another learned costuming when working as a wardrobe assistant while in school; a few years later, she costumes small companies while dancing. She considers costuming part of her dance work, but that's not performing. Dancers construct symbolic boundaries, some stronger than others, between performance and other dance work; other dance world work isn't who they are, but as they move away from performing later, it may become their regular work that they have slowly incorporated into the self.

Getting Paid

Kendell is proud of her ability to support herself in the dance world, but it is not totally from performing. She teaches, runs rehearsals, and organizes dance companies. She differentiates between exactly what her parents paid for and performing and work in the dance world:

> When I graduated, I was able to pay off my loans. That was one of the proudest moments ever. Since then, I've been able to support myself. My parents helped me a couple times with medical things. Rent has always been me, living in the city has always been me. When it comes to making money, I teach a lot. I knew that I didn't wanna graduate and then resent going to school because I was left with huge debts. I did as many work study jobs as I could find. I also was part of this fellowship where you get like $100 or $200 per performance. You put together a forty-five-minute program with musicians, actors, dancers from school. You perform at healthcare facilities. It was fun and a good way to learn how to collaborate. My last two years of school I got a teaching fellowship, which was $10,000 for me to teach.

Kendell expresses some ambivalence about dance work and money, thus, creating a symbolic boundary between performance and teaching dance. She will perform for no money, if it is real art, but responded differently to that question if it was nonperformance work. When she traveled over an hour to teach and found the class canceled, she was furious about the failure to pay and called a lawyer. Most dancers say they need to be paid, especially for nonperforming activities. The boundary is slightly fuzzy—her work is all in the dance world, which she is proud of, but it isn't art:

When I was creating work a couple years ago, I knew how uncomfortable it was to not get paid. I always wanted to be able to pay the people I worked with. I think there comes a point where sometimes you do things because you love them, and being paid just ensures that you're gonna be available and not schedule something else. Sometimes we do things because they're interesting, but the paycheck really helps. There are other times I would do this even if I wasn't getting paid because it's so interesting to me or it's really important work. Maybe it fits into my schedule. It's a hugely personal decision, which is why it's never an easy answer when somebody's like, "Well, can you do this thing?" I'm like, "What's the time commitment? What is the thing?"

Like Kendell, Natalia agrees that when your artistic side is nourished with interesting new ways of moving and the experience is good, money doesn't matter as much:

When I started working with her, she didn't have much money to pay. "I will give you this small fee if you can do this," but it was such a pleasure to do that, I didn't mind. Now she's getting more. She started a bigger fee first and then she was also able to pay me by the hour. It's good when you see someone who is going up the ladder and doesn't forget the people who helped her and gives back.

But when the dance work isn't sufficiently artistic and unpleasant, Natalia takes a different position:

It's like so many hours and at the end you're like, 'I'm losing money here." Some choreographers just pay a standard fee and that's hard because maybe it looks like you're getting more money.

When performing is seen as abusive, other sources of income can tide a dancer over if they quit. Dancers talk about being abused. Casey left two companies and enjoys the life she created by becoming an aerialist, dancing in projects, and editing films—all within her boundaries of art; but symbolic boundaries aren't fixed—they evolve. She started her career with an excellent small contemporary ballet company but saw it as abusive and quit:

I fell into doing video production, and so started making my money between bartending and producing video content. After leaving that company, I freelanced and then just stopped dancing for a year—it was such an abusive career. I had made it. I had made it to the top, and I was barely making ends meet. I was being treated like a disobedient child. I got pulled back into dance again $10 an hour standard, maybe $100, $150 performance. I quit bartending because I was juggling video production and running to rehearsals and running back to work.

I started working for [a small contemporary] company, and I'll go on the record saying the director is a narcissistic horrible person who abuses people. She'll provide visas for dancers and then either not pay them or pay less than she says. She's really manipulative.

This third company was so abusive to the dancers that Casey "took the role of trying to almost unionize the company" before she quit. She continues in the dance world to do projects with friends for her performing self and spends more of her time earning money as a video editor, which she can tie weakly to art. When the company experience becomes truly unpleasant, even dance is placed outside the boundary of art.

Small companies may have more consistent performance opportunities than project-based work, but most also require paying jobs on the side, and, after a while, the repertory may no longer challenge. Several portfolio dancers performed in small ballet companies before coming to New York City. Audrey describes her experience:

I was still making a really low wage, but that was what they offered. This gets very frustrating when you are working hard and cannot afford to eat. We performed a lot, which was the whole point. I wasn't getting paid the first year, but I got a lot of performance opportunities. I worked six days a week. I'm including the ballet. You work in cafés, coffee shops. I was cocktail waitressing. I worked at some cellphone company. Our day [ballet] was from 9:30 to 4:00. We had class from 9:30 to 11:00, and then a fifteen-minute break, rehearsals all day. I was frustrated and done with the company, although I had a really good time. There was nothing more to do, I was dancing some lead roles.

She had no trouble separating waitressing and performance, but when success in dancing good roles is outweighed by a growing routine and the performance becomes a way to make money, it was too poorly paid to live. She chose exit, moved, and made a successful transition to a portfolio contemporary career. Her main work was in a small contemporary company that traveled regularly and required creative dancers. She danced with them until her late thirties when she decided to start a family.

Dancers, such as Audrey and Casey, want to be challenged—art challenges. Sebastian also left a small company when the dancing became too routine and the relationships were stifling. He danced with a project group while still in the company and before beginning graduate school. He returned to perform it—that was art, well worth doing:

> I started out as a freelance dancer for about three years. Then I was hired to dance for this company, which really consumes a lot of my time. I'm pretty much full-time. There are six of us in the room all the time who are constantly working with each other; it gets to be a lot. Everyone is really dramatic. It's not like [freelance choreographer's] rehearsal and experience, where you show up and it's a fresh group in the space, and there's a timeline, and everyone is there to do the job, be malleable and cordial, and get the job done as opposed to the company, where I see them all, all the time. Personalities fly, and you really show your true colors. I definitely think, in the freelance project world, I've had more positive experiences having worked with people in a more inconsistent way, as opposed to those who I work with full-time.

These dancers prioritize their performance art over income, both inside and outside the dance world. But when performance or relationships are unpleasant or dance becomes routine, Casey and Sebastian exited companies to do project-based work; Audrey joined a contemporary small company whose work she found fulfilling.[12] They all wanted to be challenged by their art and to dance in reasonable social environments.

Prioritizing Dance Income

Especially for young people who have few economic supports, the economic precarity of developing and maintaining a portfolio of work may lead them to accept work that does not fit their image of art.[13] But it is still dance. Chantel's family circumstances made portfolio building risky after her conservatory graduation. She took a dance job for the summer in a Broadway revival, and then a Broadway production, but wanted something more fulfilling and felt impelled to stretch her boundaries of art almost to include commercial work:

> I just went into panic mode. Right after graduation, I was auditioning as if I was homeless and this was my last opportunity. It was intense. I cut my leg open. I had a broken mirror in my room. I was gushing out blood, but I was so desperate to get a job that I went to the audition. "I just need money. I need to make sure I'm okay so I can take care of Mom." I had to go to the emergency room that night and get stitches.
>
> Not much [pay] because he's [choreographer, summer] stingy, too. He came to our show last night, just to say he thought it was a mess. Choreographers of that time are just cuckoo for cocoa puffs. He cursed us. He comes from that generation of throwing chairs. It was crazy, but it still was a good experience overall. Before that summer job ended, I found out that I had a permanent job. I had a Broadway show. When I was waiting until it started, I would do different gigs. One asked me to be a guest artist at his company's performances at the Joyce. I did Dancers Responding to AIDS. I did a commercial for BlackPeopleMeet.com. It was good for me to freelance for a minute.

Shows, such as this one, were not, according to Chantel, fulfilling art, or a place to learn. She used the word "soul." She needed income and they were dance. She maintains a boundary between meaningful dance and her Broadway show, preserving her artist self:

> I just want to do something more, it's just entertainment. Something more meaningful and informative and more goes with the type of person I am or what I'm about. It's not really doing too much for fulfilling my soul. That's what I'm most interested in, whether it's Broadway, a TV film, or a company. Just something that's fulfill-

ing my soul more, where I'm making money, but I'm also just doing something I love and I'm really learning from. Not just that, but that people I'm around are on the same page because on Broadway, you're around a lot of people that only do stuff for money. Money directs them in every path they go.

She sees a need to create a boundary between art and commerce, but for her, it is weak. Commercial work was temporary, but others who made the transition from companies to portfolio building found it too risky and saw a need to create stronger boundaries between art and Broadway as commercial work. They distance their identities from Broadway dancers—it isn't who they are—they just need the money.

Broadway dancers generally earn more than many company dancers as they belong to a stronger union (Actors' Equity Association) than AGMA, but jobs are few, often require singing and acting skills, and the dancing is frequently routine. Broadway raises the nagging question of the degree to which the dance is art. Most classically trained dancers don't dream of dancing in the corps on Broadway, in commercials, during fashion week, or modeling. As temporary work, it pays and, for a lead, can result in recognition and perhaps thoughts of a new career, such as Robbie Fairchild (former principal dancer, NYCB) as the lead in *An American in Paris*. But a sticky identity as a classical dancer makes it less than satisfactory for some.

Tre and John left struggling portfolio careers for the money and stability of Broadway. Tre was a principal dancer with a small ballet company and came to New York to dance in several small companies and projects. He also sang, so he auditioned for Broadway where he spent time as a "swing" and on the road for a production:

> Financial stability. That's what I saw on Broadway. I've been auditioning for tons of other shows, but, unfortunately, it's not really about your dancing. It's about how you fit the persona. The stability; above all, what comes up at the very end of the day is the big neon sign saying, "Stability." I was [nervous] all the time. All the time on edge. It's draining.

Tre tried out for a Broadway musical and got a "cover position"—for three years, which meant he was on call if someone couldn't make it:

I wanted to get a permanent position contract. She would skip me. I was always in audition mode, always doing 200 percent. I wanted to prove that I belong here, and I want to have that quiet in my heart that says, "Okay, you have a permanent position. I moved over to the other guy's place to replace him. In the meantime, he came back. I did the job of two people. He didn't show up for work, she hired him for the full time. I saw it and my eyes went black. I called her, and I said, "You never, ever meant to give me that contract. You've been fooling me." She said, "But what do you think about being the vacation swing." I said, "If you need me, you can call me, but thank you." Since then, she's been using me as a vacation swing. Whenever somebody is out, I have to go, because I need money, but it's a painful story.

He secured the regular position dancing on Broadway after speaking with me and performs occasionally with a small ballet company. He still sees himself as a ballet dancer, so Broadway is a way to earn a living, distinct from art.

For someone who leaves a ballet company after several years, who then tries to develop a portfolio, holding onto a performing self is possible but earning money is more difficult. John, like Tre, did not see his decisions as choices. Broadway was a way to pay bills; it wasn't an important identity. But unlike Tre, John rarely engaged with alternative ways to affirm himself as a ballet performer.

John left a strong small ballet company to follow his wife but had problems finding enough paid work in dance. He was hired by a well-funded company that folded, and then he performed in a Broadway show with excellent dancers that closed. When I first met him, a freelance choreographer was creating a new piece on him. He was grumpy and said, "You don't want to talk to me, I'm cynical." When we finally met on his way to the Broadway theater, he was polite and friendly. He was conflicted about what to do next at thirty-five. He told me Broadway was for the money, but unlike Tre, he was angry about dancing on Broadway. Interested in design, he had no vision yet of a pathway to that career. His narrative included experience with a short-lived contemporary company and ambivalence about performing on Broadway:

She [the artistic director] just had no experience. No idea what the hell she was doing. She just was very . . . sadistic. We were supposed to do three-hour ballet classes because we had to be strong. Everyone was miserable. I was really stressed. My wife wasn't liking school, and she wanted to leave, and I was like, "Well, I signed this contract." It was just a horrible—personally and professionally. I grew a depression injury beard because the show closed [second job], and I was injured. Then I auditioned for more Broadway stuff. I don't know, I just didn't want to. I was already ambivalent about dancing and then to have to be like, "Here I am." You have to be more committed in a way. That was uncomfortable for me. Basically, I got [Broadway show], and it was ballet.

Talking about his future made him uncomfortable. Several years later, he was still in the show. For some ballet dancers, like Tre or John, dancing on Broadway does not appear to be incorporated into the self; but, for Chantel, it allowed her to stretch her notion of art at the beginning of her career. Broadway mitigated the economic risks of a performing career, but where was the artistic challenge? They all affirmed the boundary between art and Broadway (commercial and routine), and Tre and John put their work, with regret, on the Broadway side, but it wasn't who they really were. They appeared to be a bit unmoored as to who they were and unfulfilled as dancers. Chantel who was earlier in her career continued to hope for meaningful, creative work and to expand her notions of art.

For some, working in more commercial dance to make a living is a greater challenge to their self than working in a coffee shop where it is easy to separate dance and working to eat. But on Broadway, dance becomes money. Your artistic self becomes questionable. Making money to live is important, but not at the expense of remaining an artist. Struggling to achieve balance takes effort. There is no established manner of setting these symbolic boundaries; some separate art and money, and others separate art and non-art performing. Some construct stronger boundaries than others, others adapt boundaries over time, and many include social relationships on the job and challenges as part of the boundary construction. It's a struggle in the portfolio world with few formal institutions to help: it's mostly friends.

THE REWARDS OF COLLABORATION: WE CREATE THE ART

The love and challenge of performing are fed by the sense of collaboration and community on- and offstage. Some don't sit around when they
don't have performances and try other arts: making films, costume
design, photography, music, choreography. The rewards are creativity
and community. Portfolio creation opens opportunities for performing
a diversity of dance styles; sticking to one's art and performing what
one wants, sort of. Using your body in different ways and searching for
artistic fulfillment in the portfolio world nourishes dancers with innovative content and possibilities for collaboration with choreographers,
dancers, and audiences, according to Anya. She trained in Russia at sixteen and received a major ballet company offer but decided on college
before returning to dance. The portfolio market allowed diversity and
creativity through collaborative efforts for Anya:

> They had different techniques [different groups]. The movement
> itself, the other dancers, I just could learn a lot. That was a big—I
> liked working on those different dances. Then artistically, it was the
> most satisfying. I could be dancing in the Met [opera] one day and
> like at the Chocolate Factory [experimental] the next. I was really
> doing at least two extremes. The right spot for me was somewhere
> in between a creative role, like a creative dancer role, like making
> contributions to the creative process, so in a more collaborative sit-
> uation.

Dancers must work hard to maintain their opportunities, but the joys of
collaboration in the creation of the project and performance, keep many
performing.

Indelible Dance, a project-based company, illustrates entrepreneur-
ship, collaboration in creation and performance, innovative ideas, audience involvement, and community. The venue is critical to Robin
Cantrell, the artistic director. In fall 2018 she had the date set but located the venue, a former factory, only a short time before the scheduled performance. She set up bleachers on either side of the large space
with three "rings" in the center—it was a sporting event. Each audience
member received a blue or red wristband, was assigned a bleacher section, and was told to cheer one team and boo the other. The audience

was encouraged to move close to each of the three rings set up between the bleachers on either side of the room as the dancers moved from one ring to the other. One of the duets in the "boxing ring" was particularly beautiful. We all laughed at the final "race" in one ring where the dancers moved beautifully using dance versions of runner movements grunting like racers. Dancers don't grunt! Dancers hide the sweat and difficulty of the movements; dance should look effortless. I'm not much of a sports fan, but I, along with all the audience members, cheered and booed loudly by the end of the evening. No one remembered for whom. It was a true collaborative effort; several dancers choreographed, and the dancers could see and hear the audience's excitement growing.

The central figure in the following year's performance was late in her pregnancy. In a ballet company, pregnant women typically take leave at about three months but may continue to take class. The theme of the evening was her pregnancy and the community of women—she looked beautiful and danced well. Robin decided the theme when Mira Cook told her about the pregnancy. Over 125 people attended each of three evenings.

The performance, *No Man's Land*, started with men in bright leotards and tights, demonstrating exaggerated "male" movements. Everyone laughed. Some were dancers, and others didn't have dancers' bodies or movements. The audience moved their chairs or sat on the floor in a different location on the large factory floor; a photo of Mira dancing across the screen before pregnancy was projected on the back wall as she appeared walking across the stage gracefully, her large body visible but never the object on view. It was the woman as dancer on view, not the pregnancy itself. She was joined by a group of women with whom she danced; they supported her and she, them. Perhaps it was a dream of all the women gone before her and her youth; the dancers moved again, joyfully. A dancer, who returned from Europe for the performance, danced inside a contraption that resembled an igloo symbolizing as I saw it both the child growing within and the future mother feeling the new boundaries of the life that awaits her. With some of the audience pulled into her "cage," the dancers dance wildly around it before moving to the pool where they danced as Mira sat in the water. As the audience moved to surround the pool, we participated with the women dancers who floated candles that shone brightly against the dark water. My eyes teared up, and I saw that others did too.

The evening was a celebration of community and life transitions of women, one often unacceptable for women performers. A very pregnant woman is at the center of a performance, proudly showing her body and dancing with her friends around her. The next generation emerged from below white waves, and, finally together, the men and women danced happily with Mira in the center. The creation of and the performance is a true collaborative process. Each section was choreographed by a different group member. Robin had to forgo concerts with her regular company as she had this weekend planned before they found out about a tour. She said the artistic director understood her divided loyalties but had to find a substitute.

Robin has developed ways to finance the production. Admission was twenty dollars, which was the fee for many project events pre-pandemic, and ticket sales were about enough to pay the dancers. She has ideas that both enhance the evening and make money for the group; she sold drinks, snacks, and fanny packs for ten dollars with *No Man's Land* emblazoned on the front. Production values are good for the project-based world: music, lighting, different costumes, and a cool venue. They contribute significantly to the experience of the evening. At a tech rehearsal of another group at a university's poorly equipped theater, the dancers were lighted from only one side, leaving half the audience with little possibility of seeing the dancers; it was slightly better at the performance. Many performances take place in studios across the city where the lights are either on or off so little opportunity exists to use lighting to enhance an effect. Robin bought equipment such as lights, cameras, and Marleys that she rents to other small groups. One of her dancers rented the equipment for his performance, and then she paid him for her next performance about what he paid for the rental. These performances involve not only cooperation but true collaboration, including with the audience who follow the performers around the space and stay to chat afterwards.

Dancers talk about their choreographic collaboration—in performing and with the audience. Choreographic collaboration works well, Tyler found, especially with more mature dancers:

She came to dance with the choreographer and me. He saw this, I think, as an opportunity to try something new. He made a dance for us. When we were in the studio, rather than just watch us, he would close his eyes, and he would describe to us what he saw, what he wanted it to look like. He would keep them shut until we were ready to show him that expression. Then we would show it to him, and he would tweak it a little. There was a great deal of satisfaction in the doing.

Choreography is often collaborative in the contemporary portfolio world, but not all work collaboratively. They are more likely to do so partially because they often work with new dancers each time who are differently trained so they need to see what dancers can do. Involving the dancers makes it theirs. Lisha talked about the tension between some choreographers' visions and her own:

> That's always such an interesting balance, finding the balance of putting yourself into the work and setting yourself aside to be a vessel for the choreographer's vision. That's hard because you wanna stand out as a dancer. You wanna showcase your thing, but you also wanna be true to that person's vision. Sometimes, that person's vision includes you. I feel like she includes us in the vision a lot. She's like, "How do you get out of this?" I love that, but a lot of the time, working with [another choreographer], it was, "No, this is what it is, no, you're not doing it." It's such subtle things. I really thought I was doing it.

Portfolio dancers often have ideas about movement they wish to express. Ellie found that some choreographers want dancers to do exactly how they envision it; her own ideas were not important. She felt the tension too:

> It's all movement that she created and gave to me. There is variation in terms of each body moves differently—she's looking for a certain effect, so maybe I have to do it slightly differently than she does to get that effect. For the most part, it's her movement on my body. I've been navigating. I get this resistance—it's an ego thing and I recognize that. I'm working on it. This frustration because I'm being asked to embody something that I never generated. Or to find emotion in movement that—it was her movement for that emotion. Not neces-

sarily mine. In the arc of this process, I've gotten a little bit defiant. What about how I move? I'm just realizing it's an opportunity to access a new place and find a new persona through this work. I believe in her work. That's not to say that I discount her process. It's just very new to me. I've felt a little bit of pushback in myself.

Most small groups have no understudies, so the dancers need to collaborate and develop close relationships as they are always with the same people. Lars describes one such group:

I was literally crying [watching two performers]. It was so touching, and you could feel it. They only have one cast. No understudies and no second cast because he wants to create that comfort zone. You don't have a different partner every time you're onstage. You're always with the same person. You create this relationship with other performers. Of course, we learn each other's parts, so when something happens—there is an emergency scenario. I think that's something smart. Some people think that, "Oh, it's probably a financial decision not to have second cast." Maybe it is, but it does have another purpose to it, too, because we get to really bond and find this relationship between us.

Audiences in small spaces may become part of the collaborative process. Dancers can see them in small places and many in the audience are known to the dancers who feel connected to them. Audience members participate on the periphery as they do in Indelible Dance and stay to congratulate them. Eda explains one such relationship that she experiences:

It's great to see reaction to this work you've done. You perform it. Performance is great and being in the moment and connecting with the people you're onstage with. Then also to see the faces afterwards and the see the community and people who have come out and support you. Or vice versa, when you go see a performance, and you see your friends or people you know performing, it's so wonderful. Especially if you're really good friends with them and see them doing what they do. It's just really special. It's nice to feel that support in the community—even though it's such a hard life as a dancer. It's such a wonderful community.

The dancers, even while performing, feel connected and collaborate with audience members as Lars describes in small spaces:

He creates a very intimate setting. The audience is only about 160, 170. It's very intimate. You have people dancing really close to you. The way the piece is structured is not to create a general picture for an audience member who sits in the balcony. It's almost personal. There's a lot of moments that you interact for a moment with an audience member. There is eye contact, communication.

But collaboration is sometimes unpleasant and generates negative emotions, as Graham experienced in a small company whose director seemed to create or exacerbate conflictual company relationships to create a dance:

There was a section in the piece where it was this massive partnering duet where they were almost sparring. It's not like that was the only thing that was going on, but there were these very real tensions in the group that sometimes made their way into the work. Dancers were not expected to just agree with him. I remember one dancer who's now one of my closest friends, she and the artistic director almost got into a fistfight about his behavior. It wasn't the kind of space where dancers were just subservient to the choreographer. There was a real, sometimes to a fault, but sometimes in a very real way, an active dialogue between the choreographer and dancers and the dancers and one another. There was something about it in that context that felt really heightened, but I think that choreographers are using the real dynamics between people in a room in generation of their work. I think he almost got off on it.

Collaboration is deeply embedded in the world of portfolio building, in the creation of dances, production, and performance. Many of the dancers want the work to express some of who they are; their personal identities as creative artists. Many are unsatisfied to be purely vessels of choreographers. They want to contribute more to the art of creation, to have the work express some of who they are, in addition to producing performances.

The collaboration on projects may be episodic, and those who develop portfolios often perform with different groups, but some of the dancers form communities that Casey mentioned and come together for projects. Life in small, more regular companies can be as difficult or more so than large companies—with directors who treat dancers poorly, overly intense relationships among the dancers, or performances that become routine and lack challenge. Some small company members turn to building portfolios with more project-based work that enables them to explore and challenge themselves.

REWARDS OF PERFORMING AND COMMUNITY

Is it a community of people who love dance, is it a profession, or is it work? It is often all three. Portfolio dancers feel that some payment is important for performance, but most don't dance to eat. Some are willing to waive a fee if they evaluate the performance as artistically important. Most choreographers and companies feel obligated to pay something—it is work and they are professionals. All show up for the performances of friends, and the friends are sometimes people with whom they dance—it is a community of artists. I run into dancers in the audience now whom I know and meet family and partners. When Konverjdans put on a Zoom show during the pandemic that included live dance, filmed dance, and a singer, the audience of more than fifty Zoom screens (most had multiple participants) kept the chat box active with congratulatory comments. Friends and family show up for performances.

Some dance classes emphasize community. With a rotating roster of teachers active in the dance scene, NYCommunity Ballet started in 2015 offering classes for professional dancers: "Because we are the community, we recognize the challenges dancers face, including finding affordable dance classes that are high enough quality to be deserving of our time and effort. Our classes are friendly to your wallet and your wellness!" Several days after COVID-19 closed studio buildings in New York City, they began teaching Zoom classes. Technical issues arose; the music could not be heard, the internet went out, the sound and movement were out of sync, but it worked! Classes included glimpses of pets and family. One taught from Berlin. Many knew one another and waved or unmuted and said hello at first; but they are professional dancers who need to take class and they rarely chatted. At the end everyone said thank you. It is work. As all were unemployed, they charged a voluntary minimal fee for classes, and teachers were paid, so it was a business venture but deeply embedded in a community of portfolio professionals. It continued in person—masked and vaccinated when permitted. They are entrepreneurial and a community.[14]

But community and the collaboration it entails are fragile, as many dance companies are project-based, as Katie found. She thinks that it may be better in a company but hasn't found one and most have few opportunities for collaboration:

> I miss the community. I miss working on something together with people having a goal, having a performance that you're working towards. That's really rewarding. You become a little family for a time, which is why freelancing is so hard because you build these really strong relationships, you finally get to your performance, it happens, it's exciting and you've reached this point, and then it ends, whereas in a company, you're constantly building that connection with people. I really would love to be in a company because I would love to have the cohesive nature and consistency of that.

Yes, it is a community that uses its entrepreneurial skills to continue to struggle as a working community. Perhaps, some can't imagine loving to do a job so much that they do it for little money or fame. It isn't that they can't do something else—as we will see in the next chapters—they can and do many different forms of work. They love the challenges of creating and performing, and they receive social and emotional rewards from both the community and performance.

But community developed in small companies can be fractured by directors with their treatment of dancers, according to Tyler, who had enough contacts and project work to exit:

> It had felt very united. Then newer people whom I liked very much joined. It was very clear, at that point, that loyalty wasn't part of his process. If someone new came in with qualities he was interested in, you could be removed from whatever section. Fine. I wasn't interested in being treated that way. I went to the executive director, "I'm gonna leave." He asked, "Why?" "I'm just not interested. I understand that's how he works, and I don't wanna interrupt his process,

but I'm not interested in working this way anymore." I did a smart thing, which was I worked with other choreographers during time off. I thought, I'm a valuable dancer in this community. I can work for other people. It's not like I'm begging to have this job. I don't understand why I would be treated in this kind of arbitrary way. I quit.

Dancers continue performing because they love it and receive social and emotional rewards from performances. They know how to meet challenges and like new ones. Most will never become known much beyond the community of dancers and dance enthusiasts, and they don't earn much money from it. Barbara explains her love of performing:

I loved performing. The best! No matter what, I loved being onstage. I felt freer on stage than anywhere. When, I would go teach and then may be another rehearsal—go to class, go to maybe another rehearsal, go to an audition. Then we'd have a show at night, and I was like "Whew! Finally! Now I can relax onstage." I feel better onstage. I feel safer onstage. One step from the wing to the stage [snaps fingers] changes your world.

CHAPTER SIX

DISTANCING FROM THE PERFORMING SELF

Discovery and adaptation; transitions are rarely easy, but all dance performing careers must end.[1] Developing new skills, identities, and sense of self is a process, and it is particularly difficult if a central activity stops overnight. Lisa—more than ten years after performing as a lead dancer in a small, well-known contemporary ballet company—is currently a successful lawyer, married with two children, and on the board of a dance school. She looks like a dancer despite her injuries, which were the reason she had to end her performing career. She is the main family breadwinner as her husband remains in the arts. She is somewhat unsatisfied with how her career ended, despite her successes after performing. Lisa recalls that when faced with needing a second surgery to continue performing, she saw it as a risk rather than a recovery challenge, as her first surgery had been:

> It was an emergency situation. I had injured myself over and over again. It was actually quite devastating. I remember I thought, "Oh, this one feels bad." I went to bed. I woke up the next morning, and the first thing I did was wiggle my toes. Then I thought to myself, "The first thing I'm doing is wiggling my toes to see if I can feel them?" I can't do this anymore. It turns out that I couldn't anyway.

The injury actually was severe enough that I would probably have to get surgery again to dance. I couldn't do it anymore. I think because of how severe it was, I immediately thought to myself, "I better get a move on."

I think I was twenty-three or twenty-four, I had gone to college just to broaden my horizons and get started. I met this wonderful Franciscan monk who was the head of admissions. He offered me a full scholarship if I committed to going full time. For a year I went in the mornings before dance class. I hustled like that for a year. I told him I had to stop. When I injured myself the last time, as soon as I could walk, I went back. He was like, "Are you ready?" I was like, "Yes." He actually reinstated my scholarship. To this day I'm like, "Brother, you saved my life." I got into political science classes. It was most interesting. I got a history degree. That seemed a natural transition to law school.

She found it difficult to distance from her performing self, though education and new identities facilitated the process. Family, she remembers, helped her through school challenges:

I did [miss dance during my college years]. The first couple of years, I really couldn't do it. Many times, I tried to be physical, really minimally physical. I would hurt myself again. I think I even got some steroid shots just to get me back on my feet. Then at some point, I said, "Okay, that's not what I'm doing anymore." I was applying to law school. I started getting excited about that. I didn't know what I was gonna do in law school. I kept trying the arts with law. It was so funny because I remember coming home and telling my husband, "I keep getting tricked. They have an art-law society. Then it's contract law." I would just pull my hair out, "No, this is as far from the arts as I understand." I had to divorce myself from that idea.

I hated law school the first year. I applied to a dance administration program and a school of journalism. Got in. Then my father-in-law was like, "Are you insane? You got through the first year just to throw it?" I really liked the second two years. For me, I think it was really hard, because it was so divorced from anything I had done in my life before then. There's no thinking outside the box. There's no artistic element to it. I just thought, "What am I doing?"

Not much [go to dance performances]. For a while, that was something I found really hard to do. It crushed my spirit a little. Because to move on, you almost have to divorce yourself from it. Then, I think you can come back in pieces. I've seen a few performances since then. They haven't affected me at all, actually. I was even talking to somebody recently like, "I could go again." Now, I still know everything about it, but I can't appreciate it without feeling something was taken from me.

Injuries leading to exit are fairly common. Lisa also highlights the importance of a liminal period for exploration and change in which one belongs neither to the past nor the future.[2] This is a space that is betwixt and between, where dancers no longer participate regularly in the performing world and have not begun new work. It allows exploration of new identities, activities, ideas, and distance from former selves. Universities are designed for exploration and enabling transitions, but they are expensive. Others create a liminal period of exploration by talking with a therapist or a career counselor in organizations such as Career Transition for Dancers, a division of the Entertainment Community Fund (formerly the Actors Fund) that offers some scholarship money and career advice.[3]

When a dancer belongs to a company, exit is clearly defined; a dancer is in or out. For portfolio dancers, exit may be more gradual, dancing with fewer groups with less arduous dancing. The athleticism required by ballet and some contemporary companies makes it obvious to dancers through their bodies when exit is warranted, but this is not as clear for those who dance with groups more interested in acting skills or movement qualities. Portfolio dancers may often have income from activities outside of performing or have relationships with partners with regular incomes. Portfolio dancers, thus, can taper exits, making gradual transitions from performing.[4] But leaving an activity is different than adapting a self when the self is located in the passionate activity—performing. Passion needs a new locus. What are the narratives of company exit, and how do the dancers begin next steps in the processes of adapting the self? How do the narratives of exit and next steps differ for portfolio dancers?

COMPANY EXIT

Research on dancers' endings to performing careers frequently focuses on aging or injured bodies.[5] For Lisa, the decision was made for her; she physically couldn't dance without further surgery, which she was unwilling to do. She saw surgery as risky. For others, the decision is more complex; a dancer may have a series of small injuries, and it may take some time before the person interprets them as signals it is time to stop performing.[6] Or the body, even without injury, slowly indicates it cannot do what it used to do, like legs that won't go as high, backs or knees that make jumping or partnering painful, everything aching more than usual, or simply tiring of working to keep the body thin enough, muscled, and fit. But it isn't only the body that signals the end of performing.

Few dance in the corps more than ten years. Struggles encourage dancers to look beyond dance. They slowly discover they are no longer entirely satisfied with a performing career, are receiving fewer rewards or challenges such as interesting roles, and are attracted to other lives. Narratives of exit beyond the body include problematic relationships with staff, interpreting signals from staff that it is time to go, and wanting to leave before being non-renewed; lack of challenge and promotion; and few opportunities to use their voices. Dancers also expressed ideas about being drawn to education and explorations of the world beyond dance. Passion beyond dance is possible.

Today, many have a next step in mind before leaving performing. Deborah Bull, former principal dancer of the Royal Ballet, says that relatively few dancers plan for a second career, but new research finds that dancers develop ideas about what they might like to do while performing.[7] Those who attend college while dancing in the United States may develop ideas of what to do afterwards. Bull has done well in transitioning to university faculty, dance commentator, and writer:

It's not so much that it's hard to see what we might do next: it's just that it's difficult to envision a career that will provide as much pleasure, challenge, stimulation, and satisfaction as dancing. How many people have the privilege of doing what they love and getting paid for it? So where do you go from there?[8]

Bull was a principal, however, not a corps member; most corps members saw some career drawbacks. They hadn't reached the ideal and only rarely danced the most interesting or creative roles.

Most injuries are not as traumatic as Lisa's. Surviving multiple injuries may lead dancers away from the dance world, toward a search for a new career direction. Bodies give hints it is time to leave. But frequently, injuries are coupled with fewer rewarding roles and lack of new challenges; artistic directors notice changes in bodies. Paula's multiple surgeries became one of several signals to retire as a ten-year veteran of a major company corps. She also saw the lack of interesting roles as a loss of rewards and challenges and had completed her college degree while performing:

> My career was really fantastic. I feel very fortunate for it. I was injured a lot, especially the last few years of my career, which is why I retired. Because I was so injured, obviously, those last few years, I didn't get what I wanted. I knew that I wasn't able to execute all that I wanted, it was a mutual reality. I understood that. I was coming back from the second surgery, and I did a jump and broke my foot. A year and a half after that had another surgery. It was from that that I came back and had a great year. Then the last year I was just dealing with such constant pain; it was like this level of sacrifice for the kind of fulfillment and satisfaction is not worth it. There are so many other things that I could be doing in this world other than struggling to remain competitive when I feel like I've pushed my body way too much already. It was time. It had been time a while ago, and I just ignored it.

The reality of injuries as risk and the punishment of pain pushed her out, but, importantly, Paula was also attracted to the new.

Leaving before non-renewal makes exit easier. In her narrative, Allison chose to leave a decade-long career in a major ballet company; like Paula, she was no longer getting the challenge or rewards of soloist roles, and no promotion, which she could attribute to injury, not her dancing. She was also attracted to the new. She could leave on her own terms, like Paula, and thus, view her career as successful. And she decided on her immediate future during her last company year:

That was part of it [not being promoted]. Certainly, it's hard, because I had this major injury happen; I think if I hadn't gotten injured, this is hindsight, but I think that if I hadn't gotten injured, then I would've had a pretty good chance of being promoted either that year or the next. The injury took almost a whole year out. I never felt like I was quite on that path again, even though I did soloist work after. It was never with the same frequency and what I felt like enthusiasm from artistic staff. Once I started to realize that probably it wasn't gonna happen, and I had maybe hit my ceiling, you have to reevaluate and say, "Well, if I'm not gonna move to this next level here, how much more do I feel like I can really accomplish at the level?" How much would I accomplish by going to another company? I really toyed with that, you take a step back. I didn't think it was necessarily the challenge that I was craving at that point. I'm young. I wanted to be actively challenged and really fulfilled by what I was doing. I was senior corps. I got to do a lot of good things. I knew that going back to school was something I had always had in the back of my mind. I decided to attend college.

I wanted to make sure that it was the right time, just because I had given my whole life to this thing. I had a sense that I wanted something different, but I wanted to be really sure, so I think I went into the last season in my career pretty sure that it was gonna be the last one. I know some people that have left without being sure or not on their own terms; it's really hard.

Focusing on her injuries allowed her to make sense of not getting the good roles or promotion and the lack of new challenges prompted her to consider college, smoothing her transition.

Unlike Paula and Allison who felt encouraged to leave by staff who limited their soloist roles, Steven was urged to stay by the artistic director, likely due in part to the shortage of men. Steven had no traumatic injuries, but his passion was beginning to be outweighed by pain:

I was definitely throwing these ideas out. I was like, "My knees are hurting." I knew it was coming. People were a little surprised. I put the call in a little early. I remember telling the ballet master. "He's like, "No." I said, "Yep. This is gonna be my last tour." I remember him saying, "We had big plans for you." I said, "I don't think my body

did." I was moving up really well; a lot of people were like, "You were
just about to break out." I cracked thirty. I knew that clock was tick-
ing. I don't think they're gonna get out of me as much as they hope. I
felt differently. Jumping was not fun anymore.

Injury is not the only body issue that may encourage departure.
Some dancers frame their exits as more voluntary. But Natasha felt she
was treated as little more than a body that would not conform easily to a
ballerina image, and she wanted to know who she was outside of dance;
she saw a future beyond corps member in a major company, even if she
did not know what it was. She continued to love the ballet company
where she danced for five years and remains friends with her peers:

I always loved dancing, but it was really hard for me to be a dancer.
To me what that meant was when I was onstage or in rehearsal—
dancing was my passion. To this day, there's probably nothing that I
love more professionally or have ever enjoyed more. What came along
with being a dancer, the intensity of the focus on how you looked and
how much you weighed, constantly being told how I should look and
not having a say in that was really difficult and I resented that. The
insular world you live in as a dancer, felt a little suffocating to me.
The second I could even picture my life doing something else and
being happy, it was time. He [artistic director] was surprised and
I think it was maybe "Take some time to think about it," which I
did. It was really traumatic for me to leave the company. The day I
told the director that I was leaving, there was a performance. When
my part came on and it wasn't me dancing, I just lost it and started
crying. It was almost as if the second I made it, it was so painful I just
had to make a complete break.

I always worried that I would never find that passion again. That
made me doubt whether or not I should've stuck it out or if it was the
right decision, and I really didn't know who I was outside of ballet. It
was a painful time. At the same time, it was really exciting because I
could figure that out, but I worried if I stayed too connected to it, it
would not free me to explore my new opportunities.

I loved doing those types of ballets [classical] and being a part of
the corps. I thought in many ways that was way harder than doing
the soloist or principal roles because in addition to having to worry

about yourself, you're worried about everybody around you and breathing together. The thing that I really rebelled against was—I always resented—I always struggled with my weight and it was hard for me that so much of my success hinged on what I looked like versus my talent or my brain.

This narrative describes Natasha's leaving as more of a rupture than the others. Natasha separates her identity as dancer, requiring her to be extremely thin, from the act of performing and what her body could do. In her narrative, leaving was voluntary; she did not want to put up with the focus on her body's size. But it is frightening to leave behind who you were since you were seven years old for the unknown, to find something else that you enjoy doing and become valued for other skills.

The pull from the world outside dance was strong in the narrative of exit for Natasha. For Isabel, the desire to pursue other fields combined with the lack of the challenge of new roles, encouraging her to think about leaving. For her, the desire was strong to finish college, which she left during her freshman year to join a major company. She prioritized her own growth after ten years in the company:

It started to get very good, reviving a lot of ballets that I had not done and that I was longing to do. I got better and better. They were giving me more roles. Then I was approaching thirty. I had always promised myself that I wanted to finish my undergraduate degree. I wanted to have children. When I found out what the repertory was gonna be the following year, "I've already done all that." I would have killed to do that lead role, but I knew it wasn't gonna come my way. "Do I stay another year and do the same dances for the eleventh year again?" I love it, but I'm done with it.

It was like a calculation. I met with him [artistic director], and I cried. His words were, "Why is it that whenever they start to get to the point where you want them, they always leave?" I was already married. It was perfect. I got my undergraduate degree. I loved it. It was brutal to say goodbye. I think I would like to say though I feel very grateful about how I transitioned. They fired my friend. She was their principal ballerina. "All right, I've done everything I wanted to do." I don't think that happens, but I did enough.

Without the challenge of new roles and an image of her future, Isabel reentered college.

Whereas Natasha chafed over the control of how her body looked and Isabel had insufficient challenges, Anthony suffered under the autocratic control of his artistic director in his major contemporary ballet company. Anthony thought that he had too many questions, and began disengaging from his performing self while dancing and working towards his future:

> AGMA rules are created in a way to help dancers be dancers, but in doing so, you're preventing them from being other things. If you are cast in a ballet that is garbage, you have to do it. If you are told by the world's most contemptuous person to do a step that you have spent years learning how to perfect in a way that is universally agreed to be better, you still have to do it the way that person says. I needed to know more. I needed to know "Why is this like this? How did this person who is in charge get in charge?" Because there were so many different things about it that didn't add up, really lit this passion in me to look at it harder.
>
> I had to take the GRE. I got into [graduate school]. I remember just sobbing and feeling like I had received this "get out of jail free" card I had been looking for. That last minute the company was called to perform at Obama's second inauguration at the Kennedy Center, which was the highlight of my dancing career. It even solidified that, "What's left in this journey that I haven't checked off the list?" The next month and a half was one of the happiest I had ever been dancing.

The realization that his voice didn't matter was disruptive, but he put a plan for the future in place. All these dancers had well-educated parents and siblings, so it was not a great stretch to consider college or graduate school as the dancing career was ending.

As we saw in Chapter 4, using your voice and questioning staff can get a dancer in trouble, even for men. Matthew used his voice to express his ambitions for promotion. But it didn't work. He saw his lack of soloist roles the following year as punishment and left the major ballet company after seven years:

My sixth year in the company was great, and people were saying, "Aren't you going to get promoted to soloist?" I felt there was a possibility and went in to talk to the director. "I've had a really good season, and you've been treating me like you're going to promote me." He's like, "I just don't really see you as soloist material, but keep on working like you have, and prove me wrong." I did a handful of principal roles in contemporary works. I came back for my seventh season, I didn't have one soloist or leading role. "If I stay here, I'll probably burn out." I was bitter that I wasn't getting promoted. I was like, "I'll probably quit. I'll probably retire."

All dancers must deal with staff's focus on bodies and expected deferential behavior. If dancers don't recognize a "failing" body early enough or do not act sufficiently deferential in the artistic directors' opinions, directors are faced with a dilemma. Thinking as a "family," they may try hinting that careers are over by not giving soloist roles instead of non-renewing them, as several of the women perceived. Was the artistic director also "cooling the mark out" by telling Matthew to work hard and then not giving him any soloist roles in his seventh season after asking for promotion? Because Matthew "chose" to leave the following year and senior corps women "recognized" their injuries were holding them back from soloist roles or promotions, the director did not have to actively non-renew them. This narrative allows them to keep a dancer's self reasonably intact. But control over bodies and perceived lack of challenge are a more voluntary exit narrative. All these dancers had some idea about what to do next; they wanted new challenges and could leave with their performing self reasonably undamaged. But then they needed to adapt it as they exited.

A LIMINAL PERIOD

College makes it possible to distance oneself from the professional performing self while exploring other avenues for work, enjoyment, and identities. Others use apprenticeships and therapists. Without a liminal period, it can be difficult to transition after training and performing for fifteen to twenty-five years—particularly distancing one's self from performing and developing voice. This transition process requires, for most, some often difficult, emotion work.

Some suffer more, particularly at the beginning of the process and when they don't have a liminal period to work on adjusting the self. I first spoke with Matthew when he was beginning his journey away from performing. He expressed much distress and hadn't yet figured out where he was going and how to make a living. He was in the middle of transitioning. Without a liminal period, the transition from company dancer to small contemporary company to choreographer and teacher for Matthew was painful. He had earned a two-year degree while dancing. But developing an adapted sense of self—a new identity distinct from that of performer—was a struggle. When training and performing have organized lives for a considerable period, it takes time to figure out a new type of work and adapt a self. Without a liminal period, Matthew followed his partner and joined a small contemporary company. There he earned a third of what he had been making and exacerbated his back injury. That short experience ended his performing career:

> Say that your first love, they break up with you, but you wanna be with them. There's that layer of pain. I had that pain for dance, which was very weird. I was like, "I have to do this no matter what." That was really my driving force. It's funny, because it's actually parallel to my career now as I am transitioning. Because I have that sense of immense desire to have that career, and I would do whatever it took. Then once I finally made it into my career, I could calm down and enjoy my life a little bit more.

Two years after the interview, he put together his own project-based company, raised money, and choreographed enough for an evening-length performance. He teaches to earn a living. It isn't as painful anymore, just difficult.

College allows students to focus on a number of activities, which allowed Justine to take less emotional energy to adapt herself, but felt she had to keep performing. In the process of transitioning, she uses her college experiences to think more critically about her company life. Although she hasn't figured out what she wants to do and who she wants to be, she was investing in education and beginning to construct a student identity. She hung up her pointe shoes before graduation:

I love it [being in school]. Now, I have the passion for school that I didn't have in high school. Conversations surrounding our lectures and the contributions from the students come from that lived experience that I was speaking of. It's so rich. It's something I would never have gotten had I gone to college when I was eighteen. It's such a privileged career and career path and influenced my whole purpose of being here. As dramatic as that sounds, it's just true. Every single one of those [courses] has been informed by my dance career. Not in a way that I could've known or appreciated during my dance career. I'm getting this opportunity to be educated about experiences I've already had. I've had some really intriguing conversations about the direction of ballet, ballet administration, and the importance of dancers forming their own voices. It's a career where you're so used to not having control of what happens that you become resentful of the career itself, resentful of your own passion towards it.

Not only does she see herself as a more mature artist, dancer, and student, but she raises the issue of improving the voice of dancers. After leaving, both Paula and Justine see the ballet world as confining and dancers as too deferential to leadership.

Not everyone struggles with exit. Allison attributes her lack of angst to distancing herself from performing during her last year in the company, as she thought about her next steps and became excited about college:

I think people have a hard time negotiating a new sense of identity when they don't necessarily feel totally in control of the decision, because I've been able to embrace this new path and new journey in a way that's felt really exciting and really what I wanted. I've been surprised that I haven't missed it as much as I thought I would. I haven't taken class [ballet]. I went skiing for the first time in fifteen years!

I found that the experience of going back to school has really opened so many windows onto other things in my life. I enjoy that because I think you realize a bit the things that you're shutting out. As you have more friends who are not involved, you want to be worldly. You wanna be able to talk about the things that people are talking about. It's been amazing to be inspired and nurtured in a different way.

Importantly, Allison saw new possibilities, and once studying, took advantage of new experiences and explored; college offers her an entrée into a broader world and the possibility of new activities, identities, and friends. It was a liminal stage in which she could pursue new ideas and express her views openly without committing immediately to a second career stage. When I spoke with Allison during her freshman year, she had little idea about a major, but hard work and persistence led to graduating as valedictorian. She married and now works in the business world.

College not only allows a slow adaptation of self but the chance to explore what one might want to do next. Natasha was able to think about what she wanted to do while she distanced herself from performing and the surveillance of her body. She didn't want anything to do with the dance world and found her future by chance in her senior year—finance. Natasha recalls:

> I felt I didn't have control over my body, and I didn't have control over my destiny. That was really hard for me, and I think why I went so far in the other direction, which was I'm gonna, my second career, have control of my destiny. I'm gonna go into something where if I work really, really hard, I'm gonna be successful. Doesn't matter what I look like. It doesn't matter how much I weigh. If I'm good and if I work hard, it will lead to success and I found that, sort of.

As a dancer, she was her body. And she had to defer to others' assessments. Natasha experienced these assessments as constraints on who she was and could be. Her focus on what her mind could produce and hard work paid off; she adapted herself and found a high-paying career.

While Natasha used college to come to this conclusion, Michel used a therapist to make a similar decision. Relationships to their bodies were central to exit for Natasha and Michel, not injury. Michel dramatically exited class without knowing what to do next. He realized how much of his self was tied up in a dancer's body, but he was not getting performance opportunities and recognition:

> I was seeing this great therapist. When I stopped dancing, left the company, I started to guest a little bit, and I thought I don't want to be a guest. It's not for me. I stopped dancing—literally, left the

studio, which felt a little bit like a tantrum. You are suffering so much, "Okay, I quit this." I remember leaving the studio because I left during class. It was that bad. The switch went off. I took my bag, "What am I doing?" I remember the door closing and the sound of the piano. I felt good. It felt momentous for my life. I felt liberated. I thought I would never do that ever again. I think what I meant by that was not so much dance and ballet, but I think it was the fighting and the being told all the time that you're not right. I felt good instantly and lost instantly.

Then she's [the therapist] the one who said, "Okay, what next?" I went, "I have no idea." Because at this point I realized that not only did I not know what to do, but I didn't know who I was. Who I was in my mind, in my body is the dancer, because that's what I knew since before I can remember. It was not just a career change at this point I needed to think of; it was a change of identity. I became very aware of that. It's literally, you need to get out of your body—to understand that the perception of myself came through how other people perceived me, because that had to do with my body. My body is an instrument as a dancer. I experienced it through other people's eyes as an audience. It was kind of an interface between me and the world. That also influenced the way I thought of myself, I perceived myself. Because I could never go out without hearing people, "Oh, are you a dancer?"

Michel uses his therapist to acknowledge that his body that he used to perform is what is recognized by others and has consumed his life. But he wants a new identity to incorporate into his self, that of someone who produces something. The realization that the product is what matters, not his body, was transformative for him.

He decided on set design with his therapist. His evolution of self and skills continued during training. He searched his creativity—his artistic eye—and accepted challenges such as designing a set for a play without prior art training:

I had no portfolio. She said, "Well, how about you go design this play. You make a model and a set of costume drawings, and you send it to us, and then we'll let you know." I did that and had no idea what I was doing. "Thank you so much, but you're on the waiting list." I was a bit disappointed, but also thinking, I'm a dancer, I applied for the best school, and I'm on the waiting list, that's pretty amazing. They called me back and said, "We'd like to take you in." For the first time I heard the words "transferrable skills," which honestly, at this point, was Chinese.

Completely amazing, because in a way, it brought back a sense of freedom that hard work can make you do great stuff, and you can be who you choose to be as well through your work. It's not this kind of weird thing that ballet is about, which is either they elect you or not, no matter what you do, no matter what you want. I decide if you are elected or not through how I perceive you; that's ballet. That was the first time it was like, "It's your work. That's all." It was great. It was a school of really true collaboration.

Not only does Michel adapt his embodied self like Natasha—his self is not his body—but he finds something in performing he loves, collaboration, to use in his new work.

An apprenticeship also can be a liminal period. Albert, by offering to help out with research and administrative work for a well-known director and choreographer, created one. Telling the story many years later, he didn't mind not being asked to perform as he realized his body was slowing down after dancing with two major companies, and he was already choreographing and looking to the future. He needed to move on in his narrative. The apprenticeship encouraged an adaptation of self from that of performer and provided Albert with new skills and affirmed new identities:

I did research, tried to find original cast members. We needed them to be able to retrieve whatever was left in their minds about their choreography. I worked to develop materials for auditions. Then he'd said, "Well, I'm going to put you in the show." I said okay. I didn't really want to. I was thirty-eight. As he auditioned, more people in my age group came through, and he didn't pick any of them. I thought I'm not really going to be in this show. I wasn't. The research was why I wanted to be there and to get a closer look at how he worked. He said to me, "Why aren't you doing your own work?" Some people think, that must've been hard that you didn't get in the show. My leg wasn't going quite high enough in certain things, and it's like, no I'm done. I'm done dancing, done performing.

Albert used the apprenticeship to acknowledge his separation from performing, and he was encouraged to develop new directions—improve his organizational, choreographic, and directing skills.

Some are pushed into a liminal period. Philip had a rocky end to his career with a major contemporary ballet company. During a liminal period, he managed to adapt his self before deciding what he wanted to do. Performing no longer needed to define him; it became one aspect of his self. He found he was successful doing other work too. Returning to school for an MFA allowed him to learn new skills and to certify for an envisioned future career; he had already created a broader self in therapy and found new work:

I decided along with the company [after ten years], I put myself into treatment and stopped dancing completely. Took four years off. I'm back. I'm in dance now. During that time-the drugs and alcohol—I needed to get a handle on it. It was consuming too much of my life. It took a long time for me to unravel all the stuff going on inside of me. I was in intense therapy and treatment for about a year before I'd even started to wake up because we're now dealing with thirty-one years of baggage. After that, I thought I'd come back, but with the advice of some people, I became an addictions' therapist and started working in a treatment facility as the admissions director. Also, I was choreographing musicals, to get some artistic value back and then, I decided, I'm ready.

It was [necessary to keep the art] because that's where I'm most happy, when I'm doing the art thing. That's just where I thrive, so I had to have that outlet. It was part of my therapy—finding the joy for it again, understanding what it was. But also, understanding that I'm not just a dancer; it's what I do. The arts is what I do, but it's not who I am. That was part of that experience as well. It's something I love to do, and it's something that is a huge part of who I am, but it's not just who I am because I thought that's all I could do, which is not true. It's about creating the art and sharing that with people. That's the beauty of it.

Philip had a major transformational experience between performing in a company and returning to school so that he could expand opportunities in the dance world. It is a different use of education; graduate school was a requirement to get to the next step. He had already explored new identities and parameters of self, putting performing in a smaller place. His self is broader now; it is creative as he choreographs and helps others develop their talents through teaching.

Some, without a liminal period, decide on their own that it is their ballet bodies that need to change. Theo, a member of a major ballet company, felt he needed to reshape his body not to be identified as a dancer as he evolved to actor:

I definitely sensed that my history was in my way. I was labeled a particular type, and I probably was. I'm sure I was, and I'm sure my body language said everything they needed to hear or see. I wasn't your typical guy. That was really disconcerting, and, I thought, a detriment. I said to my wife, "Okay, I'm stopping [dancing]." She told me I was crazy, but I did, and it was actually a wise choice in that I needed to rewire my brain. I started training in martial arts.

All these dancers received new rewards during their liminal period. Their dedication to the tasks at hand pushed them to become successful; they enjoyed learning, made new friends, learned to look differently at their pasts, and began to voice their opinions of their pasts and futures. They began to successfully adapt their selves, partially by examining their careers critically while in class or talking with a therapist. Some experienced the transition away from performing as a rupture in the beginning, but they all appear to have moved on successfully.

FROM DANCE PORTFOLIOS TO NEW WORK

Portfolio dancers can slow down, taking fewer or less physically demanding roles. Most danced with several small companies and projects; they can leave some of them. Women may first stop wearing pointe shoes, enabling them to dance longer and with less chance of injury than ballet company members. Additionally, many have college degrees, and they make much of their income from nonperforming activities. Some have work that they can slide into or that keeps them afloat while developing new skills or envisioning what they would like to do next.[9] They have less need for a liminal period but must decide on their own as exits are not framed for them.

With the possibility of slowing down and less arduous dancing, some portfolio performing careers are longer than those of ballet corps company dancers. Lack of money becomes a critical issue, but some have partners with steady jobs, and others have reasonably paying side jobs. Some choreograph, compose music, make or edit films, photograph, teach dance or Pilates—all while dancing. These activities may become a new focus.

Transition is possible while dancing by adding other art forms. Kelly majored in dance and social science. She had regular work with a small international traveling company for nine years, which she gave up two years after the interview. She has a vision of what she would like to transition to yet continues performing without pointe shoes. One of her goals is to expand the dance audience by producing videos:

> My strategy is to just keep producing media: videos and other things so that there's just more content out there, so when you're looking for things and it can get you interested. I guess, if I wasn't dancing with them, I would want to put myself in more things in my own work. Just because I'm not ready to be done dancing yet. I feel like I'm still doing fine. I have all these ideas for what I wanna do with my own work. I think unless I'm devoting more time to it, it can't become what I want it to be. I just love it [dance world]. I love dance so much.

Several years later, Kelly still takes daily class and performs with a choreographer she admires. She stopped dancing with other groups. She has produced evening-length live performances and three short dance films and choreographed for her former company. She has ideas for several new creative projects. She is slowly adapting herself.

Bodies are still an issue for some. Portfolio dancers may not have a specific person surveilling bodies, but some struggle to maintain a "performing body" that leads to decisions to exit. Graham had to fight to maintain a dancer's body and made an undramatic exit unlike Michel. He wasn't under surveillance; it was his decision. The change in how he viewed his body developed slowly; gradual exit was possible by moving to less athletic performances and fewer of them. Graham worked to dis-

tance himself from a dancer's body and, instead, developed what he considered a healthy body:

> I thought to myself, this is the last time I'm ever gonna take ballet
> class. It was just like I don't need to do this anymore. I enjoyed class
> because I just enjoyed moving. I enjoyed the performative aspect of
> class like going across the floor and dancing for all these people. I
> guess there just came a time where I stopped enjoying it or it felt
> more like a burden than a pleasure or I didn't feel like I needed to
> practice picking up my legs anymore; it just wasn't that applicable
> to what I was doing. I started to find that there were more efficient
> ways to keep my body healthy and strong.
>
> When I shifted away from dancing, I just emotionally needed to
> shift away from training spaces that were about having a dancer-ly
> body. There was something about that, that was kind of painful for
> me. I now have a thirty-minute thing I can do. I feel like I've actively
> made the choice.
>
> I wanna maintain a healthy body. I feel like that's a big shift that
> I've been negotiating from my years as a dancer where it's all about
> being thinner, more muscled with more range, able to jump higher.
> To move away from that for my internal life has been a very positive
> shift.

Graham worked to distance himself from his performing self by actively
changing his body regime. But he didn't leave performing yet.

Like Michel, Graham started the process of distancing himself from
performing with a therapist but in a much less dramatic way than
Michel. As he prepared to move on, he found performing less fulfilling—
his passion was ebbing, and his feelings about his body created a desire
to separate from performing. He uncovered what he liked about the
dance world, which helped him decide what he wanted to do. Graham
danced less, finished his BFA, and obtained the research experience
he needed to attend a clinical psychology PhD program. He supported
himself through his office work:

> When I first started the transition, it was less clear, I think because
> it just felt scary to let go of it, but the longer I've been committing
> myself to this other kind of work [preparing for graduate school]

and basically not regularly being in kind of a creative practice that's rooted in dancing, I can just feel that it's not the thing I do anymore. The years of dealing with difficult feelings about my body, and I just noticed that that was becoming more intolerable for me. I could not deal with people telling me what to wear, when it became time to wear tight clothing. And this is not the only factor that contributed to the transition, but it was certainly a major part.

I feel very inspired by the creative people that have come into my circle while working as a dancer. So, I feel committed to staying inside of the creative community here. I just notice I don't want to perform anymore. That has been a real surprise. It feels less about a body's inability and more just about wanting to get some distance from those spaces of being observed.

I started to notice over time that the creative process and the psychotherapeutic process, started to feel more similar. I started to locate what I think was left over in my interest in dancing; the process of working with people. Working with people in these pressure-cooker spaces where you really are working to discover something. I saw this moment where two major projects I was working on were both ending, and it just felt like an opportunity to start to actualize a shift. I wanted to be done with school by the time I was forty. Young people are benefiting because in dancing, you learn so many amazing skills. You learn how to communicate nonverbally. You learn about touching people. You learn about being looked at. I just think that dancers are thinking and perceiving on many levels all the time.

In his narrative, passion for performance was dissipating as he worked through his body concerns. As a portfolio dancer, he was able to curtail performances slowly, and his work with a therapist helped him figure out what he liked most about the dance world and what he wanted to do next with his life and career: it provided him with liminal space to distance his self from his performing body, but he continued to dance. He recognized his body was no longer a dancer's body; no artistic director told him. He saw positive aspects of dance, that dancers were not just an object to view but have social/emotional skills that others may not. I ran into him at a theater; he was enjoying his classes.

Financial concerns matter. After ten years as a portfolio dancer and feeling like he never found enough dance work, Adrian's injuries and financial precarity led him to stop seeking performance opportunities and search for a career with financial security. Lack of money was becoming risky, not merely a challenge, so he sought a salaried job:

> I had another back injury. I already knew that I was moving out of it [dancing]. The doors were gonna be closing soon. I think just from the very beginning I was always worried about my future. I was always worried about a retirement plan, health insurance. I auditioned again for [small major contemporary company], made it down to the last dancers, and didn't get the job. Then the back injury happened. I just knew it was over. I just thought, "I don't want to be doing this anymore." My mom was saying, "Physical therapy is a good job." Biology, physics, chemistry, "There's no way." I was really poor in these subjects in high school. I decided to take a biology class, and if I did okay, that was gonna be my green light to go ahead. I did very well, because I was older and you apply yourself.

For portfolio dancers who have never earned much money, finances may begin to play a role in thinking about the future as it did for Adrian, especially for those who extend their performing careers by doing less dance or less demanding roles. As the body begins to tire, many start thinking about the future. Alyssa's partner had a good job but is also an arts freelancer. She dances in a small company, does some of their organizational work, and runs rehearsals. Currently working backstage for a new show, finances still worry her:

> There's no retirement plan, no 401K, none of that security. I'm in this place where looking at the future—I need all these things to be set up for my later years. I really want them to be great.
>
> Seeing what my mom went through [illness], you need to have that health insurance. I've got a Roth IRA, thankfully, but that's nothing—finding that modicum of security that allows you to get up out of bed without being terrified. I'm researching all these potential new careers.

Portfolio dancers do not necessarily take a period of liminality or retraining. Portfolios include remunerative work, and some drift into careers they started to support themselves while performing. It is reasonably easy to drift away from performing as Tara found. She worked as a personal trainer while performing and continued with her own business into her late sixties:

I guess I was still dancing in my late thirties. Then I wanted to have a child and had a baby [at forty-one]. I was nursing in the wing. Then would hand the baby to the techie and go out onstage. I thought, "Okay. It's enough." That marriage didn't work out. Then, I became so invested in being a single mother that I created this business, which I still do to this day. I had started to do it even before I had her. I worked for a company. It was before personal training. I was still choreographing then, and this woman would farm people out to work with people in their homes. I segued into just having my own personal business. I never meant really to do that. It just kind of happened. Frankly, it worked very well for being a single mother.

With her successful career as a trainer, Tara was able to put her daughter through a private college.

Skills and knowledge are one part of the transition; the self requires adjustment too, just as it does for company members. But the process may evolve differently, as portfolio dancers often begin new work, especially in the arts world or body training, while they perform. Not all continue in the direction they start. Some appear to exit and partially adapt their selves while not dancing as they construct liminal periods by attending school or working. But they return to dance on Broadway and work on blurring the boundaries between art and commerce.

REIMAGINED REENTRY: BROADWAY MUSICALS

Some who love dance and value the challenges of performing transition to the for-profit world of Broadway musicals after first appearing to exit. Had I interviewed Ariel and Josie in their mid-twenties, I might have said they had exited performing careers. For Ariel the lack of reward, in fact the pain, of the life of a ballet dancer in a major company had overwhelmed her after five years, and she left. After completing college, she slowly returned to dance—first as a principal dancer in a small ballet company where she couldn't support herself except by doing some commercial work on TV, and finally, by making a home on Broadway to extend her professional dance career and support herself. Josie maintained her passion through injury and more than four years of recuperation, but she knew she could never do the work of a company ballet dancer with her injuries so she tried Broadway. Both Josie and Ariel needed to deal with the issues of what to do with their ideas of art. They blurred the boundaries between ballet companies and the commerce of Broadway unlike Tre and John in the previous chapter, who separated ballet companies (art) and Broadway (income),

Ariel sees herself leaving performing in her late thirties. Her story involves making a living and using her body—"being physical." But she still has a passion for dancing. After the trauma of her five years in a major company, she loves performing on Broadway. Her time in college allowed her to figure out who she was and what she liked doing:

> Well, I went through a huge depression because I completely quit. I couldn't dance at all. I was just so, so burnt out, I decided, "I'm not dancing at all. I'm just gonna go to school." I graduated with a BA in English and was premed because I thought maybe I should do something with orthopedics or physical therapy, since I know so much about injuries. I took the MCAT and I hated it.

She decided that she enjoyed moving and did not have to end her dance career; her love of dance remained, and the memories of suffering faded. Ariel received social and emotional rewards from dancing but decided she needed to support herself. Her dedication and persistence paid off:

> I think being so physical for so long, I was going stir crazy sitting with books, so I started teaching ballet. I wanted to start dancing again. I was twenty-six, and I thought that I had peaked too early. I didn't wanna regret having quit when I was that young. That's why I started taking class in a very safe environment with people who didn't expect anything from me. That was perfect because they were like, "You're so good." I got the positive compliments I needed that I think I lacked for so long. I was able to start getting better again, healing emotionally and physically, and started dancing again because I loved it. I was like, "Maybe I wanna start auditioning again." I got a contract with [a small ballet]. I got to do some really fantastic leading roles that otherwise I probably never would've done.

The paycheck was $300 a week. After taxes, $270, and I was a principal dancer. I'm glad I danced again, but you just can't make a living doing this. I was teaching ballet. It was a lot of work, but I'm glad I did it. I only danced for one year there. They offered me a raise to $440, "No, I can't do that." I auditioned, not because I wanted to be on Broadway, but because they were looking for classically trained ballerinas, and I realized that's really where I had pigeonholed myself.

Ariel still loves ballet, and, while sometimes conflicted about it, ballet remains an important part of who she is. The Broadway show has allowed her to continue ballet and also make a living:

My relationship with ballet has morphed over the years. It has just been like this lifelong marriage, where sometimes you separate. Sometimes you come back together, love/hate. I've gone through all those mixed emotions with my thirty-three-year relationship with ballet, and I have to say I love it more now than I ever did because of where I'm at, because I'm not in that competitive stage. I don't mind that my career is coming to an end. I've had a full experience, and now I can just love it as a gift that it has brought to my life. I have sustained myself and made a living for myself, which is a hard accomplishment as a dancer. I'm really grateful for that.

My fiancé got me tickets [to see a ballet] for Christmas, and I thought, "Is he crazy? What if I have a nervous breakdown?" I absolutely love it and it's gorgeous, and even though I can't do it to that level anymore, I don't care because it still inspires me. "Oh, I'm gonna try to do something like that in the studio tomorrow." I'm grateful that I'm at this place, this stage in my life, and that I can just love it in a different way now.

Ariel and Josie both use their Broadway careers to extend what they are passionate about: performing dance. Josie's dance career was shaped by her injuries. She had a forced liminal period of working outside the world of dance for four years. After largely recovering from her injuries, Josie tried out for Broadway. A friend taught her the choreography—she was excited she could do it and it was ballet on Broadway. Although she missed what she refers to as art (a ballet company), hard work and persistence allow her to dance again:

My teacher was a little unconventional. I was on pointe by the time
I was eight. By the time I was twelve, I was constantly injured.
Whether or not those injuries were because everything started so
early is very probable. I moved when I was fifteen [to a major company school]. Almost immediately, I injured my hip.

To be a professional ballet dancer, you have to have this super
tunnel vision your whole life. It makes you a little bit crazy. You
have to have a drive like no other. The doctors were like, "Well, you
might not walk properly on that foot again." "No, I'm probably gonna
dance again." That's the mentality that you have. I was on crutches
for almost two years with that [new injury] because it wouldn't heal,
and I'd be on one crutch, and then I would re-tear part of it, so I was
working at a doctor's office as a receptionist. Then the second two
years I was working for a catering company.

I auditioned five times over a period of a year and a half, and I got
different reactions. The first time I was too tall. I had my hair up.
The second time I wore my hair in a lower bun, and they were like,
"How come we've never seen you before? You're beautiful." Totally
different. This is six months apart. The third time, they didn't hire
anybody. The fourth time my boss offered me the tour. I was a freelancer at that point. I was really lucky, but I was on a mission. I had
so many setbacks and so many disappointments.

She faced more challenges than most and succeeded.[10] She remained in
the Broadway show for many years and took time off to travel to explore museums and to dance occasionally in performances that met
her demands for art. She loves dancing, but Broadway was only one of
several identities, including political work and studying paintings. She
had the reward of reasonable pay and other interests that nourished her
creative side that compensated for the routine and lack of challenge of
Broadway dance.

Broadway is a way to extend dance careers by letting dancers perform.[11] The shows allow dancers to soften the boundaries between art
and commerce but not all like John and Tre soften the boundaries.
These dancers' extended careers were possible in part because of the
social habits developed as children—persistence, meeting challenges,
and dedication in pursuit of their passion. Josie rejoined the show when

Broadway reopened after COVID-19 closures. Ariel married and was teaching ballet.

TIMES ARE CHANGING

Unlike earlier generations, many more dancers are aware early that their performing careers are finite and they prepare. Carson, still in his twenties, has a BFA, dances with several companies, and recognizes that he will arrive at a future point where his body will not be able to do the same things:

> My cousin works in Silicon Valley. He was trying to explain, "Oh, yeah. I'm turning thirty this year and trying to think about what is my long-term plan." I was like, "You don't understand. The longer I do this, the less valuable I am. Sure, there's a maturity, and your résumé. You've worked with more people, but you're that much closer to not doing it. Your expiration date is creeping a little closer." He didn't understand that. "You work for so many companies. You keep getting a pay bump." I was like, "No. If I leave my company, then I start at the bottom and don't get to dance as much and don't get paid as much."

Exiting the world of performing is a process, though a dramatic event may initiate the process, as it did for Lisa. For many, a confluence of factors, including nudges from company staff, begin the process of thinking about the decision to exit a company. College or therapy, for those who have the resources, provide a liminal period to distance the self from performing or classical ballet, consider options, develop new identities, and learn new skills. It is often more of a situational rupture for company dancers who have fewer outside activities that they might develop into something more. But distancing from the performing self is rarely easy even for the portfolio dancers who ease themselves out.

For most, transitions are still difficult, as Anita recounts:

> Performance is embodying yourself. I don't know. It's a whole different thing. That is one thing I'll say. Nothing compares to performing. I feel like a piece of me is gone right now without having that, definitely. I don't really know what to do about that at this point.

Anita illustrates both why some fight to stay and the difficulty of exit. She teaches Pilates, is a mother, and started to work in her husband's business; yet, she will always be a dancer. Liminal institutions helped transitions for some, but adapting the self was a difficult task for many and involved a process of discovery and rupture. It was more difficult than getting A's in college. For some, there are rigid boundaries between dance and everything else, but all those I spoke with, after pain and a lot of effort, managed the transitions; they used the habits cultivated as children to find and develop new occupations aided by schools, therapists, family, and their creativity. They are accustomed to challenges, and, as we will see in the next chapter, chose a variety of new work. They used the knowledge, experiences, and habits of dance performers to link their new lives to their lives as dancers.

CHAPTER SEVEN

NEW WORK

New Identities and Adapted Self

What do you do with that performing self after you stop performing? Marian Horosko told Joysanne Sidimus, "If you decide to stop dancing, don't mourn the loss of your dance career because it isn't lost. It is still within you, and the qualities that were developed and the talents you had for that career are still there."[1] And Kathleen Bannon, another notable performer, reminds dancers that "You never stop being a dancer!"[2] These dancers separate the performing self from an identity as a dancer with memories of performing, with the social skills and habits learned as children and affirmed as professionals, and with the posture and walk that allow others to identify them as dancers. Many of the habits, experiences, relationships, and skills of a professional dancer are useful in new types of work, sometimes in surprising ways. Doing multiple *fouettés* may not be, but observing others' efforts to turn, being able to see the problem, and explaining how to improve it are important to dance teachers and stagers—as is the ability to deal with challenges, the dedication to work, the persistence to improve, and skills of collaboration for all. But some habits, such as unquestioning acceptance of the authority of others and not using one's voice to express opinions and point out the poor behavior of others, need to change. The love of the art remains, experiences linger, and self-discipline carries over into new fields.

In the course of their performing careers, dancers form life skills and develop habits that help them navigate post-performance challenges. Boundaries between performing dancer and dance teacher appear permeable and fluid while those between dancer and lawyer appear more significant, but all face challenges; these changes require not only new work skills and behaviors, but new types of relationships with others, whether as doctors or Pilates instructors. This chapter explores what habits get in the way, what habits and knowledge are surprisingly useful, and what connections they can make with their dancing past. Challenges vary somewhat among the types of work, but the dance performing identity recedes in importance, becoming more embedded in memories.

The lifelong habits of hard work and persistence serve dancers well in their new work. Lisa reflects on how her work habits help her current work as a lawyer:

> Dancers are very driven human beings. It's the type A of the arts in a way. I think if you're gonna be a real successful dancer, it's just every day. The craft is honing it all the time. It translates into being quite a good student if you can hone that and put it into your classwork, then into being an employee.

Natasha highlights the skill of dealing with competition and persistence in aiding the challenge of establishing a place for yourself in a new work situation:

> Just the fact that you can transition to another career at a pretty young age, which dancers have to do, speaks volumes to how talented and wise dancers are. I can see it in my daughter already because from a very young age you are trained to be nimble, and you're trained to seek excellence and to be disciplined. You're in such a competitive environment that you have to be open to finding your niche, finding what makes you unique, and finding your strengths. That, later in life, is a really good skill to have.

Changing types of work or occupations in a career is not unusual. Athletes all need new work;[3] and all PhDs cannot find university jobs. Coders cannot always keep up with all the new computer languages and, after a while, seek other work. Some jobs become obsolete such as word processing or industrial work moves to other countries. Now AI threatens other work. Some people become bored with their work, are attracted to something else, or their life circumstances change.[4] These transitions are rarely easy, and it is often difficult to see in advance how the first work, in this case, training and dancing professionally, may inform the second.

Dancers do all sorts of things after their performing careers; some appear more related to their former careers than others. First, drawing on their artistic skills, they become designers, choreographers, artistic directors, videographers, or photographers. They use their knowledge of performance, storyline, and movement to choreograph, design costumes and scenery, or develop dance programs. A second option is to emphasize knowledge of bodies, which makes teaching dance or Pilates, staging dances, or training to be a physical therapist a sensible route. Some peoples' careers don't fit comfortably in these categories; there are overlaps. Daniella teaches dance (body) and choreographs (arts), but she sees herself as a choreographer. While Barbara choreographs and directs opera, she earns most of her income and spends most of her time teaching and thinks of herself as a teacher. Teaching dance uses the body to further the art. A third possibility is to leave the world of bodies and art—to emphasize verbal, interpersonal, and analytical skills. At a national meeting of physicians, I was chatting with an OB/GYN when he asked me about this project. When I told him, he excitedly explained that his two best residents had been professional dancers with outstanding work habits; they listened carefully both to him and to patients, did their work on time, dealt with each case thoroughly, and were always pleasant. He continued for several minutes extoling their performances as residents, not dancers. Whatever past experiences, new work requires fresh skills and knowledge, new styles of relationships with others, and self-adaptation.

Market analysts tell us today's workers must be nimble, ever ready to move between jobs and cross occupational boundaries. The boundaryless model suggests that large organizations where people could make their entire careers are becoming less dominant and that occupation-based employment with short-term work in more agile organizations is becoming the dominant model.[5] Transitions between worksites are seen as smooth, relatively easy, and frequent, as fluid transitions. Others focus on "rupture"—for example, when young people, especially without much education, begin their work careers and move from job to job or a job type disappears.[6] Neither description is particularly concerned with where the workers start, with the experience of the process of transitioning as we saw in the last chapter, or with the lived experiences of those who enter new types of work.[7]

Boundaries separate professional dancer and practicing lawyer, but they also separate performer and dance teacher. Some occupational boundary crossings require education and licensure (for example, for becoming a lawyer or physical therapist), whereas a ballet teacher needs no official training, though some like American Ballet Theatre or Royal Academy of Dance provide certification. Some colleges require a BFA or an MFA for employment as a college dance teacher. Pilates or yoga often requires certification as well. But the new work experience itself often demands new skills and new styles of relationships, which can shape experiences. All have to contend with an evolving sense of self and new forms of relationships at work, learn new workplace routines, and figure out what the expectations are. While certification and licensure are formal boundaries, others are more interpersonal such as learning to lead or how overemphasis on the "ideal self" or perfectionism may trip up the worker in a new environment. The informal boundaries may be just as difficult as the formal boundaries of education and licensing.

Another boundary to cross is changing the type of labor market—from companies to freelance work or vice versa; this can create ruptures for some, such as struggling to find work after leaving a company, or for former portfolio workers, learning how to work in large organizations. Additionally, training does not include all they need to know, and they have to figure it out on their own—do "stretchwork."[8] Although some of the new work may appear unconnected to their past work, many dancers use metaphors or images from dance to connect the two, weakening the boundaries and smoothing out ruptures over time. Change is a process to get to a new career stage and to make sense of that new employment; it takes time. Some situations feel more like rupture, while others, they find, are more fluid than expected.

Of those I interviewed who danced professionally, thirty-eight will probably stay off the professional dance stage.[9] Broadly categorized, fifteen continued to work on the body, including teaching dance and other body training or physical therapy; thirteen worked in the art world including artistic directors, painters, scene designers, choreographers, and costume designers; and ten transitioned to the world of analysis such as finance, law, or business. How did they deal with the challenges of new work? Which skills and habits are transferable, and which must be learned or adapted?

TRANSITIONS IN MODERN TIMES

Today both men and women dancers transition to paid work, but in the last century, women often felt the most significant option was marriage and children. Ann Jenner, a Royal Ballet principal, born in 1944 and married in 1980, envisioned such a transition when interviewed by John Gruen in 1975:

"I think that if I did Giselle, then I could quite happily retire. In a funny sort of way, I'm quite looking forward to having my freedom. It would be such absolute bliss not to have to live on schedule. . . . In the meantime, I'll go on. I think that when one reaches the age of thirty-five, then that is the time when you should start thinking about retirement. . . . I will have children, and perhaps do something in a hospital."[10]

Taking on roles that become identities and often essential aspects of self makes the transition easier. The role as "wife" provides an identity alternative for Maria Tallchief, New York City Ballet principal (1947–1965), and can become an important aspect of self:

I felt a sudden pang of fear. The future, spread out before me like that limitless expanse of clouds, was a world I was about to enter as a dancer no more. A ballerina, retired. . . . My priority was being Mrs. Paschen, not Maria Tallchief, prima ballerina. Frankly, it was a relief. Buzz needed me.[11]

These women's performing careers were unusual at a time when many women did not have careers outside their homes.[12] Then they joined others in what were valued roles as wives and mothers. Nevertheless, Maria Tallchief later founded and directed the Chicago City Ballet, and Alicia Alonzo, after dancing as a principal with ABT, directed the

National Ballet in Cuba from 1948 until she died in 2019. Some women, who were not principals, did fashion careers outside the world of dance. After three years with the NYCB corps, Judy Kupersmith completed her medical degree in 1969 and became a psychiatrist.[13] While dancing in the NYCB corps in the 1980s, Linda Hamilton started an undergraduate degree in psychology and completed her PhD in clinical psychology in 1989. She only stopped performing when she did her internship. After immersing herself in issues hobbling dancers and theater people, Hamilton wrote several books (1998, 2008) and an advice column for *Dance Magazine*. She also speaks with trainees and students of dance about health issues, in addition to her private practice. These dancers met the challenges of major transitions, used their work ethic and organizational skills, and were able to find their voices to make careers that were relatively unusual for women at the time.

Bear in mind that career options in dance aren't based on equal opportunity. Men who were principals are usually first in line to become artistic directors, ballet masters, company schoolteachers, or stagers. Peter Martins joined the NYCB as principal dancer from Denmark and then took over the NYCB company for more than twenty-five years when Balanchine died, and Kevin McKenzie danced with the Joffrey Ballet and as principal at ABT before he became its artistic director also for more than twenty-five years, a year and a half after he finished performing. Neither had much time to think about what to do next. Angel Corella, principal dancer of ABT, returned immediately upon his retirement in 2012 to Spain to direct his company before he took over the Philadelphia Ballet in 2014.

Until recently, few women worked in dance leadership positions. Lourdes Lopez, principal dancer of New York City Ballet, was hired by Miami City Ballet in 2012. The Washington Ballet hired Julie Kent, principal dancer of American Ballet Theatre, as artistic director in 2016, who then moved to the Houston Ballet in 2022. And the NYCB hired two former principals, Jonathan Stafford and Wendy Whelan, in 2019. Susan Jaffe, former principal dancer, was appointed artistic director of ABT in 2022, and Tamara Rojo joined the San Francisco Ballet from the English National Ballet and planned her first season for 2023–24. Of course, not all principals find or want a place in the dance world.

Developing new identities and acquiring unfamiliar skills while the body retains its communication skills is hard. Whether twelve or seventy, dancers communicate with their bodies, and that form of communication rarely appears to leave the body. In 2010 Damian Woetzel, New York City Ballet (1985-2008) who became president of Juilliard in 2018, and Violette Verdy, principal NYCB (1958-1977) who became a professor of dance at Indiana University, coached New York City Ballet principals Tiler Peck, Joaquin de Luz, and Daniel Ulbricht. Verdy, in her seventies, moved gracefully as she demonstrated the movement nuances required. Joaquin was injured, and Daniel did not know the entire role, so Woetzel danced too. It looked to me as though they couldn't help themselves but move.[14] Kevin McKenzie, in his sixties, up on the stage in a break from an ABT dress rehearsal, demonstrated the artistic aspect of a movement for the dancers. Even after their performing careers ended, they continued as "stars" in major artistic roles. Corps members and portfolio dancers face other challenges as they plan their futures but are increasing aware of the challenges they face.[15]

KEEPING OTHERS' BODIES IN SHAPE AND LEARNING TO LEAD

Work that appears as a natural follow-up to performer, such as dance or Pilates teacher, is not necessarily that much easier to figure out than work such as physical therapy with more formal boundaries: a college degree and license. Knowledge of the body learned in dance is useful in all these professions, but the knowledge and skills necessary to do the work is different from performing; it involves communicating how to do movement verbally, how to lead the interaction, and how to understand the bodies of those who are not dancers. Non-dancers who take Pilates or dance classes are often unaccustomed to imitating demonstrated movements as dancers do; they need verbal instructions and can't do what dancers can. Dance teachers must learn that on their own; physical therapists learn it in school. For all, what their bodies do is no longer as important as figuring how out how to explain bodies to others. To do the work well takes determination. Boundaries from performing to current work are often informal but take effort to cross.

Economic and social life may still be precarious after stopping performing for those who work on the body. More often than not, a salaried teacher in a major ballet company school is a former principal dancer—a similar position in college often requires a master's degree. Many who remain in the world of bodies continue as portfolio workers. Teachers are often paid by the number of students taking the class. Barbara continued her portfolio career teaching dance in several locations and also directing operas for small venues:

> I am mostly teaching ballet classes and after-school programs with little children. They're basically kindergarten through second grade. Then I teach at a private school once a week, also ballet. I do a little directing. Right now, I'm directing an opera. Their summer intensive [dance school] is three weeks, and I just got an email saying, "Please let us know if you're interested—." I did that last year, teach ballet, once a day. They're very nice, and they pay more than the regular school [where she teaches several classes a week].

Rushing between schools, she ekes out enough to live on, frugally. Barbara learned how to verbalize movement but always demonstrates and now teaches students of many levels; small children, preprofessional, and hobbyists. She acquired the knowledge of how to teach various groups by doing stretchwork. Teaching adult hobbyists as though they were professionals doesn't succeed. Her college degree gets her access to some schools but did little to help her teach different groups. That, she learned on her own.

Learning to lead the interaction is critical and different from deferring to authority. Anita, who danced with several well-known small contemporary ballet companies, recognizes the challenges she faces as a Pilates teacher and the extensions of and differences from her experiences as a performer. She stretches her performing self to add healer and teacher and realizes that she now leads the interaction instead of an artistic director or choreographer. She develops an ability to explain by thinking about her experiences, not by training:

> Part of it [performing] being just like your sense of self is really wrapped up in what you're doing with your physical body, and how you're communicating with your physical body. Now, what I do is I put my attention on other bodies. I'm not focused on my body. I do gain satisfaction from working with other people and that exchange

of energy, and that almost like a healing type of modality. It's like a complete role reversal, you know? A lot of times, as a dancer, you are the student. Now I'm the teacher. I'm still adjusting to it.

Learning how to speak up can be a challenge and is not necessarily intuitive to people who learn to communicate with their bodies. Ariel, a college graduate after dancing in a major ballet company, emphasizes the importance of verbal communications in teaching:

I think it's because you're so used to using your body to express yourself that it's like the words aren't going to explain it to people, so that you wanna keep using your body. It's hard as a teacher to find the words that's gonna be effective to help them understand it. How do I explain this again because what I just said didn't work? Let me think about how to articulate myself so that something can sink in. That's a challenge. That's the real challenge of teaching.

During the years of concentrating on the body, dancers cultivate an understanding of the way the body functions so feel they can use that knowledge to help others with theirs, but they also need to understand how movement regimes work on non-dancers and older or injured bodies. They, like Alyssa, enjoy sharing their knowledge and develop ways to explain it verbally to non-dancers, unlike some dance teachers who continue to demonstrate without speaking much. Alyssa appreciates the challenge of figuring out the best ways to teach movement to non-dancers but has a self-imposed barrier to teaching ballet:

I like teaching physical therapy yoga. I do not like teaching dance. I think it's that I don't really know how I do what I do [as a dancer], and I like it that way. I like it that it's a mystery to me how things come out and how things are expressed. To be a good teacher, you have to break things down. You have to analyze them. They're the building blocks of learning, and I just don't want to do that [with ballet]. I love doing that with other types of movement.

I teach private clients and yoga for PT. There's just so much information in here [points to head] that I like sharing, transposing it into someone else's world of understanding. I like that kind of challenge. I work with a lot of people that have some sort of complex issue. I worked with one woman who had MS. Those are my favorite types of clients. As a person, I've learned the frailty of the body, the tempo of the body, the frustrations.

Alyssa has taken the challenge of teaching movement to people plagued by body problems and taught herself to work with them.

The changing labor market matters. Transitioning from companies to portfolio building requires new skills to find enough work: constant job searches, building networks, and speaking up. Alicia found her training and company membership helpful for developing organizational skills and dedication that she would like to pass on to children. In her narrative, she says she never learned to speak up, nor is she good at networking. She realizes she is too deferential to become a bigger success but sees herself as a teacher and creative artist inspiring others:

I teach every day—ballet classes I'm teaching four times a week. Today, I teach at [small major company school], and I'm teaching little ones. I'm teaching a Mommy and Me class, which is ballet, but it's more creative. I've been pegged into doing this early childhood, because I'm good with children, but at the same time, it's not as fulfilling—I mean, it is fulfilling in a way, but I love teaching older kids as well. I can get into the meat of dancing. With children, I call it my community service—because I'm inspiring. You never know. This is how Misty Copeland got into dancing. I do wanna hand over that spark that ignites somebody. They may not even be a dancer, but it may ignite them. I feel like I have this discipline. I can handle a lot of things, but I'm not one for marketing myself very well. I'm not one to ask for more money. I should speak up. I'm not good at networking. Those are my weaknesses.

Again, finances have become a more significant issue in her life as she has not developed voice or networks, but Alicia worries that one of her sons is deciding his future career based largely on the financial rewards of the work (perhaps as a result of her financial precarity). She sees the importance of passion that she can pass on to others.

Unlike most dance teachers, physical therapists (PTs) attend university programs for professional training. They use their experiences with the body but need new skills of diagnosis and treatment for those who

lack the ability to move easily or are injured. They gain training in relational techniques. Adrian and Steven are physical therapists with keen
senses of body fitness and rhythms. Both see themselves as goal oriented, pondering their futures earlier than many dancers of their generation. Steven, a company dancer, was willing to take more economic
challenges than Adrian, a portfolio dancer. Steven used his knowledge
of dancers' needs, a "take charge" perspective, to determine if an injured dancer could go onstage in one job and often employed his dance
connections in his varied PT career. He opened his own business after
working on the road with various dance companies. Steven recalls:

> The transition was perfect for me. I was a very goal-oriented person.
> Before I picked PT—I knew I was thinking about it, what to do after-
> wards. I was like, well, maybe I could be a dance critic. I went on the
> road as a Broadway show's physical therapist and toured with them
> for a year and a half. I did that after working for [major company]. I
> was with that company for a couple years. I quickly grew out of that.
> I wanted to do my own thing. I was offered the job as the director
> of PT at [another major company]. Did that. That's why I love this
> career. You can keep shaping it and changing its surroundings.

Steven uses his creativity and desire for challenge to keep changing his
work environment; as he tells his story, he experienced all his work
transitions as smooth or fluid. He said about working for one company,
"I was as much a part of the company as a dancer was." His self is embedded in a dance institution, but more in his knowledge of the body
and helping others, not in his body. His dance world referrals fuel his
current private practice. Although Adrian too had attended college
before dancing professionally, he had been a portfolio dancer and saw
portfolio building as a financial risk. He became a salaried physical
therapist. Neither found the transition as much of a rupture, but Adrian
later found work in a large organization as a bit too routine without an
outlet for his creative energies. He started to write.

   Whereas all the body-oriented workers liked what they did, only
some talked about it as a new passion. Renée used her creative skills to
invent new body work, long after she gave up aspirations to dance professionally. Drawing from her life and skills as a preprofessional dancer
and the critical skills gained in college, Renée created her body-oriented

career after college and working in corporate communications for several years. She used her creativity, her understanding of science, her voice, and her years of dance training to develop a new specialized exercise program:

> I decided to get certified in Pilates so I could make some money on the side. This was the calling that I'd been wanting. I remember going through the training and feeling excited for the first time since I'd quit dancing. I felt alive again in a way I'd not felt for a long time. I had already been doing Pilates for my own injuries. I was offered a job immediately at the studio where I went through training. I worked my butt off building a practice while I was teaching and was invited to join the teacher training faculty. That's where I discovered I really enjoyed educating.
>
> My Pilates training was very anatomy heavy, so it answered all these questions I'd had that nobody would respond to previously. They encouraged questions. That brought me back to my college style, which was very much the opposite of my ballet world. In the ballet world, certainly at the time, it was "Don't question. Do." College was the opposite; it was all about critical thinking, and I became good at it, but it wasn't second nature for me to question stuff. I was diagnosed with osteoporosis, which led me into the specialty with bone and joint health I have now and creating this exercise system and teaching other instructors.

Although she struggled at each turning point, in the end she was able to connect many of the previous activities and ways of thinking she loved, and Renée developed a new passion. Her career combines body skills, dedication, and persistence with a knowledge of academic routines and critical skills, which are the core of her self-image.

Renée and Steven talk about new passions, as did James when he became a massage therapist. Dance and dancers continue to excite him into his sixties. Dance freed him to do many things he did not anticipate growing up, but, knowing that performing doesn't last forever, James needed to find something else to do with his life. When his back problem was improved by massage, he decided to train first as a massage therapist, then, thinking he wanted more challenge, trained as an occupational therapist. James enjoyed his massage work more and has continued to find massage jobs through his dance connections. His knowledge of the dancers' bodies comes in handy as he continues to perfect his skills and moves easily among worksites:

Then one of the dancers who was familiar with my massage work, calls me one day and said, "Would you come on tour with [a small important company]? You'll massage [artistic director] and we'll see how it goes." They flew me. I massaged him. The physical therapist went in. He came out and said he loved it. He said you're on for the rest of the tour. Then I was touring with [them]. I have to say, what I liked most about that job is being able to take class; that focused my massage practice into a more medical massage where I would have to work on specific injuries. I wanted more of that. This whole thing is just a massage therapist's dream. I'm working on these incredible artists. They're fun, and it's like I can relate to them. They say, "It's like my *arabesque*, it hurts when I do *arabesque*." You just know where to go.

James saw few boundaries between performing and massage and fluidly moved among worksites.

Still, the continuity between two career stages can carry you only so far. But, by examining experiences rather than just formal boundaries, it is an ability to deal with challenges that allow dancers to manage the identity changes and interactional skills that work change entails. All had to deal with taking charge of interactions, explaining movement verbally, and deciding whether to work in an organization or remain in the portfolio world. Willingness to meet challenges and occasionally fail in the process is a big part of a successful transition. Although one might imagine that the worlds of body and art are mere extensions of performing, they require real changes and asking, "what do I need to change" and "how can I make that happen" rather than seeing change as risky. These challenges, along with dedication and persistence, allow necessary transitions despite some ruptures in the process.

ARTS: STRETCHWORK, MAXIMIZING CREATIVITY, AND HONING MARKETING SKILLS

Former performers settling on artistic pursuits face additional challenges. Much work necessary to make a career in the arts requires stretchwork—learning skills that are neither taught in schools nor from dance experience, such as grant writing or sewing leotards.[16] For body work, much of the stretchwork is adapting the self to communicate verbally, rather than learning new body skills. At times dancers have to confront their tendency for perfectionism when learning new skills on the job. Whether choreographers, designers, or artistic directors, they need to think of themselves also as entrepreneurs. Because much arts work and some body work is project-based, the dancers must learn to build networks and relationships to find and do their work, with the exception of the artistic direction of large companies. Many dancers don't see themselves as entrepreneurs, valorizing their love of art and downplaying their need for money. Additionally, they all need to learn to lead to organize others in addition to themselves. Collaboration with a diverse set of people—such as dancers, administrators, and boards of directors—is a recurring theme when they reflect on their current work lives.

Stretchwork is essential. It takes a lot more than creative imagination to create dances and sustain the life of a choreographer. For example, choreographers must think through the dance design and change the choreography to meet the needs of a particular group of dancers or location. They must also obtain contracts and commissions and sometimes write grants to support creating work. Often they design costumes and lighting—all while earning a living in the process. For artistic directors, the tasks strain one's skill set, even as a salaried employee, particularly in a small company. Not many take naturally to the never-ending job of raising money, developing boards, organizing dancers, managing labor relations, hiring and developing dancers and choreographers, planning productions, and cultivating audiences. People running businesses may earn an MBA, but few programs teach how to be an artistic director. Larger companies do have executive directors with management experience; those working for small companies often are on their own. Stretchwork is critical.

How do you choreograph when dancers have different skill levels and different training? No one teaches that. A choreographer's life is often like that of the portfolio dancers described in Chapter 5. In New York City, a busy choreographer often works with several groups in different locations—in the course of one day. At 10 am, Daniella, a contemporary choreographer, arrives at a midtown studio, teaches a class in the movement style she developed, then continues choreographing with these preprofessional, ballet-trained students. One young dancer refuses to participate in the dance, but an injured dancer sits on the side tracing the movements with his hands. The dance proceeds slowly, but Daniella never raises her voice. She has developed her own strategy for choreographing dancers with different training by, for example, asking the dancers questions about movement and having them make up some parts in order to see what they can do. Additionally, she has had to learn to write grants for funding her company dancers to perform in different places around the city. Schools of dance or experiences don't teach this.

Creative people challenge themselves to figure things out. Maya, artistic director of a small classical ballet company, kept her company afloat for some forty years through diligent fundraising, spotting promising choreographers before they were established, teaching classes for children, learning how to manage lighting and costuming, and doing social media work. Major challenges for Maya were creating an active board and generating audiences and donations. With no formal education in management, she taught herself relevant skills by trial and error and assiduous collaboration:

I beg and beg and borrow [find theaters and money to pay dancers]. I'm out just about every night, trying to meet people. I meet people at the ballet; some of our biggest funders are people who just happened to sit next to me, and I try to introduce them to what I do. I have no shame. Fundraising is very difficult. It's difficult for a company like mine, because we're in one of the capitals of the art world, and we're a small company. Must we survive? Probably not. People forget what we can offer; what we do, those big companies can't. It's a different theatrical experience; you're involved in the piece because of the intimacy. It's a different viewing experience.[17]

People would rather give their money to a big company where it's socially more prominent. With us it's nitty gritty, like having a board that can really work with us. I try to do a thirty-five-week minimum [her company]. I don't always, I think we're almost thirty-five this year. We're gonna make payroll in the next two weeks, and then we are broke.

Putting together a board for a small company like Maya's is difficult. A board member's status reflects on the arts organizations; a board member's stature, in turn, is enhanced by being asked to join a prominent arts organization. Lincoln Center or the Metropolitan Art Museum are very choosy when it comes to prospective board members, inviting those able to make large donations and underwrite fancy balls at the season's opening. Little status is gained by joining Maya's board. And she needed them to collaborate.

Like others, Michel found his school-based design education lacking, drawing instead on his experience as a performer. When someone he knew asked to meet with him, his first response had been, "Thinking designing for dance, I wouldn't even know how to start that. I had not studied this." But he was so successful, he continued to receive design commissions.

Costume designers are also left to their own devices to learn new skills. Tyler started while finishing his design degree. But he needed skills not covered in design school: working with stretch fabrics. He did not shy away from asking questions of established dance costumers, adding to his understanding of designing clothing that enhanced the performance rather than overwhelming or constraining dancers. He sewed costumes on his own, correcting his mistakes as he went along. Tyler liked a good challenge and let go of his perfectionism so that he could learn by doing and asking questions. He accepted making mistakes:

On top of learning at school, I was also taking on these projects, which was causing me to make so many mistakes. Learning how to deal with stretch fabrics, which you don't learn at school. There is a knit section, but you don't learn how to make a leotard—you just have to figure those things out. I would visit the costume shops of these companies. I would ask questions. People were always very giving with information. Then commissions just kept coming. With each one, I just kept trying—I would figure it out. I would work late into the night in my apartment, make huge mistakes, burn holes in things with the iron, and start all over again. It was so weird. I didn't even know it was happening until it had already happened.

Tyler somewhat belated learned to speak up about contracts and getting paid, solidifying his entrepreneurial self:

"Oh, this college is performing my dance. Can you send them the designs?" Well, no. We would need a contract first. They're like, "Oh, what do you mean?" We would need a contract that lays out what our royalties are, licensing fees.

To become and remain entrepreneurial, networks and new styles of relationships are important. When Michel, a company dancer, began to develop his career as a scenery and costume designer, he had to work hard on developing new relationships with dancers, choreographers, and artistic directors in the ballet world; he thought that he did not have strong enough networks to launch his career:

He [artistic director] said, "Okay, leave your portfolio, and I'll let you know." He is not someone I was close to. He said, "Well, actually, it's bad news. We're not doing the workshop this year. But I would love you to design my next world premiere." Good news? It was great. It was a short one-act ballet for him. It was really lovely to work with him. Very strange to be working in the company where I had been danc- ing and that was tough, because some dancers were still my friends or people I'd danced with. Made me quite tough. Then after that, I was doing theater and opera. Then I bumped into [major choreogra- pher]. I'd never thought I'd be flown to show my design. I would never have thought actually I would become a designer, to be honest, but someone's assistant. [The choreographer] came in and looked at the work and very much liked it. He said, "Listen, I've been asked to do a premiere—would you like to design it?" I couldn't understand what he meant. I said, "Yes, of course," thinking it's gonna be the small space, which is like a ballet studio with three rows. No, the main stage, blew my mind. That was the first piece we did, which went really well.

Good reviews of the choreographers' work for which he had done the designs, with positive mention of his designs, also burnished his reputa- tion, which led to additional opportunities.

Choreographers and designers typically rely on dance world net-works. But Michel was afraid that he didn't have a broad enough net-work and worried constantly about getting enough work, unlike Tyler, who had a plethora of personal contacts in the dance world:

In my last year of school [major choreographer] got in touch with me. I didn't know him at the time. He was starting to do small things. [A company member] had seen some of my work. She said, "You [the choreographer] should get in touch with this guy [Tyler], because I think he knows what he's doing."

As an entrepreneur, in order to do a project well, it was also import-ant to develop strong relationships with many people in different roles. Michel recognized what he liked best about his dance experiences—collaboration. As a designer, he works with, not for, the choreographers, artistic directors, behind the scenes workers, and dancers:

What was amazing is that it was a collaboration [working with a par-ticular choreographer], which is really what I do today as a designer. Don't come to me if you want me to tell you how we should do things. I'm interested in collaboration. I'm not a designer who comes from the visual arts or from architecture or from fashion. I collaborate on what are we doing, not what I wanna do.

Michel argues that the process of design is different than that of an artist. It is one of collaboration. To do the job, Michel realizes, he has to become more assertive and ditch his instinct to defer to develop collab-orative relationships. Although his entrepreneurial abilities have im-proved over time, the challenge of landing the next job is still a source of anxiety for him; his self is vested in his success as a designer, and he needs income. To stay in the game and ensure that artistic achieve-ments are matched by financial rewards, he has to keep networking too.

Tyler also used his collaborative skills to establish a long-term part-nership to develop his business:

He's [well-known choreographer] like "I'd like to see some of your work." I then went to my closest school friend—we'd always talked about collaborating. I thought this is a perfect opportunity. Maybe we could get it done quicker if we do it together. In a couple days we put together a tumbler of some of our school projects. I asked him if there was a dance in the company repertoire that he didn't like the designs of that we could redesign, to show him what that might mean.

He used the collaboration with his design partner and then networked successfully to find opportunities and create work.

Choreographers and artistic directors of smaller companies, thinking entrepreneurially, use some of the techniques devised by large companies to help them build audiences and finances; they invite donors to a rehearsal. I watched one rehearsal with about thirty people in the loft of the choreographer where a group of four men and four women worked to put together sections of a dance. The choreographer/artistic director entered the room explaining to the audience that the first section was reasonably set, but the rest was still in fragments and not set. He was not going to show us one section; it was surprising, dark, and special, and we could see it in several weeks during the performance, perhaps a strategy to encourage us to buy tickets. It worked. The costume designer sat in front of me holding colorful drawings of the elaborate costumes. I peeked over her shoulder before she passed them around. During a break, the choreographer said we could leave as the next section was still rough; it was unpolished as the dancers stopped several times to ask questions and adjust their movements. It looked substantially different at the performance. Here the choreographer had created an event—it was a rehearsal, an audience generator, and, potentially, a fundraiser.

Organizing self and others is a critical skill. The daily life of a choreographer can be particularly complicated and also means organizing others. With the preprofessional group mentioned above, the work goes on until 3 pm, with a twenty-minute lunch break that Daniella uses to schedule rehearsals for the next several days while munching on nuts before creating a new section of the dance. Next, she takes the subway to another studio to choreograph a piece for a student graduating from a college program. After that, she can use the studio to rehearse a new project with her professional dancers. Several months later, she choreographed two new dances for different groups, but had to leave the theater immediately after her senior conservatory students performed to catch a 6 am flight to a college halfway across the country where she was commissioned to create a new dance. After a flurry of activity, little may happen for several months, with teaching providing the only income opportunity.

The choreography process itself requires that Daniella not only organize her own schedule to meet the needs of several groups, but the schedules of her company dancers who performed for multiple companies and juggle sundry jobs to keep themselves in food and shelter. Schedules dictate some of the structures of a dance. One dance I saw had two sections with two separate groups of dancers. When I asked why dancers in part one didn't pass the torch to dancers in part two to make a clearer storyline, the response was, "I couldn't get the dancers together for one rehearsal!" This is a fairly common problem; even choreographers creating for a major company may also have to compete for dancers. They need to compose solos, duets, and trios separately to accommodate each dancer's rehearsal schedule. It can be difficult to get the group together to create an ensemble section. The final dance form may be as much an expression of the dancers' shifting schedules and the venue as the choreographer's artistic sensibilities.

Artistic directors need to extend their ideas of collaboration beyond performance to working with very different groups of people: the board, donors, dancers, and other staff members. Albert, an artistic director, turned around two troubled companies with his executive director. As we saw in the last chapter, he apprenticed himself for the sake of learning managerial skills in finance, production, and coordination. Albert emphasized the importance of cooperation and collaboration with dancers, his executive director, and board chair. He used the pronoun "we" to underscore the fact that collaboration is key to success:

> It was so challenging in my first company [as artistic director]. When you talked to the board and tried to set it straight and then you meet with the dancers when you're a candidate, you try to get a feel for the place and what do people really want because you're serving the company. Change has to be very calculated and—not slow but—at a pace that they can handle. My second company was really smooth because the former artistic director was living in the community, and I had full support. The company [first one] was in debt, but we got them out of debt, and I never had to reduce the amount of reper-

tory. We got lots of new pieces, and we kept touring internationally. We fixed it. Then we went to [medium size ballet], and I was there for seventeen years. They also were dead in the dumps.

There's just some of us come in when the chips are down, and our job is to make it better and to, well in this case, get them into a new theater, without wrecking the repertory or cutting weeks. We're not starting companies. There was no place to learn how to do that. You just try to get all hands on deck and for the board to understand. I worked with the same executive director in both places. Our responsibilities, which we decided, were such that I would come in later in the process or I'd make the original proposal with the executive director. Then we'd present it [to the board], then they'd get to work on it.

Having an executive director allows for some division of labor. The artistic director may concentrate on artistic decisions and not get bogged down as much in fundraising and supervising staff. Albert's apprenticeship gave him a chance to hone his managerial and directing skills.

The precarity of their labor (arts and body workers) affects them at different times, but at the end of a career without much retirement money or when a partner becomes ill, it may become most important. Maya continues to deal with many challenges, especially her own financial situation. She isn't the only one. Others in the arts and body worlds also begin to experience financial precarity as risky with life changes and age. Theo found he needed a regular job to earn a steady income after leaving a major dance company for acting. With a growing family, he decided, "I had to get a solid job, something that was not flighty and crazy, so I got a solid job at a university." The same was valid for Adrian who took a salaried job as a physical therapist.

As an artistic director of a large company, Albert has some retirement benefits. Freelancers—designers or choreographers working for smaller companies—may have little money set aside for a rainy day. Doing a good job as a company and school director doesn't ensure a comfortable retirement, as Maya confides. She was not good at securing a pension, nor does she have the finances to recruit and pay additional staff. For the company to survive, she must find someone to run it and raise money:

I'm hoping that in January I'll be gone from the company. I'll keep the school. That's the board's job who takes over the company, not mine. I'm seventy-one years old, I'm tired, you know, I'm sick of washing the floors. But I have no savings, I have no retirement, so I have to work.

I'M NOT MY BODY: VERBAL AND ANALYTICAL SKILLS

It is not uncommon among dancers leaving performing to become weary of being constantly judged by the shape of their bodies or how they move. They are eager to foreground their verbal savvy, writing skills, and analytical abilities. Some intentionally distanced themselves from their bodies even as they continued dancing; others wanted to separate their new identities from the pliable bodies controlled by others after leaving the stage. They are still creators but of a different kind—people unafraid to raise their voices and fight for their creative visions. Finessing a job outside of the arts often means going through a liminal period to secure an education and refashion their self and, for some, a license to practice the new craft. But importantly, once they begin their new work, some stretchwork is necessary that brings them back to their roots or some situations might require them to moderate a habit that had been an important part of their lives as performers.

Before he assumed a position as executive director for a small well-known dance company, Anthony, after dancing with a major small contemporary ballet company, earned a master's degree in arts management and then worked for a consulting company with an expertise in art world financing. He also learned to moderate his ideal self when he took on a small project during graduate school and made some mistakes. Anthony loves his entrepreneurial role. His work remains central to his identity, but he strongly identifies with the company, not with his performing skill:

[W]hat I missed most about not being in a dance company was not having something by which to latch my identity onto and say, "This is the thing I care about. This is what I believe in. This is what I love." That was a turning point. I went to my boss [consulting company in the arts]. "I'm thinking about doing this [applying for the position as executive director, small dance company]." It turns out the board had been scheming for how to get me to join them.

I've been having a great time [as executive director]. It has turned my life into a blender, but this is the level that I like to work. The work is so excellent, and the company was so well-known, and no one had ever asked any of these wildly influential and, quite frankly, wealthy individuals for money. "Let's do a discrete campaign. Let's say we need a capital infrastructure. What do you need?" She said, "I need a . . ." We raised $60,000. People were lining up. I've loved every moment of it. The artistic director and I have created a really fabulous connection that is really special. I work ten-hour days. I travel all the time. I work on weekends. I love it.

When Anthony felt the need to stretch his skills, he looked around for someone on whom to model how to improve his communication skills with potential donors. "I was in the lobby talking to people, just like tight as a guitar string, saying hi to this person. Then he [his model] walks around the corner. He looks at me and he goes to me, 'This guy . . .' Oh, that ease, I thought." Anthony has become an entrepreneur for the arts; that is who he is. He raises money, boosts the artistic director's creativity, explores performance opportunities for the company; being an executive director is at the core of his self-image. He did not like moving from job to job, even for one consulting company. As a dancer, he was invested in a company, just as he is as an executive director. His voice brims with enthusiasm and confidence. He has become passionate about it.

Unlike Anthony who remained inside the dance world and learned how to deal with not being perfect, Paula had to earn her stripes outside the dance world after ten years with a major ballet company. Her ideal self was something of a barrier to her success. Even with college credentials, accomplished while performing, she had to start in a low-level office position:

You know that you want to take some distance from your identity as a dancer in a world that once valued you so much. I think it's hard because people in this "real world" often don't know how to handle someone who comes in for an interview and says, "I danced professionally with one of the best companies in the United States for ten years," and they're like, "Well, have you had an office job?" You're like, "No, I haven't." There's a translation barrier that happens, and it's a question of figuring out all the skills we hone as dancers and how those transfer and translate into a new environment, but it's still a totally new environment, and making that switch is a transition that will take error and failure and training and support.

Her colleagues like to remind Paula of her seamless career. Little do they realize how much trimming her ideal self had to undergo before she settled more comfortably into the new role:

I'll give them credit for hiring a dancer. There's a very high expectation when someone knows what it takes to be a dancer. It can't be the expectation of perfection, and I think that can sometimes come more from the dancer side. I came into this job knowing it was an entry level job, that my real skills and experience are higher, so I expected to just have it be a total ease and be perfect, and that's totally not been the case. That's been hard for me. I make mistakes, and I do not like making mistakes in something that I've deemed to be an easy job.

Although Paula experienced this new work as a bit of a rupture, after our interview, she used her skills at dealing with challenge, creativity, and "body performance" to establish a consulting company to teach the presentation of self to others, for example, in negotiations. Employing her performing skills, she has developed a system to teach non-dancers how to perform in high-pressure situations and how to connect with others in person and on the internet both verbally and using their bodies. She found a way to use her past creatively and to focus on others' bodies and on developing a new passion.

Successfully exploiting her conceptual and critical skills, while embracing skills learned in performing and her identity as a dancer, Anya, a portfolio dancer, had a difficult time after receiving her MBA figuring out how to integrate performance and the work world outside of dance. At times the transition felt like a rupture, but once on the job, she began to integrate her performing experiences and critical skills by creating conceptual bridges. Entry was difficult, but the work itself became more fluid:

I'm a social innovation consultant at a boutique consultancy. It is a virtual company. I get to work with clients on their social initiatives that usually involve a lot of community building and making creative platforms. There really is nothing like working with a group of dancers and collaborating in that way. I found that people I would meet in business school and in professional settings didn't really have any knowledge about dance. One thing I wasn't prepared for was how little they knew about the intellectual aspects and the creative process that goes with dancing. The dance background was both a liability and an interest catcher. That didn't help me to get any opportunities in business school.

I met a professor who encouraged me, and I think I also encouraged myself, to embrace my identity as a dancer and try to stand up for all the things I knew it was. Just like how organizations or brands can articulate themselves, I felt like now I had to articulate myself in what dance had to offer. I ended up using my knowledge of dance and my identity as a dancer to talk about collaboration, strategy, and innovation, and try to make parallels. I couldn't really ever leave my identity as a dancer. I remember our professor told us about this approach where you strategize. It might be like you go where there is the least competition. It's high risk. I was like, "I can do that. I can be high risk." I know a lot about dance and the process of making dance as in helping people work together. If I can talk about that and articulate it, I can defend myself when I have that one second where I can see people are dismissing me. I can come back. I can convince them. It also helped me reflect back on dance.

From her experience of dancing and creating, Anya understands how important it is to cultivate a proper self-image, or as sociologists call it, deploy "impression management." This technique became handy when she set out to organize a conference. And by using the trope of choreographing a performance, she designs a successful conference:

[My job] is really interesting because it's in emerging technology and hardware startups. I produced a women and data event. It's like making a performance because you design the structure of the day; how you want the ebb and flow of the emotions and activities to feel, and you identify really great people who can speak and create moments in the room, according to what you and the client decide is necessary. Giving people things that they can think about, so that when they can create a talk; it's like driving toward an overall goal that you have for the event. That feels like making a performance. That feels like a lot of the skills that I have.

She creatively bridges dance and business as a business innovator, sensitive to the dance world. She knows how to adjust to new challenges but hasn't entirely distanced herself from performing. Working in the portfolio and contemporary dance world, Anya learned to get along with a diversity of people, an experience that prepared her to meet new challenges in her post-dance career:

> Anyway, it's because of working in dance I think that made me believe in diversity, which now I am a big advocate of and am hyperaware of in my work in business, too. Clearly, we have some work to do there.

After her injury, college, and law school, Lisa became a successful appellate lawyer, a world that little resembled her familiar artistic environment, but, like Anya, she did see connections. She argues that she uses her arts and dance experience to think outside the box in her defense work:

> It's actually a lot of writing. It's tracking a story that's with the facts as they are, but for your client. I think the storytelling is quite artistic. They've really appreciated my outside-the-box thinking. You start to realize your artistic brain is not just for dance. When you find a place that appreciates it, you can be quite successful there. They really encouraged me to be that person that's like, "What about this idea?" They're like, "Go for it."

Not only does dance ready people for the challenge to explore beyond their comfort zone, but the passion can be experienced in other work, as Anthony and Lisa found. Lisa explains:

> Studying with somebody while they're choreographing, watching their process, trying new things. It does make you brave in a way to explore outside of the confines of what I think some people could

think were very stringent. It's actually not at all. It's a moving, breathing thing.

I feel encouraged by that experience because I feel when you're in it you don't know whether you're gonna find something you love again because it's such a deep love. You have to know when you're fourteen that this is what you want to do for the rest of your life. You have to make that decision then. I think it's really hard to get out of that mindset and think, "Well, that's over and you'll never love anything ever again." That's so not true. Maybe you will. That's my takeaway.

Their narratives link performance with new work. And they focus on learning how to stretch their knowledge to fill in the gaps needed to proceed; they never back away from challenge. The sticky self as a performer evolves, for some slower than others, as they develop new skills and take on new work identities, use what they know from dance and performing, and find meaning in that work. They readily cross many boundaries of education and licensure to get where they are and create links with the past. For many, the biggest rupture is with the sticky self as performer.

YOU ARE A DANCER, EVEN WHEN YOU NO LONGER PERFORM PROFESSIONALLY

Despite the end of performing careers, all are still dancers. They may take no classes, rarely see a performance, or associate regularly with former dancers, but most can be identified by others as dancers and consciously use what they learned and the language of dance and performance in their new work. Performing experience, habits, and skills don't disappear upon retirement from the stage. The past stays with them in more than memories, as many use their experiences of performance to remain connected to their former life.

Even those who work outside the dance world maintain these connections: Natasha's daughter is studying dance seriously, Lisa sits on the board of a dance school, and Anya choreographs and occasionally performs with her husband's group. Barbara Milberg Fisher performed with Ballet Society and then New York City Ballet (1946-1958), rising to soloist. After marrying, she joined Jerome Robbins's Ballets U.S.A. Divorced with three children, the college had a child-care program that enabled her to complete an undergraduate degree and, in 1980, her PhD in English. Her works span from typical academic publications to writing about dance: *In Balanchine's Company: A Dancer's Memoir*. She reconnected late in her professorial career with her dance roots.

Some nurture future dancers or help current ones. Steven remembered how his boss allowed him to leave work for rehearsals or tours. To pass on that generosity, Steven allows his physical therapy office staff to take "paid performing" leave:

> I said, "That's not a problem." She was like, "Why?" I go, "Because someone did that for me; we're going out on the road for a couple weeks. I gotta go." I never asked him why he was doing this for me. It was amazing. I thought maybe he liked the fact that he had this struggling dancer—but I waited tables. He had a restaurant.

Well into retirement from performing, some welcome opportunities to perform again. Anya, who works outside of the dance world, or Tyler, who is still in that world, dance on occasion, but they don't think of themselves as performers anymore. Maya, in her early seventies, describes her recent performing experiences. "I still dance with the company; I do the old lady roles. I love being onstage; it's great fun."

Alicia likes to continue moving and performs once a year, but she doesn't think of herself as a performer. "If we're at a party or a wedding, I always have to get up and dance. I perform with my flamenco group now once a year. That's a high for me." James and Barbara occasionally perform together, just for fun and sometimes for extra money:

> One day I got this postcard from the Waldorf Astoria inviting me to New Year's Eve, to the Grand Ballroom, $500 each for dinner and dancing [pay for performing and dinner]. I said, "Barbara, get your résumé over here. We're gonna do this." She said, "James, we don't know a foxtrot from the sun." We had a friend who had some ballroom training. She taught us some basic ballroom stuff. Barbara and I had done so much stuff together. It was so much fun.

When I asked Tyler, in his late thirties, whether he still considered himself a performer, he replied:

I don't know. That's a strange question. I just was in my friend's show again. The show was about ballet. It was a commentary on being a ballet dancer in a company in this very comic way. I had to do ballet in it. I had to put on footed tights and straighten my knees—I think people just automatically assume of me that that's very easy. Did I feel like am I a dancer? Is this total fraud? What am I doing? Some people are like once you're a dancer, you're always a dancer. I think you're a dancer when you're dancing. I don't think dance has to define the person you are.

Despite performing, it is no longer central to Tyler's self; these activities don't define him, but he suspects others still identify him as a performer as he is asked to dance and usually accepts.

Most people whose narratives animate this chapter have no illusion about the fact that their performing careers are over. They have new identities, have adapted their selves, and have moved on, spicing their lives with an occasional invitation to perform or serve on a dance school board. None found their dancing past irrelevant to their new work. Dedication to their craft pays off, sometimes in unexpected ways. Neither rupture nor fluidity adequately describes the experience of new work. All are confronted with new challenges, some more difficult to resolve than others. But thoughtful stretchwork bridges boundaries and fills in what they need.

Most bring the dedication and persistence they learned as children and use their creativity and knowledge in a different context. Collaboration helps. These skills and habits help to make a more fluid adaptation to new work. Others experience some rupture, especially if they haven't had a liminal period in which to learn new skills: leading instead of deferring, using their verbal skills to communicate instead of their bodies, and networking. But those who want to retire at a typical age of about sixty-five and have continued as portfolio workers or in the body or arts worlds sometimes experience a new rupture when they haven't earned much money. Rupture and fluidity describe situations that dancers and most people experience while changing work and in new types of employment. Dancers meet the challenges of change as they have met challenges since they were children. They still ask, "How can I do that?"

CONCLUSION

PASSIONATE WORK IN PERSPECTIVE

I have some kind of grim determination that the show must go on no matter what . . . even if I don't feel like doing it! To not perform is a sign of weakness.

—*Artistic director/choreographer, summer 2023*

That performance was set to take place outdoors at 7 pm in 90-degree heat and extreme humidity. Spurred by the work ethic bred into the dancers' bodies, they are consummate professionals used to defying adversity and pushing themselves to the breaking point. On that occasion, however, good judgment prevailed: the artistic director canceled the show. Several other performances scheduled during that steamy summer were called off as well, including two of the five evenings of the Baand Together outdoor stint at Lincoln Center featuring five major New York companies. Such prudence isn't always demonstrated by artistic staff, and few dancers would likely raise concerns. It may be a sign that the times are indeed changing.

Starting in the 1970s, young people searching for careers were advised to follow their passion in *What Color Is Your Parachute?*[1] Today's critics suggest that taking more conventional jobs allows time for one to pursue avocational hobbies, to secure a steadier financial existence, and to bring a balance to life. Moreover, other critics of passion-seeking careers argue that women are likely to take low-paying jobs such as teaching and social work, impeding their economic equality with men.[2] People passionate about their work are also vulnerable to exploitation by unscrupulous bosses who are only too happy to load them with extra assignments and conscript them to work overtime. A steady job with regular hours and good pay leaves time to pursue additional interests, some studies show. It allows people to hedge their bets, make fresh commitments, try their hand at new things outside of work. Yes, work is mainly a way to earn a living in such arrangements, and it may also stave off burnouts.

Art without passion sounds like an oxymoron, but professional art-making is also work that doesn't always allow the artist to pay the bills. Conventional work may keep sanity in the long run. Whether a project-based dancer looking for the next gig or a major company performer on a one-year contract, these artists will be confronted with the prosaic implications of their occupational choices. Poets, painters, and writers can follow their passion at almost any time of the day or week. They may develop a following late in life, and some will continue to make their mark after death. Professional dance careers, by comparison, tend to be short, with little assurance that they will continue past age thirty. And their days and weeks are scheduled around classes, rehearsals, and performances. All of this complicates long- and short-term decisions dancers are forced to make from early on in their careers.

Artistic passion is not just a quality found in a particular individual. Passionate commitment is fanned by families, teachers, and mass media, and it depends on funding, training opportunities, and organizational resources unevenly distributed throughout society. Training is expensive for families. Dancers are also always under surveillance. Starting with parents and teachers, and later working under supervision of artistic directors and artistic staff, dancers will be nurtured by those who will feed the flames or others who will douse their artistic passions. Passion must be channeled and directed if it is to produce a seasoned dancer who may be chosen by the gatekeepers for intensives, competitions, schools, and work. Early commitments will help future professionals overcome obstacles and persevere in the face of poor odds. Passionate habits acquired through countless hours in studios will stay with aspiring dancers for the length of their lives, even if they never make it as professionals. Disciplined passion helps navigate through academic education, during performing years, throughout the waning years of a dance career when the dancers are ready to put their performing days behind them, and during the process of developing new interests and skills for the next stages of their lives. Many are able to relocate that early passion into new work in the arts, in body work, or into work involving analytical, writing, and verbal skills.

That passion enables thrilling evenings of performances for performers and audiences. But, as I tried to show in this book, artistic passion has a dark side. It breeds the habit of deference to authority figures that compels dancers to follow orders and to the pursuit of the ideal, which can be detrimental to their mental and physical health. Unbridled passions can breed bad habits, nurture self-doubts, and silence voices that can't find adequate outlets. Aware of that, many dancers now stress the need for "a separation between the identity dancers have as artists and the identity they have as individuals in society. She can also be developed to be a person who can advocate, make decisions, and lead as well," as Paula claimed.

In her years as a performer, Paula failed to express this sentiment to the artistic staff of her major company, though it was the topic of her thesis written while performing. Anthony, frustrated with the lack of opportunity to raise his concerns with the artistic director, chose to exit his company early. Others chose to work on short-term projects rather than stay in abusive companies. Today more dancers find strength to voice their opinions and grievances. The hardships imposed by COVID-19 restrictions and the Black Lives Matter and #MeToo activism played a role in this shift. Companies looked around to hire choreographers of color and those interested in different gender identities, and dancers participated in making films and dancing new works both inside and outside their companies. Books and news articles document sexual harassment and lament lack of diversity in the dance world. And dancers speak out on social media in increasing numbers.

These changes are fueled by the experiences of dancers outside the world of their companies and dance. A growing number of dancers are now attending college while dancing or have graduated before becoming professionals, especially in the portfolio market; they are more steeped in critical thinking and capable of analyzing society's ills, which gives them more knowledge and courage to speak out. Company members are increasingly dancing with contemporary choreographers in the portfolio world and taking part in performances extending their movement styles. They get involved in challenging projects that allow them to express who they are as human beings. Both company and portfolio dancers forge ties with people outside the dance community and thus expand their perspectives on cultural niches outside the dance world. They now have a greater understanding that they are more than their bodies and should not remain totally subservient to artistic directors, staff members, and choreographers the way that they did in the past.

Still, traditions such as ballet discipline remain largely entrenched, even though they may be out of sync with the social and political currents of our age. More than in the past, but still rarely, do professional dancers ask why they were passed over for promotion, complain about unprofessional behavior of staff or peers, or refuse to work in dangerous conditions. Portfolio dancers are more apt to speak up than company dancers and are more actively involved in the creation of the choreography and dances representing new social and political topics.

Old habits die hard. Learned from childhood, deferential behavior keeps many dancers from voicing their concerns. They know from experience that speaking out may jeopardize their chances for getting a plum assignment. In their pursuit of excellence, many have not learned to set boundaries in relationships with the staff or to set limits on how far they can be pushed without endangering themselves physically or mentally. Most dancers today have some experience bargaining with their parents and making strategic decisions in regard to their careers, but they don't always use them. Negotiating skills are crucial in such circumstances but not always accepted in the dance world. After all, what brings notice and accolades to a professional dancer is not an articulate voice but a body gracefully moving across the stage. Without the ability and place to articulate needs, passions can be harnessed to questionable causes. That "grim determination" can push dancers to disregard the heightened risks of performing on a slippery sweat-covered stage floor, of lifting other dancers drenched in sweat, or of swinging into action with their bodies dangerously overheated or dehydrated. Injuries are unavoidable when dancers squelch their fear, when artistic directors or choreographers push them beyond reasonable limits. The habit of pushing toward an ideal works against the performers under such conditions. Struggling to maintain a perfect body may impair judgment, especially in young dancers who develop poor dieting habits, who are overwhelmed by too many new roles, or who are working too hard. Given that an ideal is usually beyond reach, how do you know when to stop and tell others that it is necessary to do so? A key to good judgment is the ability to cast professional training as an acquisition of life-affirming skills and to reframe competition as a set of challenges extending beyond one's dance career.

James Whiteside, principal dancer with ABT, accentuates a special role that the cultivation of multiple abilities played in his life. He has learned different styles of dancing, he tries his hand at choreography, and he performs in drag. He even composes music and wrote a book. All that was before sustaining a serious injury in 2022 and struggling successfully to relaunch his dance career in his late thirties. Whiteside explained these efforts as "delusional" in his book *Center Center* (2021); I say, he was up for challenges. The challenge of diving off the stage headfirst in *Swan Lake* is impossible without trust and practice. Somebody has to make sure the rolling mattress is placed at the correct distance from the launch spot, which is different for men and women and for those of different heights. Trust is especially difficult as a guest performer in a new theater with unfamiliar stagehands. Reframing the perilous situation as a challenge and practicing within a supportive group will build confidence for performing and for preparing dancers for future challenges that they take as they move on from performing to do many other things and create new identities whether teaching, designing, or practicing law.

Knowing that they will have a reasonable ear to hear complaints about the problematic behavior of staff or peers is every bit as important as mastering organizational resources and developing collegial relationships and networks. The ties forged throughout professional careers will remain when dancers are ready to move on from performance. Conversely, if they are too shy to speak in classes and don't raise their voices in problematic situations, they will be forever handicapped.

Not every artistic director is sympathetic to those willing to raise personal or political issues. The questioner may be marked as troublemaker. Dancers, especially in traditional companies, have stories of being singled out for retaliation after making themselves heard or of people being punished for asking about promotions, roles, scheduling conflicts, and other issues. Dancers signing up to serve as union reps may get fewer choice roles the following year. Calling out problematic behaviors by staff or fellow dancers is not always easy, especially in small companies where no outlet exists to register a complaint and the perpetrator is sometimes the ultimate authority. Voices are silenced by fear of punishment. The grievance aired is cast as insubordination. Artistic directors trained to defer to authority in their own formative years sometimes revert to familiar patterns when they reach the pinnacle of power, particularly with members of the corps. The burden is on the superiors to recognize their overbearing manners as well as on the dancers to defend their interests collectively. Some professional dancers are not afraid to criticize the company management, but it is mostly dancers who are soloists or principals.

In *Turning Pointe*, Chloe Angyal argued that dancers' involvement is crucial in furthering diversity.[3] Misty Copeland (principal) publicly called on ballet to diversify, and Gabe Stone Shayer (soloist) wrote an op-ed piece in the *New York Times* titled "American Ballet Theater Does Not See Me as I See Myself."[4] He explains he wants to be seen as a dancer, not a Black dancer. The lack of racial diversity is more common in traditional ballet organizations than in contemporary dance companies, which are notably more diverse.

Still, poor communications and poor treatment of dancers befuddle dance groups of all sizes and types. Some of the complaints involve control over bodies—for instance, pressure to lose weight (more in ballet than contemporary companies) or to go on dancing while hobbled by injuries. Some of the dancers I interviewed focus on the lack of transparency in hiring practices, role distribution, and contact renewal and promotion decisions. There are persistent grievances about inappropriate touches, unwanted sexual advances, and teasing by staff members or peers. A common concern is financial arrangements that leave dancers in the lurch when the staff determines that promised supplemental travel has to be waived or pledged pay fails to materialize. Keeping silent in such circumstances saps morale and raises anxiety.

In every line of work, there is the need to assess employee performance. This is an especially thorny issue in professional dancing where, from the dancers' perspectives, no standard protocol exists for evaluating the individual's work, where routine assessments are shrouded in mystery, and employees sometimes are left wondering about their standing in the company. The artistic director, and perhaps some members of the artistic staff, make key decisions based on such evaluations, but they are not always keen on explaining the reasons behind specific role assignments or contract renewal. David Hallberg, former principal dancer with ABT with a worldwide reputation and the new artistic director of the Australian Ballet, explained to Roslyn Sulcas in the *New York Times* that he is trying to be more transparent. He responded when asked about vulnerable, anxious dancers:

> "My office is a safe space for emotion. When we are having difficult conversations, I want them to feel like they are getting an honest answer, not just being calmed down. But emotion inside the studio . . . isn't productive. That's when time is precious."[5]

But artistic directors may, in turn, be ill-equipped to communicate clearly what they are looking for in a specific role, which artist is best suited to project strength, delicacy, sauciness, humor, or some other desired qualities. The artistic director's idiosyncratic preferences play a part here, and so do unspoken considerations. Whatever the decision, somebody is likely to be bewildered and nonplussed.

To address some of these issues, today's companies need to promote greater transparency. Some have added "intimacy advisors" to stem harassment and promote trust. Few guidelines exist in the dance world about harassment and have not gone far enough to solve the problems, however. Just setting up an office where it is safe to report bad behavior will not suffice. Sorely needed are advisory committees that bring together dancers and staff to address problematic behavior and also, perhaps, to facilitate program development and new audience outreach. A significant issue is how to create a safe place to deal with problems for the very small companies with few staff. It is possible to develop a committee within the larger dance community overseeing dancers' complaints, with the authority to weigh in on the disputes and make recommendations, even if only informally. Enhanced transparency would give performers a chance to better understand organizational constraints, the criteria of role assignments, or contract renewal. Management often operates in harsh financial environments and faces many exigencies that force unpopular decisions. Bringing dancers onto the decision-making process is likely to improve morale at every level.

Performances are collaborative, and many contemporary choreographers work collaboratively with dancers, especially in the portfolio world. Dancers know how to work together, particularly in performance and dancers know how to collaborate in work they do after performing. How might companies become more collaborative beyond performance to enable the voices of dancers to be heard, not only for themselves but for the collective? It appears that David Hallberg has become pessimistic about the collaborative possibility when questioned by Sulcas about the surprises he had in taking the role of artistic director of the Australian Ballet:

> "One of the biggest adjustments for me was how everyone looks to you for decision making about even very minor things. I always want things to be collaborative, and often people don't want that— they want you to lead."[6]

But the interview doesn't indicate whether he developed any structures, such as committees, to facilitate collaboration. Are dancers overly socialized to defer to authority so that they are unwilling or too scared to participate? Do they fear non-renewal or fewer roles for speaking out? While some dancers have articulated criticisms both publicly and during my interviews of their lack of voice, I was disappointed to learn of Hallberg's experience.

Making systemic changes is difficult albeit necessary in today's work environment as we deal with a workforce increasingly willing to challenge the status quo. Parents, teachers, and dancers must take a fresh look at their actions and reassess what they owe one another. Overly deferential behavior needs a substitute: respect. Respect is earned, not demanded or expected, both by those in authority and those who work under them. For example, union representatives are chosen by their peers and asked to stand up for them. Those with whom they negotiate for breaks or back pay need to understand that the union reps represent the dancers and are doing their job by requesting that staff meet contract obligations. Both sides can earn the respect of the others by acting reasonably. If staff won't listen to what the dancers say, they may lose respect. They earn respect when they appear to deal fairly, explain why dancers can't have or do certain things, or show they are ready to step in when dancers or staff misbehave or treat others with lack of respect. Dancers want to be able to use their voices to raise questions, present their views, take charge gracefully, and question and report others' inappropriate behavior. Teachers of children need to respect their students, not necessarily by being less strict about important actions, but by listening to the questions and responses to their queries and explaining why. In a successful environment, each person earns the respect of others. People merit respect because of their actions, not because of their status.

La *révérence* is the traditional way to end a ballet class. A bow to the teacher and the accompanist is familiar to old-timers. It is often intentionally choreographed into the final movement—a nod to tradition and deference toward teachers and musicians. Fewer professional classes end with a reverence these days. A young corps member of a major ballet company told me, "We do not usually do *révérence* . . . but sometimes it will happen! Haha. Depends on the teacher and how much time we have. Class is typically a warmup for our busy schedule/season, so as a company we are pressed for time." A contemporary portfolio dancer explained, "It's mostly just ballet. Some contemporary teachers will do a bit of a cool down at the end of class though, so, kind of similar." But this cool down has little to do either with respect or tradition, although physically *révérence* may do something similar for the body. A contemporary choreographer who teaches both ballet and contemporary dance observed, "I've noticed on Zoom, some class takers like it and stick around just for that [*révérence*]." When I asked whether it included the professionals, the response was, "I think nonprofessionals are charmed by the antiquity of it. Professionals, both ballet and contemporary dancers, learned it very young, so no particular interest."

This may be a sign of ballet culture in transition. We live in a time when dancers are better integrated into mainstream culture and are less concerned to show deference to authority. Nowadays, perhaps, a *révérence* for professionals marks respect for a class well done rather than reverence for someone in charge.

GLOSSARY

Actors Equity Association (AEA)   A union formed in 1913 for actors, singers, dancers (largely Broadway). and stage managers.

American Ballet Theatre (ABT)   Based in New York City; the second-largest U.S.-based company.

American Guild of Musical Artists (AGMA)   Formed in 1936 for singers, dancers, and staging staff in opera, concert dance, and concert choral performance. Twenty-eight dance groups belonged in 2023.

Artistic director   Develops the program and may choreograph, choose new choreographers, hire and fire the dancers and artistic staff; most were principal dancers, and most do not have management degrees.

Ballet positions   There are five ballet positions of the feet and arms. Many ballet classes start with *pliés* in each position (bending the knees first so the heel does not come off the floor and then *grand pliés* in which dancers lift the heels as they descend towards the ground). Each foot position has arm positions. These positions are the same around the world. The positions are both used in warm-up and as the basis for much of ballet choreography.

Ballet steps   The steps are codified and used as the basis for much choreography. In traditional ballets, each step can be identified by name in the dancer's performance; for example: *glissade, rond de jambe, tour jeté, assemblé, pas de chat, tour en l'air, pirouette,* and *arabesque.* For a verbal description of many of the terms written by Juliana Barbosa, see https://www.learntodance.com/online-ballet -dance-lessons/

Ballet styles and teaching techniques

George Balanchine   A Russian émigré in New York City, Balanchine (1904–1983), who founded the New York City Ballet with Lincoln Kirstein, developed his own technique that emphasizes rapidity, deep *pliés,* and hiding preparation for steps such as *pirouettes;* the technique is known as neoclassical and sometimes contemporary. While in other approaches, students learn the steps they will use in performance, Balanchine used classes to develop the qualities he wanted them to use in performance. Some people say that Balanchine dancers "eat space."

August Bournonville   **The Danish** style was inspired by the French style after Bournonville (1805–1879) returned to the Royal Danish Ballet where he danced, choreographed, and was ballet master. His style is characterized by lightness, small fast footwork, and natural grace.

Enrico Cecchetti   An important dancer and ballet master, Cecchetti (1850–1928) developed a system of training classical ballet dancers that emphasizes poise, strength, and elasticity. A series of exams allow students to progress through the levels. The American Council (a ballet organization) maintains the standards and methods of learning.

French   The French style was first developed in the seventeenth century by Louis XIV (Académie Royale de Danse). The style is characterized by fluidity, elegance, clean lines, and grace.

Royal Academy of Dance (RAD, British Royal Ballet)   The RAD dates to about 1920. It has a syllabus and ten levels in the training program. The emphasis is on character dancing and merging of other styles.

Agrippina Vaganova   The Vaganova method is a ballet technique and training system devised by the Russian dancer and pedagogue Vaganova (1879-1951). It too involves a syllabus with a progression of levels and a series of exams. It emphasizes the development of the entire body and differs in some terminology from Cecchetti.

Conservatory This is a college-level institution, sometimes independent from a university, where students may study music, dance, or theater. The students can earn BFA or MFA degrees. Students take few courses other than their arts specialty. Juilliard is one of the major conservatories today. College programs in dance performance often do look a lot like conservatories, but students may mix socially with students across the disciplines and take more courses in the humanities, social sciences, or sciences. Some double major. Some colleges have programs in dance education.

Exercise programs
Gyrotonic   Developed by Juliu Horvath (b. 1942), this program is aimed at increasing strength, balance, flexibility, and joint mobility. Horvath, a dancer who came to New York in the 1970s and danced with the New York City Opera and the Houston Ballet, thought of it as yoga for dancers. While Gyrotonic uses some of the same equipment as Pilates, Horvath developed some of his own to enhance circular and spiraling movement—more flow.

Pilates   Joseph Pilates (1883-1967) was a German physical trainer who moved to New York City in the 1920s. He believed in the interrelationship between mental and physical health. The training he developed was intended to stretch, straighten, and align the body, while developing core strength. The apparatus Pilates created helped with flexibility and muscle control too. The training became popular in the dance world when Balanchine and Martha Graham used it.

Marley   Flooring to protect dancers' feet, knees, and hips; it is usually made of durable vinyl or PVC plastic. It is often placed in dance studios above the sprung flooring and on stages.

Modern, post-modern, and contemporary dance

Gaga   Technique developed by Israeli choreographer Ohad Naharin (b. 1952), who danced in New York with Graham, at Juilliard, and with SAB (School of American Ballet at Lincoln Center). Gaga is a movement language intended to help people raise physical awareness by focusing on (or in Gaga terms, "listening to") the rhythm of their bodies, letting them direct their movement and the pleasure that movement brings. Naharin was director and is currently the choreographer of the Batsheva Dance Company in Israel.

Martha Graham   Often considered the founder of modern dance, Martha Graham (1894-1991), who was taught by Ted Shawn and Ruth St. Denis (Denishawn), developed her very specific movement style. The classes are uniquely fitted to enhance the dancer's ability to use her movement. Graham classes are taught in many countries around the world (they use all the same movements), and the company is still producing her works. She started her company in 1926, which still performs under the direction of Janet Eilber. Both *Paul Taylor* (1930-2018) and *Merce Cunningham* (1919-2009) (post-modern) danced with the Graham Company and then started their own companies. The Paul Taylor Company, founded in 1954, continues after his death. And although Cunningham started his company in 1953 and it closed on his death, his technique is still broadly taught.

José Limón   Limón (1908-1972) was born in Mexico and immigrated to California as a child. He started his company in the United States in 1946, which continues today. He joined the faculty of Juilliard in 1951. His technique has become an integral part of many college and conservatory programs. It emphasizes natural rhythm, fall and recovery, and the interplay of weight and weightlessness.

New York City Ballet (NYCB)   Based in New York City, the NYCB was formed by George Balanchine and Lincoln Kirstein. It is the largest U.S.-based ballet company. Its School of American Ballet (SAB) trains many of the NYCB dancers, as well as those who perform in other companies. It also trains dance teachers who work around the country.

Ranks in many larger companies

Corps de ballet   While terms may vary by company, this is the lowest rank in a ballet company. The corps is often the swans, shades, or peasants in large classical ballets.

Soloists   The next higher rank is soloist. Soloists perform alone or in small groups.

Principals   These are the highest rank (sometimes referred to as étoiles (stars or prima ballerinas). Their pictures appear in performance programs.

Répétiteurs/coaches   These instructors work with dancers to ensure that a performance is based on the tradition that they learned when they were taught the role. A *regisseur/stager* usually comes in to ensure that the performance is as it was intended by a choreographer. Sometimes they come in and contribute to the choice of dancers and teach the roles too.

Street dance   Includes dance forms such as locking, hip-hop, popping, house, and breaking. Jookin is a form of gangsta walking that originated in the 1990s in the African American communities of Memphis. Lil Buck was the initiator of many moves that included tip-toe footwork, ankle breaks, and slides or glides. Lil Buck has performed with Yo Yo Ma and at the Vail Summer Dance with ballet dancers.

NOTES

Preface

1. Gruen 1975, 1988; Newman 1992, 2014; Sidimus 1987; Upper 2004.
2. Hallberg 2017: 244.
3. Bentley 2003: vii; Bentley was writing about her experience in the late 1970s, early 1980s. See also Milberg Fisher 2006.
4. Several books focus on a particular company at a specific time: Neale 1982 (American Ballet Theatre and New York City Ballet); Temin 2009 (Boston Ballet); Mazo 1974 (New York City Ballet); Stevens 1976 (American Ballet Theatre); Wulff 1998 (a study of the "backstage" of four international ballet companies and the only academic book—anthropology—in this group).
5. Handy 1989. Cohen and Mallon (1999) further specified this concept.
6. Jan Veen and Hellmut Gottschild brought Mary Wigman (German, 1886-1973) modern dance to the United States.
7. For an excellent discussion of what is dance across cultures and types, see Hanna (1987).
8. The quotes that I use in the book have been lightly edited for clarity and brevity.

Introduction

1. Becker 2008.
2. Homans 2010: 17.
3. Homans 2010, esp. chap. 1.
4. Anne Witchard (2011) describes the evolution of British ballet in the last half of the nineteenth century when it was "music hall ballet" with a corps of minimally trained poor young women who also had to become courtesans to

survive and prima ballerinas from Italy or France who rarely communicated with the corps. Then the traveling Russians worked to transform British ballet and work in legitimate theaters. Also, see Kelly 2012.

5. See Homans (2010) for a detailed and complex account of ballet history. Also, see Wainwright, Williams, and Turner (2007) on the effects of globalization on dance.

6. For a fascinating account of early twentieth-century traditional ballet and "contemporary dance" in Europe, often by Russians; the rise and fall of many companies; the struggles for funding; and the efforts to develop "national" styles, see Garafola's *La Nijinska* (2022).

7. She started her company in 1926, and it is still a major company today. Her movement technique has been passed on and spread around the world with the systematic classes she developed.

8. St. Denis was the co-founder in 1915 of the American Denishawn School of Dancing and Related Arts. She introduced eastern ideas into dance and paved the way for other women in dance. Both Graham and Humphrey studied and danced with her.

9. Her style of movement is often referred to as "fall and recovery." Trained at the Denishawn School, she went on to teach at Juilliard and Bennington. She also helped José Limón set up his company and choreographed for him.

10. A political activist who had two different companies and went back and forth between Broadway and concert dance, she ran the Federal Dance Project for the Works Progress Administration from 1935 to 1939.

11. She studied anthropology in the early twentieth century at the University of Chicago but left after starting her master's degree to follow her passion, dance. For almost thirty years, she maintained her company, the only major American Black dance troupe at that time.

12. For interesting essays on gender, see Thomas (1995).

13. With the exception of Agnes de Mille's *Rodeo* (1942 for the Ballet Russe de Monte Carlo, now danced by several companies) and dances by Twyla Tharp, few women choreographed for the major ballet companies until the twenty-first century.

14. Wainwright, Williams, and Turner (2007) and Wainwright and Turner (2006) show how ballet has become internationalized (and homogenized) through the movement of dancers and exchange of ballets. This is somewhat valid, but when you watch Jerome Robbins's *Fancy Free*, the American Ballet Theatre's performance is athletic; the characters appear to be having fun. New York City Ballet's is a bit less rough with an emphasis on relationships, and the Paris Opera Ballet's sailors are smoothly elegant. It is clear which performance belongs to which company. The styles of performing are different, but then again, it depends on who is dancing. See also Wulff's (1998) study of multiple ballet companies.

15. See Homans (2022) for a detailed biography.

16. Women's participation in the labor force in the United States is actually low compared to countries like Denmark (77 percent in 2016), where there are social supports for motherhood. It dropped from 71 percent in 2000 to 67 percent in 2016 in the United States (see Kalleberg 2018).

17. The "great resignation" started before COVID-19, increased in 2021, and is predicted to increase even more in 2022. Many have returned to work; some resigned and returned when employers in hospitality and retail offered higher wages—a financial decision; other decisions appeared to have been made to improve organizational issues such as child care or poor work environments, and still others sought more meaningful or passionate work. See Ellerbeck 2022; Fuller and Kerr 2022; Gittleman 2022.

18. From 2005 to 2015, 94 percent of the net employment growth in the U.S. economy appears to have occurred in alternative work arrangements, which grew during the period from 10.7 percent to 15.8 percent (Katz and Kreuger 2016).

19. The differentiation among classical ballet, contemporary ballet, contemporary dance, modern and post-modern, and experimental dance is debated by dance writers, critics, choreographers, and dancers. I will not engage in that debate, but all fit into the rubric of "concert dance" and require specific and generally long-term training in schools of dance. Not only do they use movement and space differently, but they tend to tell stories differently or different types of stories. For an interesting series of essays about what contemporary ballet is, see Jill Nunes Jensen and Kathrina Farrugia-Kriel's "Conversations Across the Field of Dance Studies" (2015). For an attempt to define the parameters of contemporary dance, as distinct from contemporary ballet, see Bakka 2020.

20. Lena (2019) has analyzed organizational transformations and the development of the arts in the United States that have become more inclusive of different art forms but are still elitist. Some of these dance forms are less elitist, and the performance spaces are often free for the audience members.

21. "Street dance" includes several styles including locking, hip-hop, popping, house, and breaking. Jookin developed in Memphis from gangsta walk in the late twentieth century. Lil Buck has now performed around the world including Vail Summer Dance and the Kennedy Center (available on You Tube).

22. It was more exciting live than their film sponsored by the Guggenheim's Works & Process series during COVID-19.

23. Garafola's biography La Nijinska (2022) shows how a prolific dancer and choreographer, beginning in the 1920s, had to go to extreme measures to find work around the world, often leaving her family in France, where she settled, to work in Buenos Aires and around the world. Baldwin's Martha Graham (2022) documents the long journeys of one-night stands of Denishawn Dance and then Martha Graham's company across the United States.

24. This is unlike Europe, which offers much more government support.

25. Menger 1999, 2014.

26. Freidson 1986, 1990.

27. Freidson 1990: 151.

28. Schwalbe 1986.

29. McRobbie 2002.

30. Cech 2021.

31. Studies of religious leaders or nuns (Ebaugh 1988) focus on a "calling." For an analysis of the lack of work as a central identity of people working in a British call center, see Lloyd (2012). Vallas and Christin (2018) deal with precarity and its effect on identity.

32. Becker 2008.

33. Bechky 2006.

34. Bennett (2009) found that few dancers in Australia dance in almost full-time companies and that the others do need to develop portfolios of work.

35. Kalleberg 2009, 2018; Kalleberg and Vallas 2018.

36. Kalleberg and Vallas 2018: 1.

37. Throsby and Zednik 2011. According to *Freelancing in America 2018*, a study conducted by the Freelancers Union, there are about 57 million freelancers in the United States.

38. Some research demonstrates that musicians, passionate about their careers, can deal with precarity by relying on family support (Umney and Kretsos 2015). Friedman, O'Brien, and Laurison (2016) extend the importance of class origins of actors to better roles because of demeanor and accents (cultural capital).

39. This idea was first developed by Arthur and Rousseau (1996), but Barley (1989), among others, challenges this use of "boundaryless" as boundaries exist both in entering a bounded organization and people experience boundaries in otherwise more fluid careers—developed by them or created by regulation, organizations, or self. Research shows how variable and inconsistent the constructed boundaries are between work and nonwork in "boundaryless careers" (Hatton 2015; Reissner, Izak, and Hislop 2021).

40. For a discussion of ideas about boundaries, see Rodrigues, Guest, and Budjanov 2016; Inkson 2006. Several projects have found little problem with movement across boundaries. Barley and Kunda (2004) found that experts tend to enjoy the flexibility of freelancing. Guest et al. (2006) concluded that among a sample of professional workers (pharmacists), those with atypical employment contracts report experiences and attitudes that are at least as positive as those of workers with traditional employment contracts.

41. Coser 1974.

42. Csikszentmihalyi 1990.

43. Barley and Kunda 2001.

Chapter 1

1. Search conducted on January 18, 2018.

2. The directors closed Aspen Santa Fe Ballet as a company during COVID-19, and it became a production company of other dance companies. Aspen Santa Fe dancers had a fifty-two week contract, the only ballet company to offer one in the United States.

3. Kourlas 2017.

4. Fisher 2003: 51.

5. Ballet West had slightly smaller expenses.

6. The number of college programs in many arts started accelerating in the 1970s (Frenette and Dowd 2020).

7. See the Glossary for a description of the different styles.

8. Cunningham declared the end of his company with his death, but his technique is still taught.

9. See, for example, his article with pictures: https://www.nytimes.com/2010/12/09/arts/dance/09nutcracker.html

10. Fisher 2003.

11. Kessler 2015.

12. Lena's (2019) analysis of organizational transformations supports the idea of greater inclusivity, particularly in the development of free outdoor programing and City Center's Fall for Dance.

13. Final Bow for Yellowface (https://www.yellowface.org/) includes many of the well-known and important people in the dance world who have signed on to change the representation of Asians in dance, ballet in particular. The organization was founded by Phil Chan who wrote *Final Bow for Yellowface: Dancing Between Intention and Impact* (2020).

14. Homans (2022: 388) argues that a number of the Balanchine dances had themes connected with the Cold War.

15. Gottlieb's essay "Free Spirit" (2018: 295) explores the impact of Isadora Duncan on society. "And for decades she startled respectable society—even as she helped transform it—with her flouting of conventions, both onstage and off."

16. Jacobs 2015.

17. Kourlas (2021) explained that in order for the NYCB to produce *Nutcracker* during the pandemic in 2021, they used older, taller young people to protect the younger children. Information on the Ballet West *Nutcracker* was found the company's website: https://www.balletwest.org/

18. Kessler 2015: 67-68.

19. Atlanta Ballet: https://www.atlantaballet.com/

20. Jacobs 2015.

21. Temin 2009: 15-17.

22. "Music: Ballet's Fundamentalist" 1954. Balanchine appeared on the magazine's cover.

23. According to Sussman (1990: 25), *Dance Magazine* saw a 322 percent increase in college dance degree programs, including performance and educational programs, between 1971 and 1978 (553 programs). She also found using a survey that the families of modern dancers in the early twentieth century were more highly educated and higher status than those of ballet dancers. Although my sample was not constructed for that reason, most of the dancers who joined ballet companies came from families that were as well-off as those who attended college for dance.

24. Some have separate teaching and performing degrees.

25. Ross 2000: 130.

26. See Klapper 2020, chap. 8; Sussman 1984, 1990.

27. List from *Dance Magazine* (July 15, 2015), the College Guide Search. The number difference is likely the number of dance education programs that are not performing degrees or not BA or BFA degrees. The 2023 list includes about 600 programs, but when I narrowed the search to performance, choreography, and BA or BFA, there were about 200. See https://collegeguide.dancemagazine.com/

28. Thomas 1995: 119.

29. "Dancers and Choreographers" n.d.

30. See Lena and Lindemann (2014) or Menger (2014) on the problems in using this data to compute the number of artists.

31. The New York City metropolitan area includes New York City, Jersey City (NJ), and White Plains (NY).

32. These numbers include teachers (university and schools of dance), Broadway dancers, and others, not just dance companies. They do not include the self-employed.

33. Bull 2011: 167–170.

34. Posted on December 5, 2021.

35. Hallberg 2017.

36. Garafola with Foner 1999.

37. December 2017 email from ABT.

38. Pazcoguin 2021.

39. Turning on one leg on pointe while whipping the other around at waist height to *retiré*.

40. Di Orio 2023.

Chapter 2

1 See Pagis 2009; Wellard, Pickard, and Bailey 2007. Although debates are unresolved about the extent to which the self arises from the social/verbal interaction and directly through the body, it may be that dancing sends messages through the body that are then shaped by teachers, parents, and peers. Gardner (2008) argues that we have multiple intelligences; those who take to movement

rapidly have kinesthetic and musical intelligence—learning quickly to dance, which feeds their early passion. Additionally, they practice looking at the teachers and themselves regularly.

2. See Klapper (2020) for a history of ballet classes.

3. Quoted in Gruen 1975: 201.

4. Page 1984: 25-26.

5. Milberg Fisher 2006: 10-11.

6. Time is so important and embodied that I received an email or text if a dancer was going to be more than three minutes late for an interview.

7. See Lareau 2003 and Kohn 1969. Sociological studies show that independence of opinion is taught to children in upper-middle-class families.

8. According to Homans (2022: 477), Balanchine told his staff to fire dancers who violated his idea of appropriate weight.

9. Klapper 2020, chap. 10. It is difficult to tell to whether the lower rates indicate that the problem is under control or whether those with serious problems leave dance.

10. See Wainwright, Williams, and Turner (2007) for a very interesting analysis of how the international exchanges of people and choreography have affected the local styles.

11. By the mid-1920s the young women joining modern dance companies were ordinary middle-class young people (Kendall 1979: 155). Prior to that (Duncan and St. Denis), most were from the marginal middle classes (Thomas 1995: 80). Most of my female interviewees under age forty came from families with two working college-educated parents who could afford the expensive classes, pointe shoes, and costumes for performances. Actors in Britain are also largely from well-off families, and their social and economic capital shape actors' responses to challenges such as extra financial support and favorable typecasting in the allocation of roles (Friedman, O'Brien, and Laurison 2016).

12. Homans (2022: 290-300) documented that many of the dancers who started in the New York City Ballet in the 1950s and 1960s grew up in families of recent immigrants, bohemians, the less educated, and single parents. That appears to be less the case today with the time and expenses necessary to train a dancer.

13. As Lareau (2003) argues, middle-class families encourage many after-school activities and allow and often encourage their children to contribute to decision making, so when their children insist upon ballet classes, they allow it, pay for it, and take the time to drive their children to classes.

14. Cissoko 2017. Also see Aalten (2005) for an exploration of pursuit of the ideal and its often negative effects on the body.

15. NYCB email May 4, 2021, announcing their virtual spring season.

16. Aalten 2005.

17. Forsyth and Kolenda 1966.

18. Van Delinder (2000) argues that ballet is a valid consummatory experience integrating reason and emotions.

19. Quoted in Winship 2015: ix.

Chapter 3

1. Becker (2008: 375) sees careers evolving with small steps and reversals, rather than always with a single progression:

[P]eople do not respond automatically to mysterious external forces surrounding them. Instead, they develop their lines of activity gradually, seeing how others respond to what they do and adjusting what they do next in a way that meshes with what others have done and will probably do next.

2. Bentley (2003: 58) argues that ballet dancers don't have a choice. I would say, many don't see a choice.

3. Clegg, Owton, and Allen-Collinson (2016) explore the relationship between dance and gender and masculinity and male privilege. Men are more often in positions of power. Some argue that as dance is very gendered—men's steps are very different than women's—making it important to train men separately.

4. According to Wagner (2015) the competition for a violin soloist career has some similarities. First, it is a soloist career, and each person studies privately. They each need to seek out more important teachers and supporters and play concerts early. Without backers, it is hard to win a competition. The hard work and grit it takes is similar. For an examination of gatekeeping in the arts see Hamann and Beljean (2021) who focus on the perspective of the gatekeepers in cultural fields rather than the people being evaluated.

5. Winship 2015: 7.

6. According to national research on arts graduates (Frenette and Dowd 2020), women, persons of color, and lower- income (greater student debt) arts majors are less likely to stay in the fields of study and, in the generation studied (those over thirty), wanted more than anything else information about how to access the labor markets they would enter (business and networking skills). The more recent arts graduates said they had more business and network information (Lena 2014). Tepper et al. (2014) found that arts graduates were among the happiest.

7. See Ravn (2016) for an understanding about how contemporary dance and ballet use space differently.

8. Alexander Technique is a method to improve posture habits that improve performance, relieve chronic stiffness, and ease tension.

9. Cech 2021: 39.

10. Lindemann (2013) shows how those who do not become professional artists use their love of the arts and the skills and habits they've developed in their future work.

Chapter 4

1. Gordon 1983: xviii, xix, xx.
2. Aalten 2004.
3. Coser 1974.
4. Bentley 2003: 20.
5. Bentley 2018.
6. Quoted in Gruen 1975: 178.
7. Perlmutter 1987.
8. Quoted in Neale 1982: 113.
9. Quoted in Newman 2014: 167.
10. Gray 2015.
11. Kourlas 2018.
12. Freeman 2017.
13. Larson 2022.
14. Hamilton 1998, 2008. Dr. Linda Hamilton, a psychologist and former corps member of the New York City Ballet, consults with companies and has brought new awareness to the problem of eating disorders.
15. When a person allows another to save face by "choosing" to leave rather than enduring the embarrassment and shame of being non-renewed, they are "cooling the mark out" in Goffman's (1952) terms.
16. See Pazcoguin (2021) for a description of what she saw as her typecasting at the NYCB.
17. Wainwright and Turner 2004.
18. Stevens 1977: 177.
19. Bull 2011: 61–62.
20. Bentley 2003: 14.
21. Lee and Hunt 1998: 73.
22. American Ballet Theatre's new three-act ballet, *Like Water for Chocolate*, choreographed by Christopher Wheeldon (spring 2023), demonstrates lack of adherence to rank. Many of the principal roles were danced by soloists and corps members, demonstrating the depth of corps talent. Corps members, even new ones, also danced soloist and principal roles in *Romeo and Juliet, Giselle,* and *Swan Lake.*
23. Quoted in Neale 1982: 121.
24. Quoted in Winship 2015: 141.
25. Quoted in Neale 1982: 128.
26. Bull 2011: 176.
27. Forsyth and Kolenda's (1966) efforts to understand competition and co-operation do not emphasize the friendships, the identity repair work, or the way collaboration and "the flow" of performance brings company members together. Instead they focus on the strict rules of ballet, the drive to do well, and the cooperation necessary to put on performances.
28. Csikszentmihalyi 1990.

29. Homans (2022: 318) describes performance as the freedom from the efforts in NYCB by Balanchine to exert control over the dancers' lives—"freedom from him." They freed themselves with the tools he gave them—the dancers did it together.

30. Bentley 2003: 127, 42.

31. Quoted in Gruen 1988: 20-21.

32. Kourlas 2019.

33. Here what is important is that there is increasing space to develop personal identities, beyond dancer in a specific company. For example, Kreiner, Hollensbe, and Sheep (2006) found that ministers also struggle with a personal identity. Ministers don't even have to deal with the deeply embodied self as dancers.

34. This video was posted during the pandemic by Vail Dance Festival but is no longer available. Damian Woetzel had taught Hernan Cornejo the Robbins's dance, which was first performed by Baryshnikov.

Chapter 5

1. Randall n.d. This blog excerpt is no longer available. It was originally posted August 20, 2015, and accessed January 2, 2018: https://blog.lifeasamoderndancer.com/artist profiles/

2. See, for example, Reissner, Isak, and Hislop (2021) on boundary maintenance strategies.

3. According to a research report by the Freelancers Union in 2017, 57 million in the United States worked as freelancers, but not all of them were full-time freelancers. Many loved the control over the work/life balance, and many worked that way by choice, appreciating the flexibility and independence; but they were also challenged by healthcare, insurance, and taxes.

4. Barley and Kunda 2004; Osnowitz 2010.

5. While Balanchine (Homans 2022: 422) choreographed Hollywood films, Broadway shows, and dances he thought were "interesting," they were longer-term projects than many portfolio dancers today. By using the terms "interesting" and "commercial," Homans appears to affirm the symbolic boundaries between art and commerce.

6. Cohen and Mallon 1999; Throsby and Zednik 2011.

7. According to Lingo and Tepper (2013), creating opportunities for themselves is a part of much of the art world.

8. In their study of jazz musicians, Umney and Kretsos (2015) argue that precarity and the experience of portfolio work is different, which is supported here. Many have some support from family, and they do find work that will pay the bills, which I argue is separated by an identity boundary from their passion: dance. Not all of the dancers prolong life transitions much more than others of their generation, though that is more often true for women who marry men with regular jobs.

9. The efforts to develop projects is related to the development of artist communities (Cornfield 2015), though the dancers see their efforts as establish-

ing professional companies. Their audiences, however, are often made up largely of their communities.

10. Skaggs 2019.

11. But it takes a while to change styles from, for example, the Paris Opera Ballet to the Russian style (Vaganova) or Balanchine. Modern dancers such as Martha Graham had her own technique, taught around the world today, that requires different use of the body than Paul Taylor, José Limón, or Merce Cunningham, who each developed distinctive techniques and classes.

12. Umney and Kretsos (2015) found that the jazz musicians much preferred project work as it allowed them the most creativity.

13. Studies of how people deal with economic precarity show that many of them can deal with it by developing narratives that reduce anxiety—such as in Spain, holding on to their achievement ideal (Ayala-Hurtado 2022) or manipulating the subjective experience of time (Skinner 2004). Here the dancer is pushed out of the very precarious portfolio market as she had to earn money immediately.

14. Dancers were aided by Katherine Disenhof's website *Dancing Alone Together.* Launched on March 16, 2020, Disenhof, a ballet turned contemporary dancer, listed classes of all styles of dance and levels and new dance videos to watch. By early April 2020, it listed about seventy classes a day and had become a sophisticated website. It ended December 2020.

Chapter 6

1. Kerka (2003) argues that up to 30 percent of workers change the type of work they do.

2. Turner 1969; Van Gennep 1963.

3. See https://entertainmentcommunity.org/services-and-programs/career-transition-dancers. This organization has branches in several U.S. cities. In Toronto, Joysanne Sidimus founded the Dancer Transition Resource Centre in 1985 to give career advice and grants (Sidimus 1987). Britain has a similar type of organization as do some of the European countries; they tend to have state money for scholarships, while groups in the United States must fundraise.

4. Here we are interested in the modes of adjustment to transition and the individual-organization interaction in transition—that is, the process (see Nicholson and West 1989).

5. Aalten 2005; Turner and Wainwright 2003.

6. For a dancer's elegant account of injuries and the end of a career, see Russell Janzen (2023).

7. Bull 2011; Baumol, Jeffri, and Throsby 2004.

8. Bull 2011: 204.

9. Bennett (2008) describes a similar process in Australia.

10. Most teachers do not put girls on pointe before age ten.

11. Wilson (2014) links her Broadway experiences of an earlier generation with her ballet start and the freedom dance offered.

Chapter 7

1. Sidimus 1987: 75.

2. Sidimus 1987: 44.

3. Cacciola 2022. Athletes need to make identity shifts as do dancers, but many have accumulated substantial resources before retiring.

4. Studies in the United States at the end of the seventies showed that between 10 and 30 percent of the economically active population had experienced at least one career change in a five-year period (Teixeira and Gomes 2000).

5. Arthur and Rousseau 1996.

6. Fenton and Dermott 2006.

7. Barley and Kunda 2001; Connell 2020; Skinner 2004.

8. O'Mahony and Bechky (2006) use stretchwork to talk about how freelancers learn enough about the work of those above them in the hierarchy to ask for promotion. In organizations where several are doing similar work, they might ask their colleagues, but here they must seek out others to help them with tasks they have been hired to do.

9. Several additional dancers have stopped performing in the years since I interviewed them.

10. Quoted in Gruen 1975: 156.

11. Tallchief 1997: 312-313.

12. Wilson (2014) found that dance provided freedom for women that was not permitted in the late 1950s and 1960s. Her parents objected to much of that freedom.

13. Sidimus 1987: 93-104.

14. New York City Center 2010.

15. Baumol, Jeffri, and Throsby 2004.

16. O'Mahony and Bechky 2006.

17. The importance of small theaters is seen by a number of companies. The Paul Taylor Company, a major contemporary company now performing in large theaters, announced performances at the smaller Joyce (canceled by the pandemic) to revive Taylor's early work from the late 1950s and 1960s, which was choreographed for small theaters and would become lost on a large stage.

Conclusion

1. First self-published by Richard Nelson Bolles, it has been republished every year since 1975.

2. Cech 2021; Tugend 2023.

3. Angyal 2021.

4. Stone Shayer 2023. This guest opinion piece was given a half page in the *New York Times* editorial section.

5. Sulcas 2023.

6. Sulcas 2023.

REFERENCES

Aalten, Anna. 2004. "'We Dance, We Don't Live': Biographical Research in Dance Studies." *Discourses in Dance* 3 (1): 5-18.

———. 2005. "The Presence of the Body." *Dance Research Journal* 37 (2): 55-72.

Acocella, Joan. 1993. *Mark Morris*. New York: Farrar, Straus and Giroux.

Aloff, Mindy, ed. 2018. *Dance in America: A Reader's Anthology*. New York. Penguin Random House.

Angyal, Chloe. 2021. *Turning Pointe: How a New Generation of Dancers Is Saving Ballet from Itself*. New York: Bold Type Books.

Arthur, Michael B., and Denise M. Rousseau. 1996. *The Boundaryless Career: A New Employment Principle for a New Organizational Era*. New York: Oxford University Press.

Ashley, Merrill, with Larry Kaplan. 1984. *Dancing for Balanchine*. New York: E. P. Dutton.

Ayala-Hurtado, Elena. 2022. "Narrative Continuity/ Rupture." *Work and Occupations* 49 (1): 45-78.

Bakka, Egil. 2020. "Can 'Contemporary Dance' Be Defined?" *Academia Letters*. https://doi.org/10.20935/AL15

Baldwin, Neil. 2022. *Martha Graham: When Dance Became Modern*. New York: Knopf.

Barley, Steven. 1989. "Careers, Identities, and Institutions: The Legacy of the Chicago School of Sociology." In *The Handbook of Career Theory*, edited by M. Arthur, T. Hall, and B. Lawrence, pp. 41-65. Cambridge, UK: Cambridge University Press.

Barley, Steven, and Gideon Kunda. 2001. "Bringing Work Back In." *Organizational Science* 12 (1): 76-95.

———. 2004. *Gurus, Hired Guns, and Warm Bodies.* Princeton, NJ: Princeton University Press.

Baumol, William, Joan Jeffri, and David Throsby. 2004. *Making Changes: Facilitating the Transition of Dancers to Post-Performance Careers.* Teachers College, Columbia University, Research Center for Arts and Culture. https://stiftung-tanz.com/wordpress/wp-content/uploads/2013/02/Facilitating-the-Transition-of-dancers.pdf

Bechky, Beth. 2006. "Gaffers, Gofers, and Grips: Role Based Coordination in Temporary Organizations." *Organization Science* 17 (1): 3-21.

Becker, Howard S. 2008. *Art Worlds.* Berkeley: University of California Press.

Bennett, Dawn. 2008. "Dancer or Dance Artist? Dance Careers and Identity." *International Journal of the Arts in Society* 3 (3): 73-77.

———. 2009. "Careers in Dance Beyond Performance to the Real World of Work." *Journal of Dance Education* 9 (1): 27-34.

Bentley, Toni. 2003. *Winter Season.* Gainesville: University Press of Florida.

———. 2018, September 17. "The Decline and Fall of New York City Ballet." *New York Times.* https://www.nytimes.com/2018/09/17/opinion/new-york-city-ballet-decline-fall.html

Bolles, Richard N., with Katharine Brooks. 2022. *What Color Is Your Parachute? Your Guide to a Lifetime of Meaningful Work and Career Success.* New York: Ten Speed Press.

Bull, Deborah. 2011. *The Everyday Dancer.* London: Faber and Faber.

Cacciola, Scott. 2022, October 3. "This Is What Life After the N.B.A. Looks Like." *New York Times.* https://www.nytimes.com/2022/10/03/sports/basketball/nba-retirement.html

Cech, Erin. 2021. *The Trouble with Passion.* Oakland: University of California Press.

Chan, Phil. 2020. *Final Bow for Yellowface: Dancing Between Intention and Impact.* New York: Yellow Peril Press.

Cissoko, Adji. 2017, May 10. "Dancer Spotlight: 'I Truly Believe That Me Being a Dancer Is No Coincidence.'" *Dance Magazine* 72. https://www.dancemagazine.com/adji-cissoko/

Clegg, Helen, Helen Owton, and Jacquelyn Allen-Collinson. 2016. "The 'Cool Stuff': Gender, Dance and Masculinity." *Psychology of Women's Section Review,* special issue on sports 18 (2): 6-16.

Cohen, Laurie, and Mary Mallon. 1999. "The Transformation from Organisational Employment to Portfolio Work." *Work, Employment, and Society* 13 (2): 329-352.

Connell, Kathleen. 2020. "Navigating a Performance Livelihood: Career Trajectories and Transitions for the Classical Singer." *Education Research* 22 (5): 569-580.

Copeland, Misty, with Charisse Jones. 2014. *Life in Motion.* New Yok: Touchstone.

Cornfield, Daniel B. 2015. *Beyond the Beat: Musicians Building Community in Nashville*. Princeton, NJ: Princeton University Press.

Coser, Louis. 1974. *Greedy Institutions*. New York: Free Press.

Csikszentmihalyi, Mihaly. 1975. *Beyond Boredom and Anxiety*. New York: Jossey-Bass.

———. 1990. *Flow: The Psychology of Optimal Experience*. New York: Harper & Row.

d'Amboise, Jacques. 2011. *I Was a Dancer*. New York: Knopf.

"Dancers and Choreographers." n.d. *Occupational Outlook Handbook*, Bureau of Labor Statistics. https://www.bls.gov/ooh/entertainment-and-sports/dancers-and-choreographers.htm (accessed November 17, 2023).

DePrince, Michaela, and Elaine DePrince. 2014. *Taking Flight: From War Orphan to Star Ballerina*. New York: Knopf.

Di Orio, Laura. 2023, November 28. "Looking Ahead to 2024: Dancers Reflect and Refocus." *Dance Informa*. https://www.danceinforma.com/2023/11/28/looking-ahead-to-2024-dancers-reflect-and-refocus/

Ebaugh, Helen Rose Fuchs. 1988. *Becoming an Ex: The Process of Role Exit*. Chicago: University of Chicago Press.

Ellerbeck, Stefan. 2022, June 24. "The Great Resignation Is Not Over: A Fifth of Workers Plan to Quit in 2022." *World Economic Forum*. https://www.weforum.org/agenda/2022/06/the-great-resignation-is-not-over/

Farrell, Suzanne, with Toni Bentley. 1990. *Holding on to the Air: An Autobiography*. New York: Simon & Schuster.

Fenton, Steve, and Esther Dermott. 2006. "Fragmented Careers? Winners and Losers in Young Adult Labour Markets." *Work, Employment and Society* 20 (2): 205–221.

Fisher, Jennifer. 2003. *Nutcracker Nation*. New Haven, CT: Yale University Press.

Fonteyn, Margot. 1976. *Autobiography*. New York: Knopf.

Forsyth, Sondra, and Pauline Kolenda. 1966. "Competition, Cooperation, and Group Cohesion in the Ballet Company." *Psychiatry* 29 (2): 123–145.

Freelancers Union. 2018. "Freelancing in America 2018." *Freelancers Union and UpWork*. https://freelancersunion.org/wp-content/uploads/2023/03/freelancinginamericareport-2018.pdf

Freeman, Scott. 2017, May 18. "The Inside Story of Terminus, the New Dance Company by Five Ex-Atlanta Ballet Dancers." *ArtsAtl*. https://www.artsatl.org/story-terminus-dance-company-founded-ex-atlanta-ballet-dancers/#:~:text=The%20genesis%20of%20Terminus%20dates,and%20make%20a%20recommendation%20to

Freidson, Eliot. 1986. "Les professions artistiques comme défi à l'analyse sociologique." *Revue Française de Sociologie* 27 (3): 431–443.

———. 1990. "Labors of Love: A Prospectus." In *The Nature of Work: Sociological Perspectives*, edited by K. Erikson and S. P. Vallas, pp. 149–161. New Haven, CT: Yale University Press.

Frenette, Alexandre, and Timothy J. Dowd, with contributions from Rachel Skaggs and Trent Ryan. 2020. "Careers in the Arts: Who Stays and Who Leaves?" Strategic National Arts Alumni Project. https://snaaparts.org/fin dings/reports/careers-in-the-arts-who-stays-and-who-leaves

Friedman, Sam, Dave O'Brien, and Daniel Laurison. 2016. "Like Skydiving Without a Parachute." *Sociology* 51(5): 1-19.

Fuller, Joseph, and William Kerr. 2022, March 23. "The Great Resignation Didn't Start with the Pandemic." *Harvard Business Review.* https://hbr.org/2022/03/the-great-resignation-didnt-start-with-the-pandemic

Garafola, Lynn. 2022. *La Nijinska.* New York: Oxford University Press.

Garafola, Lynn, with Eric Foner, eds. 1999. *Dance for a City: Fifty Years of the New York City Ballet.* New York: Columbia University Press.

Gardner, Howard. 2008. *Multiple Intelligences: New Horizons in Theory and Practice.* New York: Basic Books.

Gittleman, Maury. 2022, July. "The 'Great Resignation' in Perspective." *Monthly Labor Review,* Bureau of Labor Statistics. https://doi.org/10.21916/mlr.2022.20

Glassman, Bruce. 1991. *Mikhail Baryshnikov, Genius! The Artist and Process.* New York: Silver Burdett.

Goffman, Erving. 1952. "On Cooling the Mark Out." *Psychiatry* 15 (4): 451-463.

Gordon, Suzanne. 1983. *Off Balance: The Real World of Ballet.* New York: Pantheon.

Gottlieb, Robert. 2018. "Free Spirit." In *Dance in America: A Reader's Anthology,* edited by Mindy Aloff, pp. 294-303. New York: Library of America.

Gray, Lucy. 2015. *Balancing Acts.* New York: Princeton Architectural Press.

Gruen, John. 1975. *The Private World of Ballet.* New York: Viking.

———. 1988. *People Who Dance.* Pennington, NJ: Princeton Book Company.

Guest, David, Pat Oakley, Michael Clinton, and Alexandra Budjanovcanin. 2006. "Free or Precarious? A Comparison of the Attitudes of Workers in Flexible and Traditional Employment Contracts." *Human Resource Management Review* 16: 107-124.

Guillermoprieto, Alma. 1990. *Samba.* New York: Vintage.

———. 2004. *Dancing with Cuba.* New York: Vintage.

Hallberg, David. 2017. *A Body of Work.* New York: Touchstone.

Hamilton, Linda H. 1998. *Advice for Dancers: Emotional Counsel and Practical Strategies.* San Francisco: Jossey-Bass.

———. 2008. *The Dancer's Way: The New York City Ballet Guide to Body, Mind, and Nutrition.* New York: St. Martin's.

Hamann, Julian, and Stefan Beljean. 2021. "Career Gatekeeping in Cultural Fields." *American Journal of Cultural Sociology* 9: 43-69.

Handy, Charles. 1989. *The Age of Unreason.* Boston: Harvard Business School Press.

Hanna, Judith. 1987. *To Dance Is Human.* Chicago: University of Chicago Press.

Harss, Marina. 2023. *The Boy from Kyiv: Alexei Ratmansky's Life in Ballet*. New York: Farrar, Straus and Giroux.

Hatton, Erin. 2015. "Work Beyond the Bounds: A Boundary Analysis of the Fragmentation of Work." *Work, Employment and Society* 29 (6): 1007–1018.

Homans, Jennifer. 2010. *Apollo's Angels*. New York: Random House.

———. 2022. *Mr. B: George Balanchine's 20th Century*. New York: Random House.

Inkson, Kerr. 2006. "Protean and Boundaryless Careers as Metaphors." *Journal of Vocational Behavior* 69: 48–63.

Jacobs, Laura. 2015, January. "Balanchine's Christmas Miracle." *Vanity Fair*. https://archive.vanityfair.com/article/2015/1/balanchines-christma-s-miracle

Janzen, Russell. 2023, September 20. "On Leaving the Life of the Body, a Dancer Reports." *New York Times*. https://www.nytimes.com/2023/09/20/arts/dance/dancer-retirement-new-york-city-ballet.html

Jensen, Jill Nunes, and Kathrina Farrugia-Kriel, eds. 2015. "Conversations Across the Field of Dance Studies: Networks of Pointes." *Society of Dance History Scholars* XXXV: 1–44. https://s3.amazonaws.com/dance-studies-association/downloads/SDHSConversations2015web.pdf

Kalleberg, Arnie. 2009. "Precarious Work, Insecure Workers: Employment Relations in Transition." *American Sociological Review* 74 (1): 1–22.

———. 2018. *Precarious Lives: Job Insecurity and Well-Being in Rich Democracies*. Medford, MA: Polity Press.

Kalleberg, Arnie, and Steven P. Vallas. 2018. "Probing Precarious Work: Theory, Research, and Politics." *Research in the Sociology of Work* 31: 1–30.

Katz, Lawrence, and Alan B. Krueger. 2016. *The Rise and Nature of Alternative Work Arrangements in the United States, 1995–2015*. NBER Working Paper No. 22667. doi:10.3386/w22667

Kelly, Deidre. 2012. *Ballerina: Sex, Scandal and Suffering Behind the Symbol of Perfection*. Toronto: Greystone.

Kendall, Elizabeth. 1979. *Where She Danced*. New York: Knopf.

Kent, Allegra. 1997. *Once a Dancer*. New York: St. Martin's.

Kerka, Sandra. 2003. "Preparing for Multiple Careers." No. 29. Educational Resources Information Center. https://files.eric.ed.gov/fulltext/ED479342.pdf

Kessler, Lauren. 2015. *Raising the Barre*. New York: Da Capo Books.

Kirkland, Gelsey. 1986. *Dancing on my Grave*. New York: Doubleday.

Klapper, Melissa. 2020. *Ballet Class: An American History*. New York: Oxford University Press.

Kohn, Melvin L. 1969. *Class and Conformity: A Study in Values*. Homewood, IL: Dorsey Press.

Kourlas, Gia. 2017, November 17. "Your Week in Culture: The 'Nutcracker' Returns." *New York Times*. https://www.nytimes.com/2017/11/17/arts/nutcracker-the-man-who-invented-christmas.html

———. 2018, May 31. "Clearing the Stage for a Big Graduation Number at City

Ballet." *New York Times.* https://www.nytimes.com/2018/05/31/arts/dance
/new-york-city-ballet-dancers-graduate-from-college.html

———. 2019, March 7. "'Seraphic Track Stars,' Dancing About Freedom at the
Met." *New York Times.* https://www.nytimes.com/2019/03/07/arts/dance/
silas-farley-metarts-live-metropolitan-museum.html

———. 2021, November 26. "Why Nutcracker Kids Stand Taller This Year." *New
York Times.* https://www.nytimes.com/2021/11/24/arts/dance/nutcracker
-new-york-city-ballet.html

Kreiner, Glenn, Elaine Hollensbe, and Matthew Sheep. 2006. "Where Is the
'Me' Among the 'We'? Identity Work and the Search for Optimal Balance."
Academy of Management Journal 49 (5): 1031-1057.

Lareau, Annette. 2003. *Unequal Childhoods.* Berkeley: University of California
Press.

Lee, Sandra, and Thomas Hunt. 1998. *At the Ballet: On Stage, Backstage.* New
York: Universe Publishing.

Lena, Jennifer. 2014. *Making It Work: The Education and Employment of Recent
Arts Graduates.* Strategic National Arts Alumni Project. https://snaaparts.
org/uploads/downloads/SNAAP_AR_2014.pdf

———. 2019. *Entitled: Discriminating Tastes and the Expansion of the Arts.* Princeton, NJ: Princeton University Press.

Lena, Jennifer, and Danielle J. Lindemann. 2014. "Who Is an Artist? New Data
for an Old Question." *Poetics* 43: 70-85.

Lessor, Wendy. 2018. *Jerome Robbins: A Life in Dance.* New Haven, CT: Yale University Press.

Lindemann, Danielle. 2013. "What Happens to Artistic Aspirants Who Do Not
'Succeed'? A Research Note from the Strategic National Arts Alumni Project." *Work and Occupations* 40 (4): 465-480.

Lingo, Elizabeth, and Steven Tepper. 2013. "Looking Back, Looking Forward:
Arts-Based Careers and Creative Work." *Work and Occupations* 40 (4): 337-
363.

Lloyd, Anthony. 2012. "Working to Live Not Living to Work." *Current Sociology*
60 (5): 636-652.

Larson, Gavin. 2022. *Being a Ballerina: The Power and Perfection of a Dancing
Life.* Gainesville: University Press of Florida.

Lobenthal, Joel. 2016. *Wilde Times: Patricia Wilde, George Balanchine, and the
Rise of New York City Ballet.* Lebanon, NH: ForeEdge, University Press of
New England.

Macaulay, Alastair. 2010, December 8. "'Nutcracker' Nation: Yes We Can!" *New
York Times.* https://www.nytimes.com/2010/12/09/arts/dance/09nutcrack
er.html

Mazo, Joseph. 1974. *Dance as a Contact Sport.* New York: Da Capo Books.

McRobbie, Angela. 2002. "Clubs to Companies: Notes on the Decline of Political Culture in Speeded up Creative Worlds." *Cultural Studies* 16 (4): 516-531.

Menger, Pierre-Michel. 1999. "Artistic Labor Markets and Careers." *Annual Review of Sociology* 25: 541–574.

———. 2014. *The Economics of Creativity.* Cambridge, MA: Harvard University Press.

Milberg Fisher, Barbara. 2006. *In Balanchine's Company: A Dancer's Memoir.* Middletown, CT: Wesleyan University Press.

"Music: Ballet's Fundamentalist." 1954, January 25. *Time.* https://content.time.com/time/subscriber/article/0,33009,823252,00.html

Neale, Wendy. 1982. *Ballet Life Behind the Scenes.* New York: Crown.

Newman, Barbara. 1992. *Striking a Balance: Dancers Talk About Dancing.* New York: Proscenium.

———. 2014. *Never Far from Dancing: Ballet Artists in New Roles.* New York: Routledge.

New York City Center. 2010, November 9. "Violette Verdy on Balanchine: He Gave Valentines to Each One of Us." *YouTube.* https://www.youtube.com/watch?v=-fFK6-LsQEU

Nicholson, Nigel, and Michael West. 1989. "Transitions, Work Histories, and Careers." In *Handbook of Career Theory,* edited by M. B. Arthur, D. T. Hall, and B. S. Lawrence, pp. 181–201. Cambridge, UK: Cambridge University Press.

Nureyev, Rudolf. 1963. *Nureyev: An Autobiography.* New York: E. P. Dutton.

O'Mahony, Siobhan, and Beth Bechky. 2006. "Stretchwork: Managing the Career Progression Paradox in External Labor Markets." *Academy of Management Journal* 49 (5): 918–941.

Osnowitz, Debra. 2010. *Freelancing Expertise: Contract Professionals in the New Economy.* Ithaca, NY: Cornell University Press.

Page, Ruth. 1984. *Class: Notes on Dance Classes Around the World 1915–1980,* edited by Andrew M. Wentink. Princeton, NJ: Princeton Book Company.

Pagis, Michal. 2009. "Embodied Self-Reflexivity." *Social Psychology Quarterly* 72 (3): 265–283.

Pazcoguin, Georgina. 2021. *Swan Dive: The Making of a Rogue Ballerina.* New York: Holt.

Perlmutter, Donna. 1987, February 7. "Stuttgart's Marcia Haydée: Secrets of a Dramatic Dancer." *Los Angeles Times.* https://www.latimes.com/archives/la-xpm-1987-02-07-ca-1657-story.html

Randall, Jill, ed. and blog director. *Life as a Modern Dancer.* http://blog.lifeasamoderndancer.com/artist-profiles/

Ravn, Susanne. 2016. "Dancing Practices: Seeing and Sensing the Moving Body." *Body and Society* 23 (2): 57–82.

Reissner, Stephanie, Michal Izak, and Donald Hislop. 2021. "Configurations of Boundary Management Practices Among Knowledge Workers." *Employment and Society* 35 (2): 296–315.

Ringer, Jenifer. 2014 *Dancing Through It.* New York: Penguin.

Rodrigues, Ricardo, David Guest, and Alexandra Budjanov. 2016. "Bounded or Boundaryless?" *Work Employment and Society* 30 (4): 669–686.

Ross, Janice. 2000. *Moving Lessons: Margaret H'Doubler and the Beginning of Dance in American Education*. Madison: University of Wisconsin Press.

Schwalbe, Michael. 1986. *The Psychosocial Consequences of Natural and Alienated Labor*. Albany: SUNY Press.

Sidimus, Joysanne. 1987. *Exchanges: Life After Dance*. Toronto: Press of Terpsichore.

Skaggs, Rachel. 2019. "Socializing Rejection and Failure in Artistic Occupational Communities." *Work and Occupations* 46 (2): 149–175.

Skinner, Janne. 2004. "Temporal Strategies and Fear in the Workplace." *Journal of Sociology* 40 (4): 417–431.

Stevens, Franklin. 1976. *Dance as Life*. New York: Avon Books.

Stone Shayer, Gabe. 2023, July 7. "American Ballet Theater Does Not See Me as I See Myself." *New York Times*. https://www.nytimes.com/2023/07/07/opinion/black-dancer-american-ballet-theater.html

Sulcas, Roslyn. 2023, August 1. "David Hallberg's New Job: Decision Maker." *New York Times*. https://www.nytimes.com/2023/08/01/arts/dance/david-hallberg-australian-ballet.html

Sussman, Laila. 1984. "The Anatomy of the Dance Company Boom, 1958 1980." *Dance Research Journal* 16 (2): 23–28.

———. 1990. "Recruitment Patterns: Their Impact on Ballet and Modern Dance." *Dance Research Journal* 22 (1): 21–28.

Tallchief, Maria, with Larry Kaplan. 1997. *Maria Tallchief: America's Prima Ballerina*. New York: Holt.

Teixeira, Marc, and William Gomes. 2000. "Autonomous Career Change Among Professionals: An Empirical Phenomenological Study." *Journal of Phenomenological Psychology* 31 (1): 78–96.

Temin, Christine. 2009. *Behind the Scenes at Boston Ballet*. Gainesville: University Press of Florida.

Tepper, S. J., B. Sisk, R. Johnson, L. Vanderwerp, G. Gale, and M. Gao. 2014, February 16. *Artful Living: Examining the Relationship Between Artistic Practice and Subjective Wellbeing Across Three National Surveys*. Nashville: Curb Center, Vanderbilt University. http://arts.gov/sites/default/files/Research-Art-Works-Vanderbilt.pdf

Tharp, Twyla. 1992. *Push Comes to Shove*. New York: Bantam.

Thomas, Helen. 1995. *Dance, Modernity and Culture: Explorations in the Sociology of Dance*. New York: Routledge.

Throsby, David, and Anita Zednik. 2011. "Multiple Job-Holding and Artistic Careers: Some Empirical Evidence." *Cultural Trends* 20 (1): 9–24.

Tugend, Alina. 2023, August 7. "Is Following Your Work Passion Overrated?" *New York Times*. https://www.nytimes.com/2023/08/03/business/work-passion-overrated.html

Turner, Bryan, and Steven Wainwright. 2003. "Corps de Ballet: The Case of the Injured Ballet Dancer." *Sociology of Health & Illness* 25 (4): 269–288.

Turner, Victor. 1969. *The Ritual Process: Structure and Anti-Structure*. New York: Penguin.

Umney, Charles, and Leftris Kretsos. 2015. "'That's the Experience': Passion, Work Precarity, and Life Transitions Among London Jazz Musicians." *Work and Occupations* 42 (3): 313-334.

Upper, Nancy. 2004. *Ballet Dancers in Career Transition*. Jefferson NC: McFarland.

Vallas, S. P., and A. Christin. 2018. "Work and Identity in an Era of Precarious Employment: How Workers Respond to "Personal Branding" Discourse." *Work and Occupations* 46 (1): 3-37.

Van Delinder, Jean. 2000. "Dance as Experience, Pragmatism and Classical Ballet." *Social Thought & Research* 23: 239-250.

Van Gennep, Arnold. 1963. *The Rites of Passage*. London: Routledge & Kegan Paul.

Villella, Edward, with Larry Kaplan. 1998. *Prodigal Son: Dancing for Balanchine in a World of Pain and Magic*. Pittsburgh: University of Pittsburgh Press.

Wagner, Izabela. 2015. *Producing Excellence: The Making of Virtuosos*. New Brunswick, NJ: Rutgers University Press.

Wainwright, Steven, and Bryan Turner. 2004. "Epiphanies of the Body: Injury, Identity and the Ballet Body." *Qualitative Research* 4 (3): 311-337.

———. 2006. "'Just Crumbling to Bits'? An Exploration of the Body, Ageing, Injury and Career in Classical Ballet Dancers." *Sociology* 40 (2): 237-255.

Wainwright, Steven, Clare Williams, and Bryan S. Turner. 2006. "Varieties of Habitus and the Embodiment of Ballet." *Qualitative Research* 6 (4): 535-558.

———. 2007. "Globalization, Habitus, and the Balletic Body." *Cultural Studies ↔ Critical Methodologies* 7 (3): 308-325.

Wellard, Ian, Angela Pickard, and Richard Bailey. 2007. "'A Shock of Electricity Just Sort of Goes Through My Body': Physical Activity and Embodied Reflexive Practices in Young Female Ballet Dancers." *Gender and Education* 19 (1): 79-91.

Whiteside, James. 2021. *Center Center: A Funny, Sexy, Sad Almost-Memoir of a Boy in Ballet*. New York: Viking.

Wilson, Lee. 2014. *Rebel on Pointe: A Memoir of Ballet and Broadway*. Gainesville: University Press of Florida.

Winship, Lyndsey. 2015. *Being a Dancer: Advice from Dancers and Choreographers*. London: Nick Hearn Books.

Witchard, Anne. 2011. "Bedraggled Ballerinas on a Bus Back to Bow: The 'Fairy Business.'" *19: Interdisciplinary Studies in the Long Nineteenth Century* 13. https://doi.org/10.16995/ntn.618

Wulff, Helena. 1998. *Ballet Across Borders: Career and Culture in the World of Dancers*. New York: Oxford University Press.

INDEX

Aalten, Anna, 109
Abraham, Kyle, 4-5, 50
abuse, 93-94, 186-87, 260
Académie Royale de Danse, 2, 268
academics: dance, balancing of, 41, 44, 76, 60-65, 82
Actors' Equity Association (AEA), 190, 267
Actors Fund, 204. *See also* Entertainment Community Fund
African Americans, 32
Afternoon of a Faun, 2
Ailey, Alvin, 19
A.I.M. Company, 4-5
Alexander Technique, 280n8
Alonzo, Alicia, 233-34
Alonzo King LINES Ballet, 55
Alvin Ailey American Dance Theater, 5; Alvin Ailey Arts Center, 163
ambition, vii, 14, 81-82, 122
American Ballet Theatre (ABT), ix, xiii-xv, 3-4, 19, 20, 28, 33-34, 65, 68, 108-9, 112, 143, 145, 151-52, 163, 232-35, 262, 264, 267, 274n14, 281n22; hierarchy of, 122

American Community Survey (ACS), 25
American Council, 268
American Denishawn School of Dancing and Related Arts, 274n7, 274n9, 275n23
American Guild of Musical Artists (AGMA), 81, 113, 190, 210, 267
American in Paris, An, 190
Angyal, Chloe, 263
apprenticeships, 139, 211, 217; as liminal period, 216
art: commerce, boundaries between, 190, 223-24, 226, 282n5
Arthur, Michael B., 276n39
Artifact, 138
artist communities, 282-83n9
artistic directors, 121, 125, 130, 150, 249, 258, 262, 267; authority of, 135; body size, 117-18; body skills, view of, 119; collaboration, 248; competition, generating of, 126-27; corps dancers, 123; dancers, control of, 126; deference to, 123, 135; diversity of types, 176;

artistic directors (*cont.*)
employee performance, 264;
evaluating of bodies, 116–17;
loyalty, 137; power of, 113–14;
promotion of dancers, as reflective
of taste, 124, 126–27; repertory,
decisions about, 114–15; soloist
dancers, 128; thinking entrepreneurially, 247; transparency,
attempt at, 264
arts schools, 64
Arts on Site, 164
Ashley, Merrill, 110–11
Aspen Santa Fe Ballet, 17, 22, 277n2
aspirational dancers, 13, 41, 54, 68,
72–73; disciplining the body, 49
Atlanta Ballet, 19, 22–23; Wabi Sabi
summer troupe, 114
auditions, 29, 32, 57, 58, 62, 80, 84,
95, 105, 169–71, 178, 180, 216;
"look," developing of, 173–74
Australia, 276n34
Australian Ballet, 264, 265

Bach, xv
Balanchine, George, 3, 17, 20, 110,
268–69, 271, 277n14, 277n22,
279n8, 282n29, 282n5, 283n11
Baldwin, Neil, 275n23
ballet, 3, 6; ballet bubble, xv; ballet
mirror, 56; ballet positions, 267;
ballet steps, 2, 268; Danish style,
268; French style, 268; as internationalized, 274n14; ranks, 271;
romantic world of, 41; shaping of
body, 40
Ballet Austin, 19
ballet classes: *révérence*, traditional
way to end, 266; as year-round
activity, 116
ballet companies, 80, 83, 108, 171,
178; "company as family" trope,
14–15; corporate bodies, compari-

son to, 152; as "greedy institutions, 14, 146, 151; as hierarchies,
122; loyalty, 109, 151; social and
political issues, 4
Ballet Company, 110. *See also* New
York City Ballet (NYCB)
ballet discipline, 68; being on time,
40, 48; body flexibility, 40;
deference, 40, 44, 48; as en-
trenched, 261; ideal self, working
toward, 40; no-talking rule, 40, 49
Ballet Hispánico, 4–5, 19
Ballet Society, 255–56
Ballets Russes, 2
ballet schools, 23; the "look," 43;
presentation of self, 45
Ballets U.S.A., 256
Ballet West, 19, 22
Ballet X, 5, 19
ballroom dancing, 42
Bang Group, 20, 26–27
Bannon, Kathleen, 229
Barley, Steven, 276n39, 276n40
Bartelme, Reid, 7
Baryshnikov Arts Center, 163
Baryshnikov, Mikhail, 65, 282n34
Batsheva Dance Company, 270
Battery Dance Festival, 6, 164
beatbox, 6
Bechky, Beth, 284n8
Becker, Howard, 1, 280n1
Bel, Jérôme, 50
Bell, Aran, 65
Bennington College, 24
Bentley, Toni, viii, 110, 123, 145,
280n2
Berlin (Germany), 199
Bernard, Scott, 132
Bill T. Jones/Arnie Zane Dance
Company, 5
Black Lives Matter (BLM), 4, 260
body shaming, 92–93, 109
body shape, 50–52

body size, 1, 31, 96, 117–19, 178
Body Traffic, 5
Bolshoi Ballet School, 115
Boston Ballet, 3–4, 19, 23, 37
boundaryless careers, 12, 16, 231, 276n39
Bournonville, August, 2, 268
Britain, 279n11, 283n3
Broadway, xvi, 25, 63, 90, 136, 158–59, 172, 189, 223–25, 227; ambivalence about performing on, 191–92; financial stability of, 190; unions, 137; as way to extend dancing careers, 226
Brooklyn Academy of Music (BAM), 163
Bourne, Matthew, 83
Bryant Park, 164
Bull, Deborah, 28, 121–22, 137, 205–6
bullying, 63–64
Bureau of Labor Statistics (BLS): Occupational Employment Survey, 25

Cantrell, Robin, 193, 195
careers: choice, as shaped by others, 75; decision challenges, 73–74; end of, 202; exits, 204; management, difficulty of, 177; pathways, 105
Career Transition for Dancers, xi
Carpet Series (Pigeonwing Dance), xv, 166
Casel, Ayodele, 6
casting, 93, 122, 129, 135–36; body size, 29–31; gender, 31; race, 31
Cecchetti, Enrico, 2, 20, 45, 268–69
Cech, Erin, 10, 98
Center Stage, 65
challenges, 12–13, 16, 37, 71–72, 76–78, 89, 100, 160, 201, 243, 252, 254, 262; adversity, 94; of change, 257; difficult situations, 93; as

risks, 86–88, 97–98, 101, 184, 202, 222
Chan, Phil, 277n13
Chase, Lucia, 3–4
Chicago City Ballet, 233–34
Chocolate Factory, 193
choreographers, vii, ix, xi–xiii, xv, 1–5, 7–8, 11, 21, 29–30, 67, 92–93, 109–10, 114, 116, 123–25, 130–31, 146–47, 149–50, 159–60, 162, 165, 171, 173, 176, 179–84, 186, 189, 193, 196, 198–99, 201, 231, 233, 242–43, 245, 248–49, 260–61, 267, 275n19; collaboration, 265; dance world networks, reliance on, 246; independence of, 128–29; in labor market, 24–26; rehearsals, filming of, 161; thinking entrepreneurially, 247
choreography, viii, xv, 2–3, 20, 24, 26, 52, 67, 84, 91, 102, 147–49, 174, 182, 193, 216, 225, 242, 248, 261–62, 267–68; as collaborative, 131, 195–96; contemporary, 87, 170; flooring and space, 165
Cissoko, Adji, 55
City Center, 21, 163; Fall for Dance, 277n12
civic ballet companies, 3
classical ballet, 68, 88, 181
collaboration, 68, 72, 107, 148, 152, 160, 162, 193–96, 216, 229, 242, 244, 246–48, 257, 265; community, 121; community, as fragile, 200; friendship, 143; performance, 143; portfolio building, 198; small companies, 199; in small spaces, 197–98; as sometimes unpleasant, 198
collectivity, 138–39; performance, 143
college, 260; distancing from performing self, 211–14, 218

college and conservatory programs,
84-85, 87, 90, 92, 95-96, 105,
277n6, 278n23, 278n27
company dancers, 18, 37, 111, 223,
245, 260-61; exiting of, 227
competition, 28, 54, 80, 91-92, 126,
129, 137, 139-40, 230; with
classmates, 56; for corrections, 59;
as cutthroat, 79; friendships,
mitigating of, 58-60; with ideal
self, 55; interpersonal, 78; summer
intensives, 57-58; toxic, 82; with
unobtainable ideal, 56-57
Complexions Contemporary Ballet,
5-6, 19
concert dance, 3, 275n19; diversity, 6,
21; locations for, 6; as porous, 1, 7;
representation, 21
concert dancers, xi; world of, as
porous, 1
conservatories, 269
contemporary dance, 30, 64, 87,
101-3, 178, 254, 263, 266, 270,
274n6, 275n19; pointe shoes, 27, 35
Cook, Mira, 194-95
cooperation, 137; friendships,
facilitating of, 138
Copeland, Misty, viii, 4, 263
Corella, Angel, ix, 234
Cornejo, Herman, 151, 282n34
corps dancers, 11-12, 14-15, 37, 81,
101, 109, 114, 121, 125, 129-30, 149,
151, 160, 205-6, 208, 235, 271,
281n22; artistic directors,
dependent on, 123; as collaborative, 144; identity, 135; longer
careers than ballet dancers, 219;
loyalty, instilling of, 122-23, 128,
137, 150; as one, 143; positive
self-image, 135; principal dancers,
divide between, 138-39; promotion, 124, 126-27; repair identity
narratives, 122; révérence, 266;

standing out, difficulty of, 146-47;
starting salaries, 33; synchronization, 123
costume designers, 244, 247, 249;
dance world networks, reliance
on, 246
cover positions, 190-91
COVID-19 pandemic, x, xii, xvi, 5,
11-12, 143, 147, 149, 159, 161, 163,
165-66, 260, 275n17, 277n2;
shutdown, 116, 199, 226-27
creative tap, 6
Csikszentmihalyi, Mihaly: flow,
concept of, 145
cultural capital, 276n38
cultural entrepreneurs, 158-59, 160,
171
Cunningham, Merce, 20, 71, 88-89,
270, 277n8, 283n11
Cuthbertson, Lauren, 132

d'Amboise, Jacques, 159
dance: competition, as endemic to,
54; as expensive, 53; "falling in
love" with, 42; freedom, for
women, 284n12; as mirror, 57;
performed with others, 9; pointe
shoes, 53; practice of, 52; requirements of, 52; self-fulfillment, 9;
social habits, 71-72; summer
intensives, 53; time commitment,
52-53; as work, 9
dance companies, 21, 232; artistic
directors, 113-19, 121; collaboration, 265; collectivity, and
friendship, 138-43; competing for
resources, 113; as dysfunctional
family, 142; as "family," 116, 118,
121, 132, 138-39, 141-42, 150-51; as
"greedy institutions," 109-10, 116,
149; hierarchy of, 123, 137, 141;
intimacy advisors, 264; loyalty,
128; morale, improving of, 265;

precarity of labor, 113–15; problematic behavior, addressing of, 264; problematic sexual behavior, 4; relationships, 137; transparency, 264–65; unions, 114–15, 135, 136–39, 142–43; universities, relationships with, 113
dance concerts, 5
dance income: prioritizing of, 189–92
dance performance: as collective, 7; costumes, 7; as precarious labor, 8
dance programs: gatekeepers of, 84
dancers, 160–61; abuse, 186–87; articulating needs, lack of ability to, 261; control over bodies, 263; employee performance, 263–64; fundraising, 162; grievances by, 263; "grim determination" of, 261; inappropriate touching, 263; in labor market, 24–26; learning, 181; making decisions about future, 40–41; new work, 230, 235–36, 238–41; parents, shaping ambitions of, 13; after performing careers, 231; personal identities, developing of, 282n33; poor treatment of, 263; post-performance challenges, 230; retaliation, after voicing opinions, 262–63; safety issues, 183; speaking up, 132–33, 136–37, 210, 237, 260, 262–63; surveilling of, 109, 259; thick skins, necessity of, 93; touching and partnering, as risky, 182; treated as children, 131–32; trust, 183–84; as typecast, 119; union reps, 265; weight, as issue for, 51, 117
Dancers Responding to AIDS, 189
Dancer Transition Resource Centre, 283n3
dance schools, 18, 21; growth of, 23–24

Dance Theatre of Harlem (DTH), xiii, xv, 4–5, 19, 164
dance training, 34, 40–41, 79, 82, 83, 86, 106–8, 179; abuse in, 93–94; social habits, 71
Dancing Alone Together (website), 283n14
Dancing with Cuba, viii
Daphnis et Chloé, 7
deference, 40, 71–72, 81, 117, 123, 131, 135, 137, 151, 211, 213–14, 260; ceremonial reenactment, 49; lack of, 133; obedience, expectations of, 44–45, 47; and respect, 265–66; standing up for oneself, 133; uppity, 132; voicing concerns, failure to, 261
De Keersmaeker, Anne Teresa, 164
de Mille, Agnes, 274n13
de Luz, Joaquin, 235
Denmark, 2, 275n16
DePrince, Michaela, viii
Diaghilev, Sergei, 2
Di Orio, Laura, 37
Disenhof, Katherine: Dancing Alone Together (website), 283n14
diversity, 5–6, 21, 32, 35, 65, 84, 88–89, 149, 176, 193, 254, 260, 263; portfolio career, practical for, 90
Duncan, Isadora, 3, 277n15
Dunham, Katherine, 3, 274n11

Ear Hustle (podcast), 148
eating disorders, 51
Eilber, Janet, 270
Ellington, Duke, xv
English National Ballet, 234
Entertainment Community Fund, Career Transition for Dancers, 204. See also Actors Fund
entrepreneurs, 170, 240, 246, 250–51; cultural entrepreneurs, 158–60, 171; entrepreneurial self, 245

300   INDEX

Eugene Ballet Company (Oregon), 17,
    21-22
Europe, 2-3, 46, 76, 82-83, 105-6,
    113, 275n24
exercise programs: Gyrotonic, 269;
    Pilates, 269
exiting, 205, 221; difficulty of, 228;
    injuries, 206-8; liminal period,
    217; performing body, maintain-
    ing of, 219-20; as process, 227; as
    situational rupture, 227, 231-32;
    transitioning, 222-23; as volun-
    tary, 208-9
experimental dancers, xi

Fairchild, Robbie, 190
"Fall for Dance" programs, 6
Fancy Free, 274n14
Farley, Silas, 148-49
Ferri, Alessandra, 145
Final Bow for Yellowface, 277n13
First Position, 65
Fisher, Barbara Milberg: In Bal-
    anchine's Company viii, 45, 255-56
Fisher, Jennifer, 18, 20-21
flow, 145, 281n27
Ford Foundation, 161
Forester, Thomas, 163
Forsyth, Sondra, 281n27
Fracci, Carla, 43
France, 273-74n4
Freelancers Union, 276n37, 282n3
freelancing, 158, 181-82, 189, 232,
    249, 276n37, 282n3; flexibility of,
    276n40; portfolio approach to,
    159; stretchwork, 284n8
Friedson, Eliot, 9
fundraising, xv, 159, 162, 243, 249,
    283n3

Gaga (dance technique), 168, 270
Garafola, Lynn, 2-3, 275n23
Gardner, Howard, 278-79n1

gatekeepers, 1, 9-10, 13-14, 44, 50, 52,
    73-76, 80, 82, 84, 101, 107, 109-10,
    173, 259, 280n4
gender: boys, and dance training, 32;
    dance companies, 3; girls, 32
Germany, 103
Giselle, 281n22
Godino, Stephanie, x
Goffman, Erving: "cooling the mark
    out," 281n15
Gordon, Suzanne, 108, 143
Gottschild, Hellmut, x, 273n6,
    277n15
Govrin, Gloria, 21
Graham, Martha, x, 3, 7, 20, 88, 168,
    269-70, 274n8, 275n23, 283n11
Gray, Lucy, 112
Great Depression, 24
"great resignation," 275n17
greedy organizations, 14, 109-10, 116,
    146, 149, 151; control of workers,
    131
Gruen, John, 145, 233
Guest, David, 276n40
guesting, 33-34
Guggenheim Museum, 163-64; Works
    & Process series, xiii, 6-7, 112
Guillermoprieto, Alma, viii
gymnasts, 40

Hallberg, David, viii, 31, 264, 265
Hamilton, Linda, 234, 281n14
Hard Nut (Mark Morris Company),
    20
Harris, Rennie, 5-6
Harrison, "Maverick" LeMar, 148
Harss, Marina, viii
Haydee, Marcia, 111
hobbyists, x, xvi, 33, 41
Hollander, Jonathan, 6
Homans, Jennifer, x, 277n14, 279n12,
    282n29, 282n5
Horosko, Marian, 229

Horvath, Juliu: Gyrotonics, 269
Houston Ballet, 19, 234
Hubbard Street Dance, 5
Hudson River Dance Festival, 6
Huffman, Greg, 135
Humphrey, Doris, 3, 274n8

identity, 36, 53, 89, 91, 98, 101, 107,
    135, 171, 173, 209, 250, 252-53;
    academic, 104; aspirational, 44, 71;
    fantasy, 41, 43; negotiating new
    sense of, 213; repair work, 281n27;
    sticky, 190; upholding of, 178
identity repair narratives, 126-28;
    artistic "gray" area, 123-25
Indelible Dance, 193
injuries, 35, 108, 109, 114, 119-21, 138,
    177, 203, 221-22, 225-26, 254, 261,
    263; body, protecting of, 182; exits,
    leading to, 204, 206-8; shaping of
    careers, 36
intimacy advisors, 264
Italy, 2, 273-74n4

Jaffe, Susan, 234
Jamieson, Jamie, x
jazz musicians, 282n8, 283n12
Jenner, Ann, 233
Joffrey Ballet, 19, 132, 234
Jones, Bill T., 5
Jookin', 6, 271, 275n21
José Limón Dance Company, 19
Joyce Theater, ix, 5, 88, 163, 189,
    284n17; Joyce Theater Foundation,
    6
Juilliard, 24, 269
Jung, Harriet, 7

Kaatsbaan, xv
Kansas City Ballet, 19
Kennedy Center, 275n21
Kent, Julie, 234
Kerollis, Barry, xiii

Kessler, Lauren, 21
King, Alonzo, 4
Kirkland, Gelsey, 109
Kirstein, Lincoln, 3, 268, 271
Kolenda, Pauline, 281n27
Konverjdans, xiv, 199
Kourlas, Gia, 18, 113, 148, 277n17
Kretsos, Leftris, 282n8, 283n12
Kulyk, Andrei, x
Kunda, Gideon, 276n40
Kupersmith, Judy, 234

La Bayadère, 127; "Shades" in, 146
Lamb, Gabrielle, x, xiii-xv, 166
L.A. Project, 5, 19
Laracey, Ashley, 112
Le Corsaire, ix
Lena, Jennifer, 275n20, 277n12
Like Water for Chocolate, 281n22
Lil Buck, 271, 275n21
liminal period, 16, 204, 211-12,
    216-19, 225, 227, 250, 257
Limón, José, 20, 88-89, 270, 274n9,
    283n11
Lincoln Center, 21, 163, 164, 244;
    Baand Together, 258; School of
    American Ballet (SAB), 270
LINES Ballet, 4
Lopez, Lourdes, 234
Louis XIV, 2, 268

Macaulay, Alastair, viii, 20
male dancers, 41, 42, 43, 66-67, 81,
    159, 172, 234; ballet discipline, less
    shaped by, 68; body standards,
    leeway to deviate from, 118-19;
    greater economic and racial
    diversity, 65; lack of peer support,
    54; as less deferential, 68, 81;
    promotion, and threat to leave,
    132-33; shortage of, 14, 65
Mariinsky Theatre, 17
Marley (flooring), 270

Mark Morris Dance Company, 5,
    19-20, 92
Martha Graham Dance Company, 5,
    19, 24, 270
Martins, Peter, 234
McFall, John, 114
MC 14/22, 88
McKenzie, Kevin, 234-35
McRobbie, Angela, 10
Memphis (Tennessee), 271, 275n21
Menger, Pierre-Michel, 8-9, 11-12
#MeToo movement, 4, 260
Metropolitan Art Museum 148, 244
Miami City Ballet, xv, 19, 234
Milwaukee Ballet, 19
Missing Element, 6
modern dance, 2, 6; pointe shoes,
    rejection of, 3
Movement Headquarters, xiii
Museum of Modern Art (MOMA),
    164, 167
"music hall ballet," 273-74n4

Naharin, Ohad, 270
National Ballet of Cuba, 233-34
Neale, Wendy, 135
Nedvigin, Gennadi, 115
New Jersey Performing Arts, 21
new work, 250, 255, 257, 260;
    conceptual bridges, creating of,
    252, 254
New York City, xi-xii, xv-xvi, 5-6, 34,
    42, 77, 80, 101, 106, 158, 170, 187,
    199, 243; Brooklyn, 163, 166;
    dancers and choreographers,
    employment of, 25-26; Manhat-
    tan, 163, 166; Queens, 166; West
    Village, 165-66
New York City Ballet (NYCB), viii-ix,
    xiii, 3, 19, 20, 34, 50, 57, 110,
    111-13, 148, 159, 164, 190, 233-35,
    255-56, 268, 274n14, 279n12,

282n29; Nutcracker, 17, 21-23,
    277n17; salaries, 33; School of
    American Ballet (SAB), 270-71. See
    also Ballet Society
New York Live Arts (NYLA), 5, 161,
    163
New York University (NYU): Center
    for Ballet and the Arts (CBA), x-xi
Nijinsky, Vaslav, 2-3
92nd Street Y, 163
Nitting, Courtney, 37
No Man's Land, 194-95
Nutcracker (Tchaikovsky), xv, 39, 42,
    133, 137-38, 277n17; body size,
    29-30; Cavalier role, 33-34, 37;
    challenges, dealing with, 28-29;
    Christmas tree, 18; Clara, role of,
    20, 28-32, 58, 68; company
    members, 37; corps dancers, 37;
    costumes, 53; distinctive, at-
    tempts to make, 20; enchantment
    of, 33; as financially critical, 23;
    first full-length U.S. production,
    17; gender in, 31; hip-hop version,
    21; injuries, 35; as inspiration, to
    dancers, 13, 27-28; Marzipan role,
    35; men in, 34; as money maker,
    22-24, 26, 34; performance styles,
    range of, 26; popularity of, 21;
    precarity, effect on, 19; Prince,
    role of, 31-32; productions of, as
    diverse, 20; race in, 31-32; retired
    performers, 36; Sugar Plum Fairy
    role, 20-21, 33-34, 37
Nut/Cracked (Bang Group), 20, 26-27
Nutcracker Rouge, 20
NYCommunity Ballet, x

Oboukhov, Anatole, 45
O'Mahony, Siobhan, 284n8
outdoor spaces, 164

Pacific Northwest Ballet, 19
Page, Ruth: Chicago Opera Ballet 45
Paris Opera Ballet, xiii, 2, 274n14, 283n11
Parker, David, 26-27
passion, 86, 160, 204, 254, 258; artistic, 259; disciplined, 259-60; new work, 260; as non-work, 10; performing, link to, 68
Paul Taylor Company, 5-6, 19, 170, 270, 284n17
Pazcoguin, Georgina, 34
Peck, Justin, 57
Peck, Tiler, 235
Pennsylvania Ballet, 19, 27. See also Philadelphia Ballet
performance: abusive, 186; challenges, reinforces need to face, 69-70; collaboration, 72, 265; community of artists, 199-200; company loyalty, strong basis for, 145; ideal self, 70; non-substitutable feeling, 144; passion, 68; social rewards of, 68-70, 201, 224; teaching dance, symbolic distance between, 185-86
performance art, 10
performance sites, 164-68
performing careers, 66, 219; end of, 202, 205, 223, 256-57; extending of, 222; as finite, 227
performing self, 16, 35, 71, 102, 104-5, 125, 160, 187, 191, 203, 257; apprenticeship, use of, 211, 216-17; college, use of, 211-14, 218, 227; distancing from, 15, 100, 210-13, 220-21, 227, 229; evolution of, 215-16; holding on to, 178; liminal period, 211-12, 214, 216-18, 221, 227-28; in need of protection, 176; as sticky, 94, 98, 106; stretching of, 236; therapists, use of, 211, 215,

217-18, 221, 227; transition away from, 211-12, 218
Petipa, Marius, 2
Philadelphia Ballet, ix, 3-4, 19, 234. See also Pennsylvania Ballet
physical therapists, 238-39
Pigeonwing Dance, xiii-xi, 166
Pilates, Joseph, 269
Pittsburgh Ballet, 17, 19
portfolio dancers, ix, xii, 11-13, 18, 22, 26, 34, 50, 67, 84, 102, 104, 147, 160, 166, 168-70, 190, 200, 218, 232, 235-36, 243, 252, 260, 282n8; choreography, creation of, 261; collaboration, 193, 196, 198; in control of bodies, 178; as cultural entrepreneurs, 158-59; diversity, 90; diversity of dance styles, learning of, 193; freelancing, 159; learning new movement styles, 179-80; new skills, developing of, 15-16; non-dance activities, 184-85; performing body, maintaining of, 219-20; portfolio building, 171-72, 175, 179, 189, 198-99, 238-39; precarity of, 158, 221-22, 282n8; repair narratives, 171, 173-76; seven-day work week, 157-58; side jobs, 15; speaking up, 261; transitioning, 222-23
precarity, 11, 15, 19, 158, 221-22, 249, 282n8, 283n13; of labor, 113-15
Preljoçaj, Angelin, 88
principal dancers, 124, 126-27, 147, 271, 281n22; corps dancers, divide between, 138-39; as divas, 139; individuality, expression of, 122; interpretation, 146; loyalty, 128; self-expression, 137
professional dancers, 2, 18-19, 38, 41, 43, 68, 70-72, 75, 101, 103-4, 106,

professional dancers (*cont.*) 169, 172, 232–33, 247, 259; as contemporary, 20; gatekeepers, 107; new types of work, 229; promotion, 261; training of, 23–24

project-based companies, 178–79, 187–88, 199–200, 212, 259

promotion, 9, 11, 15, 19, 114, 132, 144, 189, 222, 238, 249, 261, 276n38, 282n8, 283n13

Public Theater: Joe's Pub, 165

Radetsky, Sascha, 65

Ratmansky, Alexei, viii, 20, 68, 112, 151–52

Ravel, Maurice, 7

rehearsals, xii–xiii, 7, 13, 18, 32–33, 41, 52, 62, 89, 113, 121, 138, 142–43, 145, 149, 160–61, 163, 168, 176, 180–81, 184–85, 187, 222, 247, 256, 259

repair: identity narratives, 122, 171, 173–76

répétiteurs/coaches, 271

reshaping bodies, 92

retirement, 15, 18, 21–22, 222, 233–34, 249–50, 256

reward system, 14

Robbins, Jerome, 256, 274n14, 282n34

Rodeo, 274n13

Rojo, Tamara, 234

Rome & Jewels, 5–6

Romeo and Juliet, 281n22

Rousseau, Denise M., 276n39

Royal Academy of Dance (RAD), 69, 232, 268–69

Royal Ballet, xiii, 28, 121, 132, 137, 205, 233

Royal Danish Ballet, 268

Runaway, The, 5, 50

rupture, 209, 218, 227–28, 232, 239, 252, 255, 257

Russia, 2–3, 12, 17, 76, 193

Russian Revolution, 3

Samba, viii

San Francisco (California), 25

San Francisco Ballet, 17, 19, 112, 114, 125, 234

Saunders, Christopher, xiii

Schert, John Michael, x

School of American Ballet (SAB), 23, 45

Schreier, Claudia, xv

Schumacher, Troy, 112

Scott, Arron, 33–34

Scottish National Ballet, 88

Seasons, The, 68

second work identity, 148

self, 76, 174, 202; adapting of, 98–100; aspirational, 43, 72; competition with, 55; commercial dance, as challenge to, 192; critical aspect of, 71; embodied, 73; ideal, 70, 78, 250, 252, 261–62; organizing self, as critical skill, 247; presentation of, 43, 45, 48, 173, 175, 252; repair narratives, 175; risk to, 86; self-image, 251, 253; sense of, 108; sticky self, 255

self-competition, 55

self-confidence, 92

self-discipline, 117, 229

Shawn, Ted, 270

Shayer, Gabe Stone, 263

Shevchenko, Christine, 28, 151–52

Shuler, Arlene, 6

Sidimus, Joysanne, 229, 283n3

Sleeping Beauty, 112, 175

small spaces: audiences, as part of collaborative process, 197–98

snowball sample, xi
soloist dancers, 126–27, 147, 271, 281n22; individuality, expression of, 122; interpretation, 146; loyalty, 128, 131; promotion, 131; self-expression, 131, 137
"Songs from the Spirit," 148–49
Spain, 283n13
Stafford, Jonathan, 234
stage mothers, 52
Stanley, Taylor, 5, 50
St. Denis, Ruth, 3, 270, 274n8
sticky self, 94, 106, 190, 255
Stiefel, Ethan, 65
Strayhorn, Billy, xv
street dance, 5–7, 271, 275n21
stretchwork, 232, 242, 250–51, 255; freelancers, 284n8
Stuttgart Ballet, 111
Suite of Dances, 151
Sulcas, Roslyn, 264–65
surveillance: of bodies, 93, 149, 214, 219, 259
Sussman, Laila, 278n23
Swan Lake, 50, 127, 137, 139, 146, 262, 281n22
swing, 190

Tabula Rasa Dance Theater, 5, 161
Tallchief, Maria, 233–34
Tamiris, Helen, 3, 274n10
tango tourism, 42
tap, 6
Taylor, Paul, 6, 20, 270, 283n11
Tchaikovsky, Pyotr Ilyich, xv, 18
Termin, Christine, 23
Tharp, Twyla, 274n13
Tokyo (Japan), 69
Tomasson, Helgi, 125
Toronto (Ontario), 283n3
touch, 44, 46, 142, 182; inappropriate, 263; as part of teaching, 45

transition, 219, 241; ballet culture in, 266; to Broadway, 223–26; as difficult, 227; as emotion work, 212; liminal institutions, as helpful, 228; liminal period, 211–12, 222; new styles of relationships, 245; new types of work, 232; as rupture, 252; of women, 233–34; between worksites, 231
Turning Point, The (film), 65

Ukraine, 149
Ulbricht, Daniel, 235
Umney, Charles, 282n8, 283n12
unions, 114–15, 135–39, 142–43, 263, 265
United States, 4, 8, 21, 33, 44, 113, 205, 275n20, 277n2; career changes, 284n4; concert dance in, 3; freelancing in, 158, 276n37, 282n3; net employment growth, 275n18; *Nutcracker* productions, 17; women's participation in labor force, 275n16
University of Wisconsin Dance Department, 24

Vaganova, Agrippina, 2, 20, 269, 283n11
Vail Summer Dance Festival, 6, 151, 271, 275n21, 282n34
Van Delinder, Jean, 280n18
Veen, Jan, x, 273n6
Verdy, Violette, 235
Villella, Edward, 159

Wagner, Izabela, 280n4
Wang Theatre, 23
Washington Ballet, 234
Weber, Jennifer, 21
Weisberger, Barbara, 3–4
Wheeldon, Christopher, 281n22

Whelan, Wendy, ix, 234

Whim W'him, 5

White Nights (film), 65

Whiteside, James, 262

Wigman, Mary, x, 273n6

Williams, Christopher, 5, 7

Williams, E. Virginia, 3–4

Wilson, Lee, 284n12

Winter Season, viii

Woetzel, Damian, 6, 151, 235, 282n34

Works Progress Administration
   (WPA): Federal Dance Project,
   274n10

Work/Travail/Arbeid, 164

Yerushalmy, Netta, 7

Yo Yo Ma, 271

Zoom classes, xii–xiii, 163, 199;
   révérence, 266